LABOUR IN TRANSITION

The Labour Process in Eastern Europe
and China

Edited by
Chris Smith and Paul Thompson

London and New York

First published 1992
by Routledge
11 New Fetter Lane, London EC4P 4EE

Simultaneously published in the USA and Canada
by Routledge
a division of Routledge, Chapman and Hall, Inc.
29 West 35th Street, New York, NY 10001

Typeset in Garamond by Witwell Ltd, Southport.

Printed in Great Britain by
Biddles Ltd, Guildford and King's Lynn

A catalogue reference for this title is available from the British Library

ISBN 0-415-08295-1
0-415-08648-5

Library of Congress Cataloging in Publication Data

Labour in transition: the labour process in Eastern Europe and China
/ edited by Chris Smith and Paul Thompson.
p.   cm. — (Organization and employment studies series)
Includes bibliographical references and index.
ISBN 0-415-08295-1.   — ISBN 0-415-08648-5 (pbk.)
1. Industrial relations—Europe, Eastern.   2. Industrial
relations—Soviet Union.   3. Industrial relations—China.
4. Europe, Eastern—Economic conditions—1989-   5. Soviet Union-
-Economic conditions—1985-1991.   6. China—Economic
conditions—1976-   I. Thompson, Paul, 1951- . II. Smith, Chris,
1953- . III. Series.
HD8380.7.L32   1992
331'.0947—dc20   92-24745
                              CIP

CONTENTS

FIGURES

NOTES ON CONTRIBUTORS

Michael Burawoy teaches at the University of California, Berkeley, and is author of *Manufacturing Consent* and *The Politics of Production*. He has in recent years concentrated his research and writing on understanding the comparative production regimes of capitalism and state socialism. His latest book in this area is *The Radiant Past: Ideology and Reality in Hungary's Transition from Socialism to Capitalism* (with János Lukács).

Donald Filtzer is Senior Lecturer in European Studies at the Polytechnic of East London and Honorary Research Fellow at the School of Slavonic and East European Studies, University of London. His main research interest is the analysis of production relations within Soviet industry. He has published a history of Soviet workers under Stalin, *Soviet Workers and Stalinist Industrialization*, and a follow-up volume on workers in the Khrushchev period, *Soviet Workers and De-Stalinization*. The third volume in the series, *Soviet Workers and Perestroika* is currently in preparation.

Jude Howell lectures on China and the politics of development at the School of Development Studies, University of East Anglia. She has taught in Sichuan Province and Shanghai and has recently spent a year in southern China conducting research on China's Open Door Policy.

David Mandel teaches in the Department of Political Science, University of Quebec, Montreal. He is author of a two-volume history of the Soviet workers – *The Petrograd Workers and the Fall of the Old Regime* (1983) and *The Petrograd Workers and the Soviet Seizure of Power* (1984) He has written and researched extensively on the former Soviet Union, including the recently published *Perestroika and the Soviet People*.

Otfried Mickler is Professor of Industrial Sociology at the University of Hannover, Germany. From his research base in the Institute of Sociology, he has written several books on technology and work, including *Technical Organisation and Work*; *Production Process and Qualifications*; *The Social Process of Introducing Industrial Robots*. His current research interests are in East–West social integration, the origins and development of technical processes and the role of technical labour in product innovation.

Chris Smith is Lecturer in Industrial Relations in the Business School, Aston University. His main research interests are in white-collar workers (especially technical labour), management strategies and work restructuring, and white-collar unionism. He is author of *Technical Workers* and co-author of *White Collar Workers, Trade Unions and Class* and *Reshaping Work: The Cadbury Experience*, and co-editor of *White-Collar Work: The Non-Manual Labour Process* (with D. Knights and H. Willmott) and *Engineers and Management* (with G. Lee). He is currently working on the comparative social position of engineers in advanced capitalist economies.

David Stark teaches in the Department of Sociology, Cornell University, New York. He has written many articles on labour market and labour process dimensions of state socialism, and is co-editor of *Remaking the Economic Institutions of Socialism: China and Eastern Europe*.

Paul Thompson is a Professor in the School of Organisation Studies at Lancashire Polytechnic. He is author of *The Nature of Work*, and co-author of *Working the System* (with E. Bannon) and *Work Organisations: A Critical Introduction* (with D. McHugh). His current research interests are in labour process reform in state socialist societies and work organization in multinational corporations. He spent four months teaching and researching in China in 1989.

Part I

INTRODUCTION

1

SOCIALISM AND THE LABOUR PROCESS IN THEORY AND PRACTICE

Paul Thompson and Chris Smith

It is in many ways an odd time to be writing about and discussing state socialism given that it is rapidly disappearing as a political and economic formation. Nevertheless the emphasis on these issues in the 1990 Labour Process Conference was extremely welcome given the insularity that has characterized a considerable portion of labour process writings. Such insularity, with obvious exceptions such as Burawoy's path-breaking work, is particularly marked with reference to issues of the state and politics (Strinrati 1990; P. Thompson 1990).

In this context socialism in any of its varieties has had only marginal consideration. Why then has it been dealt with at all? Essentially because it provides a form of comparison that illustrates the nature and distinctiveness of the capitalist labour process. Though not strictly necessary as Burawoy (1985: 29–32) shows in his use of feudalism for the same purpose, without a discussion of socialism the element of critique would be lacking. Socialism then is used in two senses. First, as a kind of ideal type, sometimes formally as in Burawoy's model of 'collective self-management'; more often as a notional opposite to capitalism at the macro and micro-economic level. So from Braverman (1974) to Bettelheim (1974; 1976) we get the counter-position of deskilling to the unity of conception and execution, of managerial control to workers' control and of market to plan. As Burawoy notes, 'In each instance the realities of capitalism are juxtaposed with some utopian constructions of socialism obtained through the miraculous abolition of, for example, alienation, atomisation, subordination' (1985: 157). As we shall later demonstrate, this kind of perspective is strongly conditioned by pre-capitalist social relations, a looking back to guild communities, handicraft ideologies and divergent interpretations of the liberatory aspects of work within modern industry.

Our chief concern here is to examine the character of the labour

3

process within concrete societies we call state socialist, rather than review conceptions of a socialist labour process within the socialist tradition. However, it is not really possible to discuss the practical examples of state socialist labour processes without in some way assessing their socialist pedigree. Using the term 'socialist' connects our analysis to a body of thought about what a socialist society should be, and the 'should be' vision of the future has an ambiguous and contradictory history within the Marxist and socialist tradition. From the time when Marx and Engels castigated Saint Simon, Charles Fourier and Robert Owen as 'utopian socialists' and counterposed their own doctrine of 'scientific socialism', there has been a reluctance to construct or speculate on the future of the labour process within a socialist or communist society. Instead of futurology there was an orientation towards immediate class struggles and a distant, relatively unspecified golden future.

Marx thought that the details of any future society were largely unknowable, it being the outcome of the material experience of real people, not ideas in the heads of philosophers. But neither could the future socialism begin from a clean slate. It was conditioned by the outcome of concrete contradictions under capitalism and a political critique of that system. In addition, in the development of Marx's writing there was a systematic learning about the future society from immediate struggles – whether over the length of the working day, or prefigurative democratic forms, such as the Paris Commune (Dunayevskaya 1975). In his analysis of English capitalism Marx highlighted features of large-scale industry as permanent not purely capitalist qualities of work organization. As such, the future is partially an outcome of the present, capitalism transitional to socialism. It is therefore a question of teasing out assumptions about the future from Marxist and socialist texts in order to understand the tension between critique of capitalism and the alternative vision. Before we attempt this, however, we shall examine the dynamic structure of the labour process within existing state socialist regimes, that is a particular type of system, which has evolved or been imposed upon specific societies, and not an abstraction, a 'socialist labour process', which remains a fiction.

THE STATE SOCIALIST 'MODEL'

The construction of theoretical or practical alternatives has not been helped by the frequently observed Soviet admiration of Taylorism and one-man management, resulting in the 'virtual elimination of self-management or producer's democracy from the Bolshevik programme' (Davies 1990: 9). The kind of direct democracy anticipated in *State and Revolution* was never extended to the enterprise. It is hardly surprising that we end up with judgements that the former Soviet Union manifests an organization of labour 'differering only in details from that of the capitalist countries' (Braverman 1974: 12). However, at a theoretical level this makes the error of isolating some particular features of the labour process under state socialism from the mode of production as a whole. Given that work relations under capitalism result from the unity of the labour and valorization processes; without a capitalist mode of production there cannot be a capitalist labour process. It also makes the mistake of ignoring the historical or national specificities of Russian state socialism.

More importantly, the emphasis of an analysis that begins with deviations from an ideal type cannot deliver what is needed – a concrete empirical analysis of state socialism as a form of society in its own right and with its own dynamics. Such a framework has been developed by writers such as Nove (1983), Rakovski (1977) and particularly the Hungarian economist Kornai (1980); later reinterpreted as an institutional analysis by Stark and Nee (1989), and for an understanding of the labour process by Burawoy (1985). The general argument is that state socialist regimes can be characterized as not only command but also shortage economies whose central force is hierarchical bargaining between state and enterprise.

The relations of production are based on the centralized appropriation and redistribution of the surplus through a strata of planners empowered by the fusion of party and state apparatuses. A ruling class combining the leading sections of administrative, economic, political and military elites emerges from these relationships. This is a much narrower group than the oft-used 'intelligentsia'[1] (the class basis of these arrangements are discussed in a later section). A distinctive state-directed character is thus given to relations between politics, society and economic processes, which 'merge into a barely differentiated system' (Davis 1989: 194). Like market economies, there are self-reproducing institutional mechanisms. In the absence of competitive markets and the law of value it is impossible to operate stringent financial criteria to evaluate efficiency. The essentially political critiera underpinning transactions between state and enterprise can create only 'soft budget constraints' which tend to encourage unlimited expansion. But though this in some ways gives management soft options, the process is still riven by fundamental uncertainties which arise from the inability of management to control the inputs and outputs to production.

So within bargaining with state structures management's inevitable goal is to use the variety of available political and economic levers to negotiate 'loose' plans which often conceals and distorts information on capacity and quotas. Uncertainties and shortages also encourage enterprise directors to hoard labour, raw materials and even investment resources to deal with actual and potential problems. Though not emphasized by all writers, such economic and political arrangements have for the most part been accompanied by a kind of 'social contract' with the work-force, at least among state employees; in which employment security and other rewards (e.g. subsidized goods and housing) are exchanged for a degree of participation or at least acquiescence in the work-place and on the broader social terrain. While not ruling out explicitly coercive aspects of managerial power, this kind of perspective qualifies theories of totalitarianism which focus exclusively on party-state elites and a quiescent population by highlighting some of the complex social networks, interest groups and organisational forms inside the economy (Stark and Nee 1989: 30).

All this has consequences for the labour processes through which goods and services are produced, or what Burawoy calls relations *in* production. Tremendous constraints exist on management to utilize resources effectively, for example studies of the introduction of new technology in Hungary (Bogdan 1989; Burawoy and Lukács 1989) show that managers, particularly at strategic level, had to look at issues purely in terms of labour supply rather than impacts on utilization or costs. On a related note, Blackburn (1991: 44) notes the inability within the former Soviet economy to make any effective use of management computers, because of 'the crudity of the calculations required by the administrative-command system'; a great irony considering the degree to which import of Western technology in the 1930s fuelled Soviet growth.

Operational management, meanwhile, has to exercise considerable discretion to deal with uncertainties and shortages on the shop floor. Dependence on key groups of workers frequently requires mutual accommodation and a degree of autonomy and flexibility in work organization to ensure continuity of production and protection from sanctions applied through middle management. Part of that accommodation results in work units as a whole exhibiting a common front in transactions with external bodies.

Overall, therefore, exercise of effective controls is extremely difficult. To achieve the necessary flexibility to deal with fluctuating circumstances managers have to tolerate 'various forms of work avoidance and indiscipline from employees' (Henley and Ereisha 1989: 65).[2] This often includes the 'right' of employees to conserve effort and dispose of their own labour power in the second or informal economy that plays a central role in mobilizing resources outside the planning system (see Stark, Chapter 2 in this volume). In practice the capacity to enforce control and increase labour intensity is limited by a range of factors, not least the double pressures of employment security and protection of enterprises from the consequences of poor performance. Work organization continues to manifest, 'predominantly pre-Tayloristic features that have preserved considerable autonomy for the workers' (Hethy 1990: 20). This also helps explain the high dependence on piece-work in many state socialist economies. Though it can be used in a punitive and coercive manner (Haraszti 1977), the effectiveness of piece-work may be undermined by a lack of connection between monetary rewards and the ability to spend the proceeds on desired goods and services.

This framework of analysis of state socialist regimes is a valuable and illuminating one. It has the added attractions of providing further evidence against traditional convergence theories and of 'softer' treatments of former Soviet-type societies which tend to see crises in terms of malfunctions (Lane 1989: 177). But it has its limitations, particularly in Burawoy's (1985) earlier version. State socialism is primarily discussed as a model. Though at a certain level of abstraction this is perfectly acceptable, there is in some writings insufficient acknowledgement of differentiation within actually existing socialisms. If we introduce a societal context, then variations based on the nature of the pre-socialist regime, levels of economic development, or nature of the state, immediately qualify the concept of state socialism and offer a guide to explaining the diverse patterns of disintegration and transformation of such regimes in recent years.

To return to Burawoy's Hungarian example, he explains Haraszti's (1977) account of the particularly despotic piece-rate system in the Red Star Tractor Factory partly by reference to internal factors (the author's status as a peripheral worker, the power of the foremen) and partly to external (withdrawal of subsidies as part of the reform process). On a broader terrain, it is argued that there is a dualism in economy and enterprise related primarily to degrees of centralization, producing bureaucratic bargaining in stronger sectors and bureaucratic despotism in weaker sectors.

While this undoubtedly has some significance, it remains too restrictive. We have to start from a clearer recognition that forms of state–enterprise relations, management and employment relations are strongly influenced also by political, cultural and spatial factors. Take the question of the reproduction of labour power which is central to Burawoy's typology of change in state socialist 'factory regimes'. Economic reforms and intensive development mean that such reproduction has become increasingly independent of enterprise control. The provision of housing, employment and other social benefits come directly from the state, thus enhancing the possibilities for greater managerial and employee autonomy. This may well be true of Hungary and some other Eastern bloc countries, but most enterprises in China remain very much mini-welfare states.

Aside from anything else the analyses are now partly outdated, bypassed by the recent revolts against Communist power. Burawoy (Chapter 6 in this volume) and other writers are re-evaluating existing models in the light of the rapidly changing political and economic landscape. It is time to draw lessons not just from the historic failure of command economies but from the failure to reform them. For the experience poses difficult questions about the possibilities for a socialist labour process.

THE FAILURE OF REFORM FROM WITHIN

Reforming responses to crises in command economies are not new. Like capitalism, with its periods of recession and expansion, state socialist regimes suffer economic crises, though it is foolish to ignore their distinctive features by reducing both to crises of the state (Clarke 1990). In a long-term and general sense, they reflect the inherent limitations in the capacity of central planning to allocate investment rationally, and to overcome rigidities and shortages in production and distribution. More specifically there have been increasing problems of low growth and stagnant productivity once the periods of intensive accumulation and industrialization have been completed. This has become especially acute in the 1970s as internal problems were magnified by the incorporation of Eastern Europe into the world economy, with its consequent rising levels of debt to the West and exposure to fluctuations in commodity prices and capital flows.

The process of reform had also been **cyclical** in character, marked by shifts back and forth between decentralization and recentralization, markets and hierarchical planning, openness and retrenchment (Stark and Nee 1989: 25). In societies based on a fusion of powers, the economic and political dimensions of crises are ultimately inseparable. As Davis (1989: 201–2) argues, the mid–1950s revolts in the Eastern bloc marked the first phase of crisis as the period of rapid accumulation, with its maximum extraction of the surplus from workers and peasants came to an end. Economic reforms spread rapidly even to the conservative heartlands such as the GDR in the 1960s as Party leaderships struggled to overcome stagnation. The end of this second phase of crisis and reform came in political repression culminating in the Soviet invasion of Czechoslovakia, as events moved beyond the control of the party apparatus.

By the end of that decade the retreat was complete with the exception of Hungary and for different reasons Yugoslavia[3] They were later joined by China (see Thompson, Chapter 8, and Howell, Chapter 7, in this volume) after its disastrous experience with the Cultural Revolution. Such reforms extended market processes much further. While the centre still controlled the commanding heights, regulated markets through fiscal mechanisms, distribution of raw materials, and control of investment and other macro-economic factors; at micro-level enterprises were given increasing powers over their own means of production and encouraged to compete in a semi-market framework, with profits as the prime indicator of efficiency.

However, despite great hopes for this 'socialist mixed economy' from reformers in East and West, the marriage of markets and planning did not work. Whether a hybrid economy *could* have worked in different and more favourable circumstances such as the Czechoslovak reforms in the late 1960s remains an open question. What we do know is that hybrids created out of the particular starting-point of the command economies of state socialism did not and could not be successful. As Thompson (Chapter 8 in this volume) and Kornai (1986) demonstrate, what tends to result is the worst of both worlds without the benefits of either. Though more specific problems can be identified, the essence of the problem was the addition of decentralization and market mechanisms on to a system that at best could be described as command-incentive, with hierarchical co-ordination remaining as the dominant organizing principle. By the time other countries, notably the Soviet Union, came into the picture in the mid–80s, the situation was beyond rescue by partial reforms.

At the micro-level reforms to democratize the enterprise were promised to accompany and in some senses compensate for the market; notably an increased role for employees or trade unions through some sort of self-management or enhanced decision-making. Ideologically and practically this embodied an important step in the direction of recognizing conflicting interests. China notionally increased the role of workers' congresses and unions, but their powers remained largely formalistic. Managers and the Party continued their dual control in the work-place. In the former Soviet Union 'self-management', even when carried out, was linked primarily to a brigade system in which workgroups were given enhanced responsibilities in return for payment by performance (Lane 1989; Van Atta 1989). The results corresponded more to Western attempts to regulate the labour process through autonomous working groups than a major change in employee rights and power integral to the reform process. Bulgaria saw changes in the labour code allowing for both self-management and work brigades. Neither led to any significant change in power relations in the firm, which was kept in an external strait-jacket (Wallimann and Stojanov 1989).

As a consequence of the failure of partial reform, there was a rapid spread of disorganization in the reforming regimes. The old-style rigidities and uncertainties were added to by new crises produced by limited marketization. In particular, the end of the 'social contract' between workers and the regime began to give rise to new social tensions and conflicts. This latter point illustrates once again the centrality of politics in state socialism. In theory this could be an advantage. Some writers (Shirk 1989) believed that the very elitist character of Leninist one-party states could be the dynamic factor for transformation.

This certainly corresponded to the political project of sections of some party elites. Zhao's faction in China promoted a perspective of authoritarian modernization which combined economic opening-up with extremely limited political reform. Perestroika and glasnost, at least in their inception, can also be very much seen in this light. Limited democratization at enterprise and administrative levels were chiefly intended as levers for shaking up the party apparatus rather than any substantial change. Yet it is precisely that apparatus which has proven incapable of delivering modernization. The fusion of powers becomes impossible to unravel and reforms are slowed down and distorted by their filtering through the vested interests of power-holders at national and local level, many of whom had an endless capacity to meet the new targets through shuffling figures and names.

As one commentator noted on Soviet work-place initiatives, 'measures to make enterprises independent fail, since managers continue to be accountable to a party whose functionaries do not have their work judged merely by economic criteria' (Rittersporn 1989: 23). The party machinery frequently cannot resist the temptation to use reforms instrumentally, for example to use newly elected representatives of collectives and other bodies as vehicles for political control (Grancelli 1989). The consequence, as Bauman (1989) notes, is that the original reform slogan – 'no political reform without economic reform' – is put into reverse. In the end, though there were considerable variations in outcome, the choice for most of the regimes was repression or abandon ship. Once the party apparatus ceased to be the factor for cohesion, the space rapidly widened for much more 'radical' policy measures and for the reconstruction of leading political and economic classes.

THE TRANSITION TO MARKET ECONOMIES

The rush to ideologically and practically embrace markets and privatization has struck many in the West as at best naive and at worst foolish. Much of the Left called and hoped for a 'third way' between the failed command economies and flawed capitalist alternative. At one stage this found echoes in the East from reform communists to factions of Solidarity. Such talk is now more or less over. As we have shown attempts to produce an alternative macro-economic framework that could aid change at the enterprise level *without* making a decisive break proved difficult. Most groupings came to believe that partial reform was no longer feasible.

Given the depth of the crisis the situation was beyond playing about with economic models. As Burawoy shows (Chapter 6 in this volume) large state enterprises found it impossible to compete effectively on world markets, given factors such as debts, antiquated capital equipment, overmanning and irrational price structures. In fact this situation was the national economy writ small. Therefore in this context it was inevitable that marketization became synonymous with economic restructuring and dealing with the crisis. However, the process was also reinforced by political factors. Any forces associated with a 'third way' were marginalized as the space closed, not only for reform communism, but also for anything that smacked of socialism, democratic or otherwise. At the same time the glamour of markets

11

and privatization were boosted by a steady stream of visitors from business and right-wing think-tanks dispensing advice distinctly at odds with the real experience of Western societies. Certainly foreign capital will not be interested in a democratic work-place, but the availability of qualified cheap labour and virgin markets.

Though there is superficially a single direction, the pace, timing and combinations of measures differ widely. Most countries have put in place some kind of anticipatory legislative framework covering questions of currency, customs, tax, ownership and employment laws. But while Hungary has led the way with recent Company and Foreign Investment Acts, reforms of the banking system and the creation of a stock exchange, Poland has gone furthest in policies with its crash programme, including price liberalization, a wage freeze, severe cuts in state aid to enterprises and a tightening of fiscal measures. The increase in social tensions following the subsequent rapid decline in real wages and industrial production, and equally rapid increase in unemployment may help to explain the slower movement elsewhere. Certainly the political costs will be high, as one assessment of the former Soviet Union by Western management writers indicates:

> Thus even under the most favourable circumstances (ignoring the likelihood of widespread bankruptcy and the prospect of massive unemployment), the majority of the Soviet people will almost certainly experience a shocking reduction in their real and money incomes, with the greatest burden falling on the working class as prices for necessities rise and the availability of non-essential substitutes shrinks.
>
> (Rosefielde and Quinn Mills 1990: 17)

In such countries which have been slower to change the process will be both more drawn out and uncertain. For example the famous 500-day plan for producing a market economy is widely regarded as unrealistic.

Nor is the situation likely to be rescued by Western business. Despite initial enthusiasm for rich pickings from cheap property and a market of 150 million potentially voracious consumers, real interest and investment has been very limited.[4] There remains considerable uncertainty over questions such as property rights, asset valuation and repatriation of profits. Nor are these mere technicalities. The problem is neatly summed up by the Chairman of Crédit Suisse; 'We may have buried Communism, but we haven't yet seen what's really

12

coming afterwards. I would like to see a little more of the shape of things to come before putting money into it' (*Wall Street Journal* 20 February 1990). What comes next will be a matter of intense political struggle. It is by no means clear that a simple adoption of full-scale capitalism is on the cards.

Large-scale privatization would have to accompany markets if that were to happen. Yet there are considerable obstacles once beyond the general statements of desirability, not least the sheer vastness of potentially disposable assets. Despite the growth of initiatives such as joint ventures (around 2,000 in Hungary alone), the state sector was still overwhelmingly dominant in 1990. When you consider that there are over 8,000 enterprises alone looking for buyers in what was East Germany, the scale of the problem can be seen. Of course one option is to break them up to produce small and medium-size units. Even that does not get round the fact that there are insufficient capital resources, both in the indigenous population, and as we have noted from foreign business.

But the problem is as much political as economic. As has been widely recognized, privatization has provided an excellent opportunity in Poland, Hungary and elsewhere for sections of the old *nomenklatura* to use their privileged power and material resources to transform themselves into an emergent business elite. In particular managers have taken advantage of new ownership laws to become 'partners' in re-shaped enterprises for often less than half the real price (Lipski 1990; Burawoy and Lukács 1991). Not surprisingly, such enfranchisement of the old state bureaucracy 'has always been taken by the employees with bitter feelings of resentment' (Kozek 1990: 15). Though somewhat less divisive, selling off state property cheaply to external capital has also proved a politically sensitive issue. Legislative caution and political paralysis have often followed.

It is clear that some privatization, indeed a great deal in some sectors, is necessary if you begin from an almost wholly state-owned economy. But given the difficulties are there any alternatives? Both self-management and employee share ownership have their adherents in Eastern Europe. As we indicated earlier, the former was a crucial part of the early agenda of Solidarity, notions of enterprise self-government bringing together the economic and political dimension of their struggle. Indeed a Bill on Self-Management was passed in the Polish parliament in 1981. Such ideas have been part of the political debate in other countries, including Hungary, the former Soviet Union and Bulgaria.

Yet as a realistic policy, self-management is even more problematic than privatization. Aside from the intense political hostility from those who believe economic democracy to be an obstacle to the rebuilding of hierarchical power in the work-place, the difficulty is that it is largely a theoretical model compared to private ownership. There is of course Yugoslavia, but that is part of the problem. The system operated through state-owned capital being lent to enterprise 'collectives' of managers and workers who took decisions and a share of the profits within a market framework. This appeared to work well and ensure adequate growth until the early 1960s. However, there were fundamental flaws centring on the substantive subordination of self-managed enterprises to political control and a bureaucratic collectivist economic environment (Nikolic 1989). The economic and subsequent political disintegration of Yugoslavia has therefore meant that in most of Eastern Europe, 'support for self-government today is far less enthusiastic than twenty years ago' (Wolinicki 1989: 68).

Self-management also crucially requires the political and material resources only a movement from below can provide. Yet even in Poland the level of interest is not high, largely due to clever tactics from the transitional government which enforced a diluted version based on limited work-force involvement. As Bielasiak (1989: 304) notes, self-management has been transformed into 'at best an organ of co-determination dominated by the power of the economic administration and pushed aside by other enterprise institutions'.[5] Elsewhere, for instance in Bulgaria, it has encouraged worker organization, but not alternative conceptions of running the economy.

The limitations of producer democracy revealed in the Yugoslav experience have weighed heavily in the minds of critics. For enterprises in a difficult transition period to distribute all or most of net earnings as wages or on worker welfare would be a dangerous risk. Therefore some Soviet reformers have advocated various share schemes as a counteracting tendency, with the aim of giving workers a long-term stake in future development (Davies 1990: 16). This is one of a number of indications that employee ownership may be seen as a less ambitious and more market-orientated alternative to straight privatization or full self-management.

One of the ironies is that a major influence has been the US experience with ESOP (Employee Stock Ownership Plan) schemes. Following the trail of privatization advisers have been alternative radical adherents of ESOP, notably Daniel Ellerman (1990) who has presented a subsequent optimistic assessment of the potential, particularly in Poland and Hungary. Such proposals have been taken up in modified form by noted market socialists such as Ota Sik (1990). ESOPs are held to be a useful counter to the appropriation activities of the *nomenklatura* and a necessary complement to any worker control measures. Despite the existence of employee shareholdings legitimized by self-governing boards in some Polish firms, isolated experiments in the former Soviet Union and a great deal of interest in a number of countries, progress in this direction is likely to be limited in the short term. However some of the new governments may go for a wider 'give away' of shares as a mechanism to speed up the privatization process, as in Czechoslovakia.

NEW SOCIAL INTERESTS AND CONTRADICTIONS

Marketization and privatization, even when counterbalanced by more leftist reforms, are reshaping class interests and creating new social contradictions. There has been much talk of divisions between the new majorities for change and old 'conservatives'. Some commentators refer to the formation of a **new political class**, which is, at least in the case of Poland, 'composed of parts of formerly opposing camps . . . with similar social status (education, prestige, affluence) united by a feeling of responsibility for social peace and by support for economic reforms from above' (Staniszkis 1989: 39). The emergence of prominent Solidarity worker activists as new 'model citizen' entrepreneurs is indicative of this trend (Ost 1989). Opposing them are populists in Solidarity and in the old state apparatus who express the interests of social groups largely excluded from marketization, including young workers and pensioners.

In some respects there is a clear resemblance to previous 'new class' theories.[6] Some commentators (Clarke 1990: 20) still cling to the reductionist view that the social basis of state socialism is the stratum of intellectual workers. Political projects such as perestroika are held to mark the culmination of long-term trends which offer the dominant class 'a favourable opportunity to convert at least a portion of their present political and economic assets into new power resources within a more efficient and stable social system adapted to the imperatives of a scientific-technical revolution' (Flaherty 1990). This would involve alliances between the modernizing elements of the apparatus, 'knowledge elites' and emergent business strata against the traditional managerial elements of the *nomenklatura*, plus

15

sections of the working-class dependent on the old social and economic guarantees.

New alliances are definitely on the agenda, but continuity of political projects should not be exaggerated. New class theories always overestimated the social and political homogeneity of the so-called intelligentsia under state socialism. Any common interests among the overlapping layers of senior state employees had been overwhelmingly a function of the cohesion and power of the party-state apparatus itself. Similarly, notions of a new political class are too simple and too economistic. As real measures replace rhetoric, **reform** can no longer act as the factor of political cohesion. Staniszkis rightly notes that 'Though everyone supports reform, each group understands it differently' (1989: 43). Solidarity has already fallen apart, as the presidential elections showed; while the other group 'umbrella' grouping, the Czechoslovak Civic Forum, shows signs of going in the same direction and both major Hungarian political formations are unstable coalitions.

Staniszkis concludes from such developments that the new political class has no reliable social base. New forms of class politics will emerge, but this tends to present interests as economically pre-formed and given. We would prefer to argue that class interests need to be **socially constituted** in the new environment. Although it is an exaggeration to say that we shall soon be observing the development of classic left, right and centre formations in Poland and elsewhere (Lipski 1990: 93),[7] the key role in this discursive process **will** be played by political parties and ideologies. The other important point is that the more such systems break up the less monolithic the Eastern bloc is. Therefore the class and social formations are already beginning to diverge in significant respects. So, for example, it would be unwise to generalize too far from the former Soviet example where there was a much clearer conservative alliance based on the military-industrial complex.

Others are equally convinced that we are witnessing the return of traditional forms of class struggle. Burawoy (Chapter 6 in this volume) sees the new workers' councils in Hungary both as a reflection of otherwise unrepresented working-class interests and the embodiment of the socialist consciousness held back and distorted by the rituals of the old regime. Evidence can of course be seen in the increasing amount of strike action in Eastern Europe, with the more notable examples such as the Soviet miners' strikes described as 'perestroika from below' (Friedgut and Siegelbaum 1990). Such events can be seen even more dramatically as embodying a logic of markets and class mobilization which can only end in 'the alternative of either working class power or the restoration of capitalism' (Filtzer, Chapter 4 in this volume).

Our judgement would be somewhat different. New independent working-class interests are certainly showing welcome signs of emerging. For example, Burawoy is right to highlight the role of Hungarian workers' councils in stepping into the breach left by the declining and compromised trade unions. But he equally correctly observes that at the moment they conceive of their role in terms of the factory rather than the wider organization of society.[8] Given the economic and political uncertainties in this period of transition, it may not be possible to go further than identifying some of the contours of a new politics of production on the road to the market.

First, there are both rival organizational forms and centres of power in the enterprise itself. Employee interests will, for the foreseeable future, be articulated by competing organizations, notably the old trade unions, independent unions and hybrid bodies such as workers' councils. In some cases the former, such as the OPZZ in Poland, who have retained a surprisingly high membership, are learning how to be oppositionists again before someone else does it for them. Enterprises also become a focus for competing interests because of the uneven progress in changing the patterns of ownership and control. Despite partial privatization and attempts to empower a managerial elite, bargaining between enterprise and state and the various work-place actors remains pervasive. As Kozek's study of Poland shows. 'Only in one fifth of the tested cases did the management have personal and decisive influence upon the functioning of a given enterprise. In all other cases, the management and the self-governing body, i.e. the workers' council, and, to a lesser extent, the trade unions, shared the power' (1990: 7). The danger being that each centre of power blocks the other one, with collective decisions and undetermined responsibilities.

Second, new issues in work-place conflict will combine with some of the old forms of production politics in a way that is still unique. Burawoy (1985) previously observed that given the inseparability of politics and economics under state socialism, any work-place struggle immediately revealed the transparency of power relations. He shows (Chapter 6 in this volume) that this is partially changing as each sphere gains a corresponding autonomy. Certainly we can expect that conflicts will increasingly reflect issues 'internal' to management and employees. Most notably there will be attempts to destroy the existing forms of worker autonomy in the labour process, as industries are forced to promote rationalization programmes (Hethy 1990). But the legacy of the past cannot be shaken off too easily. For example, many workers still see the state as protector and intervening factor in industrial disputes.

Third, the absence of systematic mechanisms to resolve or at least institutionalize conflicts and rival interests will give production politics an especially unpredictable and dangerous character. The establishment of bodies such as the Hungarian National Council for the Co-ordination of Interests, which brings together large and small employer organizations, co-operatives, private craftsmen, retail traders and trade unions, is one attempt to deal with that problem. In part this is a reflection of the wider problem of the consequences of the unravelling of hated and unsuccessful central powers. But without anything to take their place, the result will be a 'savage pluralism' (Carlo 1989).

There are therefore tremendous uncertainties in this transition period, both within and between countries; certainly too many to predict confidently the end product. Talk of a simple restoration of capitalism is premature, as are attempts to revive convergence theory in new clothes. The societies fashioned from the transition will very likely be market economies. But as that term already includes societies as diverse as Sweden, Japan and the United States, there is considerable room for variations and hybrid forms of ownership, control, planning and work organization. If this is the practical consequence of the collapse of command economies, what theoretical lessons can be learned for the possibilities of a socialist labour process?

A SOCIALIST LABOUR PROCESS?

All societies have labour processes in which people use instruments of labour to act purposefully on natural or raw materials. What gives them their unique characteristics is the combination with the principal dynamic of a given mode of production. So under capitalism it is a unity of the labour process with the valorization process, capital purchasing labour power and using its ownership of the means of production to transform labour power into profitable labour. Burawoy (1985: 13–14) makes a similar point in a different way in referring to the combination of social relations into which men and women enter to produce useful things (relations in production), with the exploitation of labour by capital through the latter's appropriation and distribution of the surplus product (relations of production). While there are no necessary features of the labour process in terms of specific ways of using skills, or forms of discipline and reward, Marx points to two preconditions. Work is under the general control of capital and the product is its property. This separation of the immediate producer from the means of production therefore sets constraints on the ability of capital to mobilize the creativity of labour and to significantly dispense with hierarchical relations.

State socialism shows that there is an alternative to capitalism. Here the labour process is combined with a specific political economy in which a dominant class based on the party-state apparatus appropriates and distributes the surplus product through centralized command planning. The dynamics of that relationship – plan bargaining, shortages and bureaucratic uncertainties – as under capitalism have varied forms and effects. But it does produce distinctive labour process characteristics as the dual control system of managers and party mobilize to meet production targets through a variety of mechanisms including an employment relationship based on a 'social contract' with the work-force; a technical division of labour frequently dependent on high degrees of flexibility and work-group autonomy; piece-work and normative reward systems.

Unfortunately state socialism has been a failure both in its own terms and as an alternative to capitalism. Though in theory, production is directed towards use values, state socialism cannot escape the inherent contraditions of an administratively determined command economy, with its attendant and generic waste of human and technical resources. Therefore we are forced to ask whether there can be another socialist alternative.

This takes us back to the socialist tradition, and the differing definitions as to how work within a socialist society should be organized. Within this tradition we can identify a number of alternative visions. These can be classified as pre-modern capitalist utopias; handicraft and craft communitarianism; and differing interpretations of what is neutral or indeed liberatory in technology, capital and labour within large-scale modern industry.

Utopian Socialists in the nineteenth century were either aiming to provide exemplars of 'model factory regimes' for other capitalists to follow, such as Owen; or detailed prescriptions for work in the new society, such as Fourier. Such visions and model communities remained tied to capitalist social relations, concerned with improving workers' conditions, education, job variety and choice – but not abolishing private ownership. Fourier, for example, wrote strongly against compulsory labour within capitalism, and the need for the future society to be based on associative labour (a principle taken up by Marx) where work was 'attractive', 'pleasurable and varied', conducted by 'bands of friends' in 'clean workshops', with tasks rotated 'about eight times a day', on the grounds that it was impossible to sustain enthusiasm for longer than an hour and a half or two hours.

However, there was a belief in the absolute necessity for the division of labour to be 'carried to the last degree', and therefore job rotation was between strictly divided jobs (Fried and Sanders 1964: 148–9). The utopians were in favour of science and the division of labour, and concerned with improvements in conditions and not transformation of relations of production. They were modern in their concern with science, and in that respect closer to classical Marxism, than socialists who identified with handicrafts, old and new, and forms of occupational community based on craft autonomy.

Handicraft visions of William Morris or the later Guild Socialists have deep roots in English industrial culture, and are deeply anti-state and scale in orientation. Work is given high moral value; it is central to life, but should be skilled and varied. Morris sought to recreate medieval crafts (carpet-making, weaving, jewellery, metal-work, glass-work) in a company were workers were thoroughly trained. He sought the restoration of conception and execution, to 'draw out the workman's initiative and intellectual power' (Thompson 1977: 105). Morris's definition of socialism was strongly against Fabian state socialism – the cult of the expert evident in the Webbs, Shaw, Wells and Stalinism of the 1930s (Callaghan 1987). He was against the specialization of labour, especially mental and manual polarization, and the deskilling and degrading effects of work in modern industry.

He was, however, aware that his company, radical as it was, could not be prefigurative of the future. Indeed, despite attempts at overcoming the capitalist division of labour within capitalism, his workers had to specialize, otherwise 'I should have disqualified them from earning their living elsewhere' (Morris, in Thompson 1977: 105). Socialist demonstrations are not islands.

Handicraft ideologies stressed the values of independence and craftsmanship, and were not necessarily opposed to property, as working in small workshops maintained the ideal of future ownership and independence. Examining syndicalism in French social thought, Ridley (1970: 16) noted:

> the syndicalist utopia clearly reflected the individualist, anarchist outlook of the craftsman as well as the familiar patterns of industry. Engaged as many workers were in small workshops, they tended naturally to think in terms of small-scale organisation. Self-regulation was not hard to visualise in a society where the factory itself was small and the worker, skilled in the techniques of production, capable of overlooking the tasks of industrial management . . . . Such workers were no more attracted by the vision of state ownership than by the economic system under which they lived. The anarchist and the liberal, petit-bourgeois pictures of the society are in some ways very similar. Both emphasise individual liberty. The liberals advocated the wide distribution of property, the syndicalists proclaimed the even wider distribution of industrial control.

Labour process visions of the future society informed by craft or handicraft production systems are therefore not one-dimensional. They can be truly petit-bourgeois, emphasizing autonomy through property ownership, not just mobile craft skills; they can also seek independence from the highly differentiated collective labourer and hierarchical labour process of modern industry – a journeyman vision of mobile skills and autonomy. On the other hand they can address questions of economic freedom and social equality which have 'considerable importance for the labour movement' (Ridley 1970: 16). They are anti-state, anti-big business and question the organization of production based on scientific or systematic principles. Communitarian, small-scale federalist economic and social principles flow from these employment forms. They can be reactionary and backward-looking in as much as they are formed on the exclusiveness of craft, and unable to resist the dynamic movement of modern capitalism, in particular the collectivizing and differentiating forces inside large-scale industry.

Conversely modern-industry, with its scale, machinery, capital intensity and hierarchically organized collective labour process holds a central place in Marxist conceptions of work in the future society. Marx, Engels and the entire classical tradition that followed them – Kautsky, Lenin, Trotsky, Gramsci – placed modern-industry at the centre of their analysis of capitalism, and the prospects for socialism.

21

Handicrafts were transitional, reactionary forms of work organization; future prescriptions for work organization were bound by what
was determined by large-scale industry. Marx saw large-scale industry
as bringing together and organizing labour and as progressive in a
way that artisan or small-scale production was not. By its very nature
it necessitates changes in work and complete adapability of the
individual, destroying the old detailed labourer and bringing into
being fully socialized labour. Similarly Marx saw modern industry
progressively destroying the differences between sex, age and other
divisions in the work-force, and hastening the decline of the reserve
army of unskilled labour.

There is within this classical literature tension over what constitutes permanent and transitional elements of large-scale industry.
Capital, in bringing into production science, mathematics and
technology, is drawing from the general stock of civilization and
human knowledge, and hence introducing something universal and
more permanent than the class prejudices and despotic work rules of
individual employers. It was moving beyond the traditionalism and
anti-scientific character of handicrafts. It was uniting labour with
civilization. In so far as modern industry forced this unity, and Marx
saw this as its special feature, then it had progressive qualities
necessary for the future socialist society. The problem with capitalism
was that such universal forces were bound by distorting and constrain-
ing capitalist relations. Socialism would not smash the fruits of this
marriage – machinery, scale and authority – but take them over for its
own ends. It would not do away with central direction, planning and
co-ordination, but replace the authority of the market-place with the
authority of 'social' production. Socialism would take-over the means
of production under changed ownership. Within the anarcho-
syndicalist tradition state socialism did not democratize or liberate the
worker in production, but merely replaced one authority with
another. For William Morris Fabian socialism did nothing to
challenge the capitalist labour process. For the classical Marxist
tradition, the productivity gains of capitalism, and the collectivization
and socialization of labour, had somehow to be preserved as these
were the fruits of civilization as well as capitalism.

In so far as Marxism saw the future through modern industry, and
not an alternative base, such as the handicrafts, then a necessarily
ambiguous view of socialism emerges. Whereas it is possible to have
and hold together two class ideologies inside handicraft and craft
communities – the liberal and anarchist, the ideal of ownership and

the autonomy of craftsmanship. Modern industry's competing class ideologies are at once starker (between owners and non-owners) and less clear-cut (within non-owners). The avenue of independent ownership is reduced, and this is why the classical Marxists saw it as progressive. Not only does it diminish the number of employers – and abolish individual capitalists through corporate forms of ownership – but it also reduces the prospects for artisans, proletarianizes, concentrates and binds labour into forced co-operative, collective and hence 'social' production. The problem is, of course, that it also creates new hierarchies, polarizes mental and manual labour, fragments labour, divides managers and owners, and in general produces more competing modes of authority and class ideologies than in handicraft production.

We have the rise of organizational specialists, experts, professional managers – what Hilferding called the 'new middle class'; we have the bifurcation of labour into skilled, white-collar/manual and productive/unproductive camps; and differentiation in owners. In other words, modern industry does not have a single authority or a homogeneous face, but a complex set of interests. The classical tradition, as we describe below, imposed on modern industry one-dimensional imperatives (typically drawn from the determinancy of technology) and hence completely underestimated and competing claims for authority of different groups. Work-place struggles of the twentieth century, over questions of workers' control and democracy, have been within the collective labourer, as much as against capital. The classical tradition could see modern industry only as simplifying class conflict and assisting socialism's future, by treating as absolute what was relative, taking as given what was contested, accepting the authority of scale, technology and capital, rather than sectional interests of a divided collective labourer.

Engels, for example, could not dissociate large-scale industry from the imperative of central authority, hence any criticism of authority, any attempt to suggest different ways of managing, was seen as non-rational and reactionary: 'Wanting to abolish authority in large-scale industry is tantamount to wanting to abolish industry itself, to destroy the power loom in order to return to the spinning wheel' (Engels, quoted in Kumar 1978: 323). The emergence of systematic forms of management were equally hard to dissociate from large-scale industry. Taylorism, instead of being treated as an ideology of the new middle class in corporate industry (Meiksins 1984), or 'a capitalist ideology' (Braverman 1974) or indeed a sectional ideology of professional engineers (Larson 1977), was seen as representing 'science and rationality' and hence civilizing forces necessary for socialism. Lenin, despite criticizing Taylorism's effect on the health of workers, undertook no thoroughgoing critique, but rather 'saw it as the last word of modern science in the organisation of the labour process' (Sirianni 1982: 255). As we argued earlier this helped legitimize a Soviet scientific-management whose effects clearly enhanced managerial control. In the 1920s critics of the Russian party's enthusiasm for Fordism who inquired 'about the monotony of labour, depersonalized and despiritualized by the conveyor belt', were criticized by Trotsky as being reactionary and 'directed against the division of labour and against machinery in general . . . . It is necessary that human labour produce the maximum possible quantity of goods' (Sirianni 1982: 256). Stalin's maxim that technique decides everything was a distortion of Marxism, but also very close to aspects of the classical tradition which lacked any critical awareness of the social construction of technology, choice of work organization, and was too wary of any criticism of conditions of production as being backward-looking or anarchist. Stalinist forced industrialization and Stakhanovism of the 1930s are in part the particular product of Russia's isolation and the failure of revolution in the West. But we cannot explain everything in terms of this societal context or special circumstances. Worker's control, self-management and reward and meaning through work were not subjects for systematic treatment by Lenin, Trotsky or the classical tradition mesmerized by capitalist large-scale industry as possessing essential imperatives, rather than competing interest groups that needed to be reconciled through political debate.

What is evident in the classical tradition is the fatalism, automaticity, technological determinism and general misunderstanding of the ways in which work could be organized. This is not surprising because analysis comes from the imperatives of structure and functions, or forms of organizing relevant to a particular time and place, but not necessarily universal. Too much attention is paid to formal ownership and systems of administration, too little to the details of constructing a labour process which is not only 'social' in a general sense, but rewarding and enriching for the individual. Too many cues are taken from the evolution of capital, management and technology; not enough to labour's pattern of differentiation and control. As mentioned above, worker's control struggles, factory occupations and general control movement from below have not simply been about a clash with management, but organizing the collective labourer. Workers' plans, for example, occurred in some industries in Britain in the late 1970s and were produced through combined committees of shop stewards representing all grades of the collective labourer, but were only ever more than paper tigers where technical and professional engineers were not a significant force on such committees.

Plans at Lucas Aerospace, Vickers and C. A. Parsons were largely sponsored by technical workers. As strategy – drawing-up designs, inventories of skills and machinery, possible new products – it utilized concerns central to professional and technical grades, rather than the whole work-force. Tensions within the combines – especially between manual crafts and technical groups – rather than straightforward opposition from employers contributed to the 'failure' of this strategy to wrest planning from management (Wainwright and Elliott 1982; Smith 1987). Any socialist strategy needs to confront this question of organizing the competing claims of different groups within the collective labourer.

The basis of individuality is also confused. Marx, on the one hand, praises the revolutionary character of modern industry which inhibits specialization and detail-labour, demands that labour be flexible, technically trained and educated and adaptable to the technological dynamism of industry. Such dynamism is constrained by capitalist social relations, but under socialism would become a basis for the full development of the all-rounded, constantly learning, flexible worker. Individuality through work is the basis of socialism. On the other hand, the concrete struggles of workers within capitalism are over bettering conditions of work – and fundamentally reducing time at work and improving their material situation to develop their humanity. 'Once the worker's material situation has become better, he can consecrate himself to the education of his children; his wife and children do not need to go to the factory, he can cultivate his mind more, look after his body better, and he becomes a socialist without noticing it' (Marx, in McLellan 1977: 537). Here, the male breadwinner increases his individuality away from, not through work.

There is the tension between reducing hours to expand workers' free time – and one sphere of individuality; and the reward of labour within a differentiating work environment – a second sphere. The same tension persists in the literature on the future society, the 'flight from work', liberation through leisure, continuing campaigns to reduce the working week, which are all premised on the inherently unrewarding, and unattractive nature of work in modern industry which cannot be changed even under socialism (see Frankel 1987 for a review). Equally, there persist modern handicraft ideologies, stressing the potential of computer technology to break up large-scale industry, disperse production back to the community, workshop and home, and rekindle artisan culture by modern means. We have the possibility of work-place utopias within capitalism (Sabel 1982; Piore and Sabel 1984), but also prefigurative forms (Kumar 1978; Frankel 1987). In fact, the three visions of socialism are equally present in capitalism today, albeit under disguises and with different supports. While we do not endorse the flight-from-work and new craft romanticism, work-place struggles over control and planning do embrace important aspects of the socialist tradition on work, namely a concern to restore creativity and individuality to work. They also highlight the anti-state tradition, and the importance of socialism getting beyond single forms of ownership, administrative systems of representation, and a purely formal definition of social labour, to more direct, immediate and tangible forms of individual control, autonomy and creativity. The necessity for new forms of work to be located within a diversity of types of production necessarily takes us beyond the work-place.

POLITICAL ECONOMY: A DIFFERENT STARTING-POINT

If the earlier idea of combinations of the labour process in general with a specific system of production is right, to ask whether there can be a socialist labour process may be starting from the wrong point. The correct question is whether there can be a feasible socialist **economy**. As none exists we can only construct working models based on identified principles and empirical observation of capitalism and state socialism.

Traditionally, the most favoured alternative within the Marxist and Left tradition is self-management.[9] This has already been discussed as one of the policy options in current Eastern Europe debates, but at the moment practice is limited and fragmented. Here we are discussing it as a systemic and theoretical model such as that outlined in a labour process framework by Burawoy (1985: 13, 158). He envisages a different form of state-factory relations in which workers manage enterprises within overall state regulation of what is produced, with what materials and from what source, itself subject to planning inputs from below through factory councils.

Most writers within a Marxist tradition are now of course sensitive to the failures of command planning, but still attempt to deal with the problems through a combination of central planning plus workers' councils. The problem is that such a model from Marx to Burawoy,[10] tends to ignore how such arrangements deal with complex forms of economic co-ordination, decision-making on pricing and products and the like; as well the construction of plans, the harmonization of interests of producers and other social groups, as well as neglecting difficult issues of management and control.

Where some detail is provided there is little improvement. Mandel (1986; 1988) is a typical example. Responsibility for determining the basic plan framework would rest with annual congresses of delegates from workers' and other 'popular councils', with responsibilities for specific branches of production taken by industry-wide equivalent bodies. Any requirement for market transactions would be minimized by the 'withering away' of buying, selling and money, facilitated by the direct free distribution of basic goods. This flows from Marx's own anti-market views in which under socialism a system of labour equivalence would operate where money would be replaced by labour tokens, certificates of which could be exchanged for goods held in a common stock (see Elliot 1987 for more detail).[11] One traditional limitation has been the exclusion of other social groups from influence over economic decisions concerning production and distribution. Mandel allows consumers into the picture through their own democratically elected bodies which liaise with workers' councils on product mix. Showrooms would be a focus for testing products such as the six pairs of shoes Mandel believes consumers should have the right to receive.

Such proposals not only fail any feasibility test, but also do nothing, as Elson (1988: 25) observes, to avoid the problems inherent in existing central planning.[12] Workers' councils in each industry would still have to make decisions on resource allocation between enterprises, and 'self-managing' work-forces would still have an interest in plan bargaining aimed at increased inputs and reduced outputs, as indeed has been the case in Yugoslavia. Considered on a global scale, the inherent problems of central planning plus workers' councils as a **national** option pale into insignificance. With these kinds of problems associated with the 'self-management' model, it is hardly surprising that as Burawoy admits (1985: 19, 112) that it has been realized only for fleeting moments under unusual circumstances and may not even be possible for more than short periods.

The above critique is not aimed at wholly writing-off self-management. But it is important to scale down expectations and end the present confusion of purposes whereby it is expected to be a method of running an entire economy, a system of political power and a means of reversing the intra-organization division of labour. Self-management only makes sense as a form of internal democratic regulation of the enterprise, with the market acting as a test of efficiency of production and quality and pricing of products. Clearly such changes in power structures and decision-making have important implications for transforming employment relations and control within the labour process. However, even in this more limited mode, self-management is not appropriate for all sizes and forms of economic unit. For example, the Yugoslav experience indicates that such participatory mechanisms are much more likely to be effective where there is a high proportion of skilled workers (Rittersporn 1989). This reinforces experiences in capitalism of advanced forms of control from below emanating from skilled workers, and underlines the importance of skilled labour for a socialist project.

This qualification ties into a more general argument concerning a feasible socialist economy. To operate effectively any social formation requires a variety of forms of ownership and control, just as it requires a combination of planning and markets – Hodgson's (1984) 'impurity principle'. But there would also be a 'principle of dominance', that is the establishment of diverse forms of social ownership as the principal regulating force in the economy, with private ownership as a subordinate factor. However, any serious discussion would have to take into account questions of scale and proportion of production and the types of commodities more suited to one sort of ownership than another. Blackburn (1991) too makes a powerful case for new and varied forms of social ownership within socialized markets, though it is marred by a somewhat over-enthusiastic description of companies such as John Lewis as 'owned by their employees' (1991: 50).

Such a recognition does not make identification of a specific form of socialist labour process any easier. For example any degree of competition between socially owned enterprises and other economic forms means that the 'indeterminacy of labour potential' remains, though it will take a different form. Therefore the development of appropriate forms of control and of management cannot be escaped. It is not enough to go on repeating the basic distinction between (capitalist) control and (socially necessary) co-ordination.

But free from the antagonistic social relations and the separation of workers from the means of production built into capitalism and state socialism, the potential is there for transforming the labour process. This could involve maximizing the development of human-centred technologies which build on workers' skills; task designs which combine conception and execution; and democratic decision-making. Constraints must still be acknowledged. There can be no utopia where everyone will have creative and satisfying work. But ways of minimizing routine work and expanding creative and rewarding labour, highlighted in the handicraft perspective on socialism, are worthwhile ideals. Nevertheless, visions of technology as a total fix, eliminating drudgery and simultaneously enhancing creativity – as suggested by post-industrial socialist utopians, such as Gorz – do not seem feasible to us. The impact of technology is likely to remain contingent, expanding and reducing skills, and we therefore cannot expect some form of 'technologized communism' to solve the problems of work. A realistic and radical labour process analysis must recognize the limits of the labour process itself as a focus for human emancipation.

NOTES

1 Some object that the term 'class' cannot be used because the 'state socialist elite' is neither closed nor in a position to become self-sustaining because of the absence of legal ownership or inheritance (see for example Davis 1989). But no ruling class operates on the basis of total closure and we should not underestimate the extent to which inheritance of power and privilege is a systematic feature of such societies.

2 Interestingly this comment comes from a study of the labour process in Egyptian state enterprises, which the authors suggest replicate many of the features of the traditional state socialist model.

3 The first phase of Solidarity-led revolt in Poland did lead to new political developments, but economic policy remained largely unaltered.

4 See for example the round-up of prospects in 'A business guide to Central and Eastern Europe', *The Times* 6 November 1990.

5 Surveys revealed that the vast majority of workers' councils – essential back-ups for any projected system of self-management – were rubber-stamp bodies barely consulted concerning management decisions (Wolinicki 1989: 73).

6 New class theorists include Diljas (1957) and more recently Konrad and Szelenyi (1979).

7 As head of the as yet relatively marginal Polish Socialist Party, Lipski clearly has an interest in the 'reversion' to left–right divisions.

8 Burawoy also acknowledges the role played by members of the Hungarian

29

Democratic Forum in facilitating the development of the councils.

9 Whether Marx himself favoured a self-management model is debatable. For a defence of Marx as the 'founding father of Workers' self-governance', see Elliot (1987). As Elliot admits the problem lies in whether Marx's penchant for central planning and dismissal of markets under socialism is compatible with self-management.

10 The neglect of such issues by Burawoy arises particularly out of treating factory regimes (of which collective self-management is one type) as a form of production politics.

11 The inequalities of such exchange would be overcome in a higher phase of communist society.

12 While Elson's critique of productionist bias is valuable, her own proposals for 'socialized markets' are, if anything, equally problematic.

REFERENCES

Bauman, Z. (1989) 'Poland: on its own', *Telos* 79, special issue, Perestroika in Eastern Europe: 10–61.

Bettelheim, C. (1976) *Class Struggles in the USSR: First Period, 1917-23*, New York: Monthly Review Press.

Bettelheim, C. (1974) *Chinese Revolution and Industrial Organisation in China*, London: Monthly Review Press.

Bielasiak, J. (1989) 'Self-management and the politics of reform: Poland in the 1980s', *Economic and Industrial Democracy* 10 (3), Eastern Europe: 203–30.

Blackburn, R. (1991) 'Fin de siècle: socialism after the crash '*New Left Review* 185: 5–67.

Bogdan, J. (1989) 'New technology and work organisation in Hungary', *Work Employment and Society* 3 (2): 239–47.

Bottomore, T. B. and Rubel, M. (1963) *Karl Marx, Selected Writings in Sociology and Social Philosophy*, Harmondsworth: Penguin.

Braverman, H. (1974) *Labor and Monopoly Capital*, London: Monthly Review Press.

Burawoy, M. (1985) *The Politics of Production*, London: Verso.

Burawoy, M. and Lukács, J. (1989) 'What is socialist about socialist production? Autonomy and control in a Hungarian steel mill', in S. Wood (ed.) *The Transformation of Work?*, London: Unwin Hyman.

Burawoy, M. and Lukács, J. (1991) *The Radiant Past: Ideology and Reality in Hungary's Transition from Socialism to Capitalism*.

Callaghan, J. (1987) 'Marxism, Fabianism and the State', in G. Duncan (ed.) *Capitalism and the State*, Cambridge: Cambridge University Press.

Carlo, A. (1989) 'Contradictions of perestroika', *Telos* 79, special issue, Perestroika in Eastern Europe: 29–46.

Clarke, S. (1990) 'Crisis of socialism or crisis of the state?', *Capital and Class* 42 (Winter): 19–29.

Davies, R. W. (1990) 'Gorbachev's socialism in historical perspective', *New Left Review* 179: 5–27.

Davis, H. (1989) 'Crisis and conflict in Eastern European state socialism', in R. Scase (ed.) *Industrial Societies: Crisis and Division in Western*

Capitalism and State Socialism, London: Unwin Hyman.

Diljas, M. (1957) *The New Class*, New York: Praeger.

Dunayevskaya, R. (1975) *Marxism and Freedom*, London: Pluto Press.

Ellerman, D. P. (1990) 'Report on a socialist reform tour: Poland, Hungary, Soviet Union and Yugoslavia', *Economic and Industrial Democracy* 11 (2): 205–16.

Elliot, J. E. (1987) 'Karl Marx: founding father of workers' self-governance?', *Economic and Industrial Democracy* 8 (3): 292–321.

Elson, D. (1988) 'Market socialism or socialisation of the market?', *New Left Review* 172: 3–44.

Flaherty, P. (1990) 'Perestroika and Soviet neo-liberalism', *New Politics* 111 (1): 74–9.

Frankel, B. (1987) *The Post-Industrial Utopians*, Oxford: Polity Press in association with Basil Blackwell.

Fried, A. and Sanders, R. (eds) (1964) *A Documentary History of Socialist Thought*, Edinburgh: University of Edinburgh Press.

Friedgut, T. and Siegelbaum, L. (1990) 'Perestroika from below: the miners' strike and its aftermath', *New Left Review* 181: 5–32.

Gorz, A. (ed.) (1976) *The Division of Labour: The Labour Process and Class Struggle in Monopoly Capitalism*, Brighton: Harvester Press.

Grancelli, B. (1989) 'Participation in economic management and the second economy: lessons from the Soviet case', *Economic and Industrial Democracy* 10 (3), special issue Economic and Industrial Democracy in Eastern Europe: 379–92.

Harastzi, M. (1977) *Worker in a Worker's State*, Harmondsworth: Penguin.

Henley, J. S. and Ereisha, M. M. (1989) 'State ownership and the problem of the work incentive', *Work Employment and Society*, (1): 65–87.

Hethy, L. (1990) 'Hungary's system on the way towards a market economy', paper to conference on Work, Employment and European Society: Integration and Convergence, University of Bath, June.

Hodgson, G. (1984) *The Democratic Economy*, Harmondsworth: Penguin.

Knights, D. and Wilmott, H. (eds) (1990) *Labour Process Theory*, London: Macmillan.

Konrad, G. and Szelenyi, I. (1979) *Intellectuals on the Road to Class Power*, Brighton: Harvester.

Kornai, J. (1980) *The Economics of Shortage*, Amsterdam: North-Holland.

Kornai, J. (1986) *Contradictions and Dilemmas: Studies on the Socialist Economy and Society*, Cambridge, Mass: MIT Press.

Kozek, S. (1990) 'An industrial conflict in Poland at the time of transition from a state economy to a free market economy', paper to conference on Work, Employment and European Society: Integration and Convergence, University of Bath, June.

Kumar, K. (1978) *Prophecy and Progress*, Harmondsworth: Penguin.

Lane, D. (1989) 'Social change, division and control in the USSR', in R. Scase (ed.) *Industrial Societies: Crisis and Division in Western Capitalism and State Socialism*, London: Unwin Hyman.

Larson, M. S. (1977) *The Rise of Professionalism: A Sociological Analysis*, Berkeley, Calif: University of California Press.

Lipski, J. J. (1990) 'Notes on Poland in transition', *New Politics* 111 (1): 88–94.

Mandel, E. (1988) 'The myth of market socialism', *New Left Review* 169 (May–June): 108–20.

Mandel, E. (1986) 'In defence of socialist planning', *New Left Review* 159 (September–October): 1–37.

Marx, K. (1973) *Grundrisse*, Harmondsworth: Penguin.

McLellan, D. (ed.) (1977) *Karl Marx: Selected Writings*, Oxford: Oxford University Press.

Meiksins, P. (1984) 'Scientific management and class relations: a dissenting view', *Theory and Society* 13: 177–209.

Nee, V. (1989) 'A theory of market transition: from redistribution to markets in state socialism', *American Sociological Review* 54 (5): 663–81.

Nikolic, M. (1989) 'Yugoslavia's failed perestroika', *Telos* 79, special issue, Perestroika in Eastern Europe: 119–28.

Nove, A. (1983) *The Economics of Feasible Socialism*, London: George Allen & Unwin.

Ost, D. (1989) 'The transformation of Solidarity', *Telos* 79, special issue, Perestroika in Eastern Europe: 63–94.

Piore, M. J. and Sabel, C. F. (1984) *The Second Industrial Divide*, New York: Basic Books.

Rakovski, M. (1977) 'Marxism and Soviet societies', *Capital and Class* 1: 83–105.

Ridley, F. F. (1970) *Revolutionary Syndicalism in France*, Cambridge: Cambridge University Press.

Rittersporn, G. (1989) 'Reforming the Soviet system', *Telos* 79, special issue, Perestroika in Eastern Europe: 9–28.

Rosefielde, S. and Quinn Mills, D. (1990) 'Transition shock: can the East get there from here?', *California Management Review*, summer: 9–21.

Sabel, C. (1982) *Work and Politics*, Cambridge: Cambridge University Press.

Sik, O. (1990) 'New perspectives on the theory of convergence', *Economic and Industrial Democracy* 11 (2): 167–78.

Sirianni, C. (1982) *Workers' Control and Socialist Democracy: The Soviet Experience*, London: Verso.

Smith, C. (1987) *Technical Workers*, London: Macmillan.

Staniszkis, J. (1989) 'The obsolescence of Solidarity', *Telos* 80: 37–50.

Stark, D. and Nee, V. (1989) 'Towards an institutional analysis of state socialism', in D. Stark and V. Nee (eds) *Remaking the Institutions of Socialism: China and Eastern Europe*, Stanford, Calif: Stanford University Press.

Stark, D. (1986) 'Rethinking internal labour markets: new insights from a comparative perspective', *American Sociological Review* 51 (August): 492–504.

Strinrati, D. (1990) 'A ghost in the machine: the state and the labour process in theory and practice', in D. Knights and H. Wilmott (eds), *Labour Process Theory*, London: Macmillan.

Thompson, E. P. (1977) *William Morris: Romantic to Revolutionary*, London: Merlin.

Thompson, P. (1990) 'Crawling from the wreckage: the labour process and the politics of production', in D. Knights and H. Wilmott (eds) *Labour Process Theory*, London: Macmillan.

Van Atta, D. (1989) 'A critical examination of brigades in the USSR', *Economic and Industrial Democracy* 10 (3), special issue, Economic and Industrial Democracy in Eastern Europe: 329–40.

Wainwright, H. and Elliott, D. (1982) *The Lucas Plan: A New Trade Unionism in the Making*, London: Allison & Busby.

Wallimann, I. and Stojanov, C. (1989) 'Social and economic reform in Bulgaria: economic democracy and problems of change in industrial relations', *Economic and Industrial Democracy* 10 (3), special issue, Economic and Industrial Democracy in Eastern Europe: 361–73.

Wolinicki, M. (1989) 'Self-government in Poland', *Telos* 80: 63–78.

Part II

COMPARING CAPITALISM AND STATE SOCIALISM

INTRODUCTION

The distinguishing features of capitalist and state socialist societies are numerous, but generally reduce to dichotomies between planning and market regulation, bureaucratic centralism versus personal control, command and scarcity versus overproduction and overconsumption. At the level of the labour process, however, we are faced with a number of paradoxes. State socialist *ideology* cloaks work in social and national ideals, tying workers to political goals and obligations beyond the narrow economic transactions of workers in capitalism. However, the actual *experience* of work in a 'workers' state' is one of economic instrumentalism similar to work within capitalism. The ideology of planning, regulation and bureaucratic efficiency also disguises a reality in which there are permanent shortages of skilled labour, materials and machinery, constant breakdowns and *ad hoc* revisions to central plans. Scientific management may be a proclaimed objective of state socialism, but in practice managers are forced to rely on workers' goodwill to maintain production, finding themselves without the environmental stability to standardize production along Taylorian lines. In other words, there are two faces to the labour process under state socialism – a proclaimed ideal and an opposite practice. If we are serious about exploring the differences between the two systems, we have to ensure that we are comparing the *experience* and not the rhetoric of socialism and capitalism. This is particularly important because there are also two faces at work within capitalism – the equal exchange between capital and labour, disguised by the wage form, and the reality of managerial control and authority over the actual labour process. This duality is manifest in the recurrent stress on workers' participation, job enrichment and involvement as proclaimed objectives of management, and yet the continued exclusion of labour from significant decision-making power. Both chapters in this part of the book are careful to compare the empirical reality of the labour process of the two systems, and not their idealized image.

The problem of comparative analysis at this very general level is also tackled. Comparing *systems* requires some societal context, and the two chapters have this focus. Otfried Mickler (Chapter 3), in particular, uncovers the diversity of state socialist regimes, especially between those which industrialized late under external guidance from Stalin's Russia – such as Bulgaria, Hungary and Poland – and those, like the former East Germany and Czechoslovakia, that had industrialized along capitalist lines before the imposition of Stalinist industrialization in the post-war period. The significance of these differences for the management of the labour process and organization of work are fully discussed by Mickler. But perhaps a bigger obstacle to comparative cross-national research in the current period is the difficulty of accommodating rapid change. Categorical statements about the nature of state socialism or particular countries are difficult to sustain in a period of radical reform, and the authors of these two chapters are careful to situate their analysis within a fluid framework, pointing out tendencies and options, not definite paths and directions.

David Stark (Chapter 2) examines the role of non-bureaucratic economic forms in both systems, the informal economy of capitalism and the second economy of state socialism. Both modernization theory and Marxist political economy, he suggests, argue that sectors of employment outside of large-scale industry are essentially anachronistic to capitalism, destined to be absorbed or eliminated by the progressive concentration of capital. Stark suggests that this perspective on the informal sector in capitalism has an equivalent in views of the second economy in state socialism by those who see it as essentially doomed to succumb to the encroachment of the state sector or else as a foreign body, brought in from the West, and anathema to socialism. Start rejects both these readings of the persistence of small-scale, informal economic activity, preferring to see both concentration and fragmentation occurring together, formalization and informalization being mutually reinforcing. With this perspective, he suggests not the withering away of the informal in the two systems, but its dynamic persistence.

He suggests, however, that the two forms of informality serve different functions in the two systems, and he is particularly interested in examining whether the second economy, which is a sphere of economic activity relatively autonomous from the state, can be a transition belt for a fundamental remaking of the economic institutions of socialism. In Hungary, his country case study, the second economy not only acts as a safety-valve for bureaucratic inefficiencies and as a provider of increased consumer choice, but also gives producers choice – self-employment, small partnerships, franchise arrangements, employment in co-operatives or as entrepreneurs. All these options exist alongside employment in state enterprises. He suggests that the second economy provides a *learning* experience necessary for a full-blown transition to a market economy. It is prefigurative of the restoration capitalist relations, and acts *against* the state sector, and not, like the informal economy of capitalism, in keeping with market principles. Stark suggests that Hungary may be moving away from a formal and informal economy, to a 'socialist mixed economy', although he is cautious about a simple transition to this new state.

Mickler's chapter uses multi-layered comparisons that engage with different levels of analysis – the system, the society and the workplace. He examines the introduction and application of computerized numerical control (CNC) machine-tools within enterprises across a range of state socialist societies and in West Germany, and is concerned to explore differences in their use and the possible reasons for these differences. He does this by examining a number of hypotheses. First, he notes that the world market for machine-tools changed in the 1970s, becoming more competitive and subject to differentiated demand, where quality and customization were more important than standardized machines. In this global climate, mass production of machine-tools was risky, and manufacturers needed to produce in smaller batches. These global market trends, he suggests, favoured working practices where there was a high degree of co-operation within the collective labourer and between management and workers. He is therefore interested in testing whether these global forces affected all the countries in the same way. Here there is a clear difference between all state socialist societies and his capitalist example of former West Germany. Mass production of machine-tools continued in the East because of the shortages of capital goods, but declined in West Germany, because of its exposure to the world market.

His second hypothesis tests the Aix Group theories about 'societal effects' on technology, in particular how its introduction and application is shaped by a country's vocational training, national employment structure and industrial relations system. These *institutional* arrangements mediate system requirements and universal forces such as technology. Here Mickler notes that Czechoslovakia and East Germany share with West Germany similar training patterns – relations between machinists and technicians are co-operative, because they share a common craft background and are part of a homogenous occupational community. They clearly differ from more centralized and Tayloristic control patterns evident in the late industrializers, such as Hungary and Poland, where training and the division of labour is more segmented and heterogeneous. Mickler distinguishes two methods of using CNC technologies – one which enhances and involves the skills of the operators, what he calls 'workshop-related programming', the second, extends the hierarchy of control and division of labour, removing skills from the machinists and monopolizing these in programming departments, this he terms 'techno-centric or Taylorist programming'.

His second hypothesis is that societies where training patterns and workshop relations are more homogenous – like the former West and East Germany, and Czechoslovakia – are more likely to adopt 'workshop-related programming' than societies with rigid divisions of labour between machinists and programmers where 'techno-centric programming' is more likely. This is what 'societal effect' theories would predict. The results of the case studies support this hypothesis for the capitalist society, West Germany, but in the case of the four state socialist societies – Poland and Hungary, and Czechoslovakia and East Germany – something like the reverse of the societal effect thesis occurred. New technologies in the latter two countries were used to extend managerial control through techno-centric programming, while in the former two, workshop programming and co-operation between programmers and machinists existed. Mickler explains these contradictions by suggesting that in Hungary and Poland, despite bureaucratic centralism the 'shortage economy' forces managers to depend heavily upon workers' skills and co-operation, whereas the relatively greater stability of the East German and Czechoslovak economies allowed management to use the technologies to extend their control over machinists and centralize programming knowledge in the technical offices. Such a conclusion points to the importance of introducing both *system* characteristics and specific *societal* features into cross-national organizational analysis, and is a corrective to the relatively undynamic nature of the Aix Group's approach. Mickler concludes his chapter with an updating of developments in Germany since its absorption of the former GDR.

2

BENDING THE BARS OF THE IRON CAGE

Bureaucratization and informalization in capitalism and socialism[1]

David Stark

INTRODUCTION

Across the diverse societies of contemporary state socialism a second economy is growing in the shadows of the central plan. From Hungary to Hunan, peasants manage decollectivized farms or cultivate household plots after work on co-operatives or collectives, private artisans run shops and transport goods, and manual workers and white-collar employees moonlight in construction, manufacturing, service and repair. This chapter addresses the question of whether and how this second economy of income-generating activity outside the boundaries of the formal, centrally directed economy of contemporary state socialism can be compared to the informal economy operating outside the officially institutionalized rules and regulations that govern the employment relation in the formal economy of capitalist society.

Until recently, the starting-point for such a comparison would have been the assumption that the private entrepreneurial activity of the second economy was alien to state socialism. Official ideology and Western analysts alike portrayed petty commodity production as a relic of a pre-socialist past: self-employment and other forms of small-scale production were hold-overs from a previous era inevitably replaced by (depending on the perspective) the superiority of socialist ownership, the technical efficiencies of large-scale production, or the irrepressible onslaught of proletarianization throughout the world system. For others, the second economy was not a hold-over from the past but a transplant from a competing social system: the private character of second economy production, its greater cost sensitivity, and its market orientation all bore the indelible mark of capitalism.

Whether as cancer or as cure, the second economy was foreign tissue in the socialist body and its growth the sign of capitalism as communism's failure. In either view, further development along a socialist trajectory would preclude the expansion of the second economy.

These assumptions about state socialism find striking parallels in the received wisdom about the tendencies of Western market economies in which the forms of petty commodity production, self-employment and various unregulated activities now often embraced under the label 'informal economy' were, likewise until recently, seen as alien to modernizing capitalism. Whether conceptualized as the laws of concentration and centralization, the dynamics of modernization, or the logic of rationalization, at the centre of modern capitalism were processes that, while differentiating functions, homogenized organizational forms. For the unilinear models of Marxism and modernization theory alike, processes of informalization were backward looking, surviving in pockets of tradition or of outdated modes of production as yet untouched by the inevitably all-embracing sweep of large-scale industrial production, corporate forms, legal norms and bureaucratized employment. Marxist, Weberian and Parsonsian analysts could agree that the problem for comparative analysis of the informal sector was essentially a question of timing and speed: destined for disappearance, in which social system would the informal economy be eradicated sooner?

Research during the 1980s, however, suggests an alternative interpretation of the relationship between modernity and informality in which proletarianization and informalization grow in tandem rather than through mutual displacement. Studies in Third World economies, for example, indicate that rates of activity in urban petty commodity production have remained stable throughout the recent period of accelerated industrialization (Portes and Sassen-Koob 1987; Rogerson 1985; Peattie 1982; Moser 1978). Far from homogenization, the growth of industrial wage labour generates diverse patterns of organizational forms as households and firms[2] adopt informal employment strategies (subcontracting, outcontracting, homeworking, undocumented work, etc.) to mitigate the consequences of the process of proletarianization itself (Portes 1983; Roberts 1989). Findings that informal activity shows little sign of stagnation and decline in advanced capitalist societies[3] such as Italy (Capecchi 1989), Spain (Benton 1989), Belgium (Pestieau 1985), the Netherlands (Renooy 1984), Sweden (Hansson 1989), and the United States (Portes and Sassen-Koob 1987; Waldinger 1986) similarly suggest

that capitalist development may actually stimulate rather than eliminate the informal sector (Castells and Portes 1989). Employers turn
to informal subcontracting, outcontracting and industrial homeworking as alternatives to factory-based wage labour and its attendant
rights and benefits in even the most thoroughly modern sectors of the
economy (Pfeffer and Baron 1988; Lozano 1989).

The comparative analysis in this chapter takes its point of
departure from the insight suggested by such recent research that
informal economic activity is not anomalous but an integral feature of
modern capitalism. It argues analogously that the second economy is
not an alien element but one of the basic economic institutions of
contemporary state socialism. In so doing, it breaks with modernist
assumptions about the homogenization of economic life in rationalized forms. Not a hold-over from the traditional and the customary, informalization is a product of the modern and the bureaucratic.
East and West, informal economic activity is reproduced in counterpoint to rationalization and bureaucratization.

But we should not conclude from this simple comparison that
capitalism's informal economy and socialism's second economy are
functional equivalents or structural counterparts. Both informal economies are responses to bureaucratization; but because the sources,
loci and forms of rationalization differ across the two social systems,
the systemic consequences of informalization differ as well. As we
shall see, despite some important similarities between the informal
sector and the second economy, the two phenomena differ
fundamentally in their causes, their reproduction, and their economic,
political and social effects.

Explaining these similarities and differences requires a strategy of
comparative inquiry that analyses relations among institutions rather
than essentialist features of a society's institutional elements. In such
a relational analysis, to understand the distinctive patterns of informal economic activity under capitalism and socialism we must shift
our focus from the informal economies in themselves to the relationship between each informal economy and the formal economy with
which it coexists. Moreover, in the analytic strategy adopted here, at
the same time that we examine the patterns of relations among
institutions *within a system*, we also compare patterns of relations
across systems. In such a comparative analysis, the specificity of a
particular institution is given by its position within a configuration of
relations within and across systems. It is not the case that the
institutions of capitalism provide the standard against which those of

socialism (or vice versa) can be measured according to the degree of conformity or the direction of their convergence or divergence. Nor is it the case that the analyst brings some universal standard to produce a priori definitions that, for all their logical rigour, reflect only the *ad hoc* circumstances of the position of the analyst within the field of debate. Instead, the effort here is to use empirical materials and theoretical insights from both cases to construct a model in which the terms of comparison emerge as properties of the overall comparative configuration. In this way, the institutional specificity of each system is revealed through their simultaneous and mutual contrast.

In concrete terms, a relational analysis of informal economic activities requires systematic attention to key aspects of the formal economies alongside which they are reproduced. In the following investigation, informality is examined in relation to (1) the dominant form of bureaucratization and (2) the dominant mechanism that co-ordinates activities across firms in the formal economy. These analytic dimensions, it should be noted in advance, do not necessarily refer to mutually exclusive processes: as we shall see, one of the distinctive features of state socialism is that the dominant co-ordinating mechanism of the economy is itself bureaucratic. In short, if informalization responds to patterns of bureaucratization that differ both in scope and in type, we must develop concepts for the comparative study of bureaucratization before we can understand systemic differences in the dynamics (causes, processes and effects) of the informal economy in advanced capitalism and the second economy in state socialism.

Anticipating the argument all too briefly, in terms to be defined and elaborated below, in market economies, the classificatory codes of regulatory bureaucratization rationalize the relations between employers and workers inside the firm, establish and monitor basic standards governing the wage–labour transaction, and provide a legal institutional framework for the broader market mechanisms through which resources are channelled throughout the economy. Formulated by an emerging class of professionals who mediate class relations from positions inside private firms and state agencies, the adoption of these official codes is promoted by an alliance of these professionals with trade unions and state managers. In response to this regulatory bureaucratization, an informal economy operates according to principles disparate from those of the classificatory rules of the internal labour market but congruent with the market principles that co-ordinate the formal economy.

In the centrally planned economies of state socialism, by contrast, *redistributive bureaucratization* is the product of a new class project differing both in scope and type as rationalized bureaucratic instruments were introduced to displace rather than complement market processes. In a modern redistributive system, the allocation of resources throughout the economy is co-ordinated through centrally controlled budgetary mechanisms. Where informalization responds to such redistributive bureaucratization, the embryonic market relations of the second economy are incongruent with the bureaucratic principles that co-ordinate the formal economy, and in fact, stimulate the institutionalization of transactive market relations inside the socialist enterprise. As an alternative institution in which skills and effort often find a higher rate of return, the second economy increases the manoeuvrability of labour and provides an opportunity for an alliance between workers and a new class of entrepreneurs.

The relational methodology of a comparative institutionalist analysis thus turns our attention from superficial similarities between capitalism's informal economy and socialism's second economy to examine underlying similarities and differences between the second economy under state socialism and trade unions in capitalist societies. Whereas the rationalization of the employment relation under capitalism was often accompanied by an expansion of citizenship rights inside private firms, the emergence of more open transactive bargaining by labour in the socialist economy is accompanied by an expansion of property rights in statist organizations as well as in the second economy.

REGULATORY BUREAUCRATIZATION AND THE INFORMAL ECONOMY

Our analysis of the regulatory bureaucratization that characterizes market capitalism (in contrast to the redistributive bureaucratization of state socialism) begins with the non-controversial observation that the history of the employment relation in capitalist development is a story of increasing rationalization. At the century's turn there were no 'labour relations' between owners and workers where the inside subcontract specified payment for a given quality and volume of production, but left supervision, wages and working conditions to the discretion of the foreman/subcontractor (Nelson 1975). Since the days of the internal markets of the 'sweating' system, supervision has been bureaucratized and almost every aspect of the employment relation is now subject to bureaucratic regulation. In union and non-union settings, work is governed by rules, output measured by standardized performance indicators, grievances formalized, and hiring, firing and working conditions subject to state regulations. Where production was once governed by the patriarchal craftsmen's moral code of 'manly bearing' (Hinton 1973), we now find the personnel department's occupational codes for job evaluations and the human resource manager's codings of job satisfaction questionnaires.

It is in accounting for this transformation from subcontracting on internal markets to supervision in routinized hierarchies that analysts disagree. Some argue that the motive for and outcome of this bureaucratization has been increasing capitalist control over the labour force (Braverman 1974; Edwards 1979); others point to efficiency gains from economizing on transaction costs (Williamson 1985). Both control and efficiency theorists, however, agree in their portrayal of employers as the primary agent of the rationalization process. In contrast to both schools, recent empirical investigations by sociologists and social historians offer an explanation of the bureaucratizations of the employment relation that casts central roles for trade unions, professionals, and state agencies. Stark (1980), for example, argues that the timing and patterns of the introduction of scientific management are best explained when viewed as a new middle-class project led by industrial engineers against the initial resistance of industrialists, senior managers and shop-level foremen.

The diffusion of work measurement schemes pioneered by Frederick Winslow Taylor, unsophisticated by our own standards but none the less critical in charting the kinds of cognitive abstractions used in today's job evaluation programmes, required an alliance of industrial engineers, trade union leaders and state officials under wartime conditions after Taylor's death in 1915. Baron et al. (1986) similarly demonstrate that the second World War was the backdrop for a wave of bureaucratization as state agencies, with trade union support, encouraged (and indirectly subsidized) the proliferation of personnel departments, formalized job definitions, and standardized wage and skill classifications. Jacoby's (1985) historical overview likewise documents how trade union and personnel professionals advocated, and employers repeatedly resisted, the kinds of bureaucratic practices we now associate with internal labour markets. The study suggests a cyclical, though cumulative, process in which bureaucratic innovations articulated by middle-class reformers in one crisis are set aside in the intervening period and come to be institutionalized only in the subsequent crisis.

If crises such as war and depression provide the setting for remaking the economic institutions of capitalism (Block 1987), this rationalization has been undertaken by a set of new middle-class occupations in pursuit of their own self-perceived interests to establish and expand their autonomy in bureaucratizing organizations. Far from a set of 'empty places' waiting to be 'filled' by contradictory class occupants (Wright 1978), middle-class professionals have had an active role in creating and shaping their new positions through a professional project that carves a new class space by offering its services as the mediator of relations between classes and the referee of relations among market competitors. At stake for the new class professionals in the multi-sided class struggle is their claim to a monopoly of the means of classification. The regulatory bureaucratization that has rationalized the employment relation operates through a set of codes – systems of classification that delineate various categories of persons and practices, and demarcate boundaries of eligibility and liability.

The new middle-class professionals and officials affiliated with trade unions, personnel departments and regulatory state agencies specialize in developing the classificatory instruments used for making these bureaucratic taxonomies. Throughout the century, they have attempted to expand their autonomy by claiming that each occupied a unique role in mediating relations between workers and managers, and that the employment relation is best regulated by the formalized structures it promoted. Whether it be in the formalized grievance procedures of the AFL-CIO, in the scientific trappings of Frederick Taylor's time and motion studies, or in Alba Edwards's conviction that his census occupational categories would be an instrument of class harmonization (Conk 1979), we see the project of class mediation expressed in the modality of formalization and codification. These and other agents of formal institutionalization specialize in the production of rationalized conventions without which the bureaucratic regulation of employment would be impossible.

The use of such rationalized conventions to regulate employment inside the firm is perhaps best epitomized in the institution known as an 'internal labour market' – the set of formalized procedures governing hiring and lay-offs, routinizing incremental wage and salary rewards, and regulating promotion along graded job ladders (Doeringer and Piore 1971; Osterman 1984). These institutional practices are curiously labelled: internal labour *markets* are, in fact, a set of *internal bureaucratic rules* that operate according to a classificatory logic (Stark 1986). Eligibility for promotion or exemption from lay-offs, for example, depends on membership in designated categories – seniority, skill grades, etc. – in an official system of classification. In such a system, negotiations at the bargaining table, in personnel departments, or in the courts often centre on the construction of categorical membership, as can be seen in the recent negotiations to alter job classifications in the auto industry (Katz 1985) or the recent comparable worth controversy over job titles and occupational sex segregation (Hartmann 1985; Baron and Bielby 1986).

The outcomes of such classificatory struggles (Bourdieu and Boltanski 1981; Thévenot 1983; 1984) can have material consequences: these internal bureaucratic rules provide protection from the market as, for example, when those in higher seniority categories are insulated from lay-offs during times of market downturns. But regulatory bureaucratization can yield protection from the market even in firms and industries where workers cannot take advantage of the job ladders of internal labour markets. The bureaucratic rules that proscribe discrimination in hiring or arbitrariness in dismissal, that regulate occupational health and safety, that govern union representation and that determine eligibility for unemployment and accident compensation are made up of codes and classifications that protect workers from the market even as they rationalize the employment relation.

In the absence of this rationalizing process we cannot meaningfully speak of an informal economy. Strategies of informalization are a response to bureaucratization; they mark the limits of rationalization. As Castells and Portes (1989) argue in an important synthetic essay, the informal economy is the product of efforts to escape this institutionalized logic. But their definition of the informal economy as 'income-generating activity unregulated *by institutions of society*' (my emphasis) fails to capture the specifically rationalized, formalized nature of this bureaucratic regulation. Moreover, it obscures the fact that the informal economy is 'regulated' – not in the statutory sense but in a sociological sense – by the cultural conventions of family, kinship, ethnic or other institutions in which, as an economy, it is embedded.

Unlike the informal codes of everyday life (without which bureaucracies themselves would cease to function), bureaucratized conventions are rationalized in a dual sense of the word. Their codification is standardized and their rationale (however much misrecognizing actual intentions and effects) is made explicit.[4] These explicit rationalizations are both a resource and an object of struggle among contending groups and classes; the informal economy is a product of their circumvention. For these reasons, we define the informal economy as a process of income-generating activities *unregulated by rationalized conventions*, in a legal and social environment in which similar activities are so regulated.

Informalization is thus the counterpoint to documentation and codification. The self-employed house painter who works for cash payment to escape the tax codes; those who take informal employment because age alone, whether too young or too old, excludes them from the job ladders of the internal labour market; the female head of household on a family assistance programme who key-punches or stitches blouses at home at below the minimum wage to evade the provisions of the welfare code; the unemployed member of the United Auto Workers who drives a gypsy cab so as not be disqualified for unemployment compensation – it is these and not only illegal aliens who perform undocumented work as each attempts to manoeuvre through or around one or another bureaucratic code.

They are joined in their manoeuvring by the sweatshop entrepreneur who disregards health and safety codes, by the politician or state official who tolerates the violations because they reduce the tensions of high unemployment, and by the corporate executive who subcontracts work to circumvent the narrow job classifications of the same internal labour market once hailed as bringing labour peace to the industry. Both these workers and these employers seek flexibility to escape the cells of classificatory taxonomies; the difference is that for the worker, the informal economy adds at best some marginal increment of manoeuvrability whereas for the employer, informalization can add considerably to profitability. Definitions of the informal economy as activities that generate income 'not included in the national accounts' entirely miss the point that whether informal activities are counted or not, they are the result of strategies to escape accountability in terms of the explicit rationalizations of bureaucratic conventions. For example, employers in unionized settings who resort to subcontracting, outcontracting and industrial homework are, in effect, saying that rules negotiated with the union 'are of no account' when it comes to informal employment. Undocumented work is unprotected work, and the evasion of bureaucratic classifications is often a means to lower the costs of labour and reduce its bargaining power.

REDISTRIBUTIVE BUREAUCRACY AND THE SECOND ECONOMY

Redistributive rationalizations

Our analysis of processes of rationalization and bureaucratization in state socialism begins with the idea, born in the nineteenth century, that socialism would replace the anarchy of the market with the rationality of the plan. A national economy, no less than a modern firm, could be managed by a visible hand. Against Proudhon's vision of socialism as self-managed co-operatives linked through market ties, Marx derided 'craft-idiocy' and argued for a single authority distributing tasks and resources to co-ordinate production for the whole of society. The modern factory provided the model for such economy-wide direct co-ordination:

> Society as a whole has this in common with the interior of a workshop in that it too has its division of labour. If one took as a model the division of labour in a modern workshop, in order to apply it to a whole society, the society best organized for the production of wealth would undoubtedly be that which had a single chief employer, distributing tasks to the different members of the community according to a previously fixed rule.
> (Marx 1847/1963: 135)

For Lenin, too, socialism's superior rationality rested in ascertaining what was scientific in capitalist methods in order to promulgate standardized rules at the level of the national economy:

> When the working class has learned how to defend the state system against the anarchy of small ownership, when it has learned to organize large-scale production on a national scale along state capitalist lines, ... the consolidation of socialism will be assured. ... Socialism is inconceivable without large-scale capitalist engineering based on the discoveries of modern science. It is inconceivable without planned state organization, which keeps tens of millions of people to the strictest observance of a unified standard in production and distribution.
> (Lenin 1918/1970: 693–4)

Lenin's call for a 'unified standard', of course, echoed the manifestos of his contemporary, Frederick Winslow Taylor, who advocated scientific measurement, routinization and standardization. But a comparison of the two great organizational theorists of the first decades of our century suffers from a misplaced concreteness if, as in most studies (Merkle 1980; Schor 1981), it focuses on Lenin's fascination with Taylor's scheme as it might be applied inside the new Soviet factories. As the above passage indicates with its emphasis on bringing millions of people under unified standards through planned state organization on a national scale, the Leninist new class project resonated with the Taylorist endeavour but differed dramatically in scope: whereas Taylor's followers attempted a rationalizing project of increasingly calculable, predictable, standardized control of the supervisory process in the microsphere at the level of the firm, Lenin's followers, in their new class project, attempted rationalization in the macrosphere as they sought to bring an entire national economy under rational control through the budgetary instruments of central planning.

Accompanying this difference in scale, moreover, was a striking difference between the legitimizing principles claimed by the new middle-class professionals of advanced capitalism and those claimed by the party elite of state socialism. Both class projects were tied to knowledge claims. But whereas the scientific management of the firm claimed legitimacy on the basis of 'laws' derived from 'time-and-motion studies', the ability to manage an economy scientifically rested on claims to knowledge of the 'laws of motion of history'.

As a consequence of the difference between these new class projects, bureaucratization under state socialism is not simply broader, deeper and more encompassing than in the West, but also differs in type. Bureaucratization under capitalism is *regulatory*; in state socialism, bureaucratization is *redistributive*. In advanced capitalism, internal bureaucratic rules and external bureaucratic regulations occur in a context in which transactions between economic units and the allocation of resources across firms are co-ordinated through markets. Within firms, resources may be allocated bureaucratically; across firms they are market co-ordinated. In state socialism, by contrast, relations between economic units are themselves bureaucratically co-ordinated and resources across them are bureaucratically allocated. Whereas regulatory bureaucratization in capitalism monitors (and reproduces the conditions for further) transactive market exchanges between private owners of various factors of production, redistributive bureaucratization in state socialism centrally allocates resources through budgetary measures linking units held in public ownership.[5] Paradigmatically, state agencies in capitalism issue regulations policing the rules of the game among market competitors and demarcating the broad parameters within which market activity occurs. Under socialism, the state issues directives specifying organizational goals and detailing economic performance criteria not as 'interventions' that might be justified over and against the rights of private owners but as the solely legitimate prescriptions for economic behaviour where the state owns (at the extreme, all) productive assets.

To be sure, the state in advanced capitalism can seek to shape the flow of resources through, for example, investment credits, sectorally varied taxation policies, and fiscal and monetary instruments. Under socialism, however, the state does not simply influence investments; it controls them directly by appropriating resources produced throughout the economy and redistributing them back through ministerial budgets (Kornai and Matita 1987). Similarly, although wage and price controls under capitalism might go so far as to include quite detailed centrally regulated wage guidelines, under socialism the state not only establishes wage level but also centrally allocates to enterprises the very fund from which wages are paid.

Redistribution and its dependencies

In a redistributively co-ordinated economy, enterprises depend to an extraordinary degree on central authorities for strategic directives, operating instructions, and the resources (funds for investments, supplies and labour) to meet these objectives. At first glance it might seem that public ownership and hierarchical authority give the central ministries enormous power to control the behaviour of enterprises under their nominal command. But dependence can frustrate rather than facilitate control, for dependants cannot be held entirely responsible for their actions. As with children in the domestic household, so with firms in the socialist economy: responsibility is inversely proportional to dependence. An enterprise whose director dutifully follows detailed instructions from the centre to the very letter of the rule can scarcely be blamed when it produces only losses. And when expenses exceed revenues, the enterprise can usually point to administrative encumbrances that justify another increase in the allowance. The paternalism institutionalized in public ownership guarantees the firm's survival regardless of its performance. Because it can acquire resources and investments without demonstrating credit worthiness or covering costs from the proceeds of sales, the socialist firm faces only a 'soft budget constraint' (Kornai 1986).

Under conditions of soft budget constraints, the firm has little pressure to use resources and investments efficiently. In fact it often has every incentive to use them inefficiently: rewarded for expansion and physical output, the socialist firm's managers seek to maximize the resources it does obtain. For this reason, the firm's demand for capital and labour is theoretically limitless. This perpetual hunger for resources, in turn, gives rise to chronic shortages throughout the economy as firms pump the state for more workers, equipment, raw materials and investments irrespective of their financial situation or ability to use those resources efficiently. In terms of the systemic limits of production at the point at which demand has ceased, the socialist firm keeps on producing at whatever the cost, stopping only when it runs out of mobilizable supplies. The problem for the socialist firm is that supply failures, far from being exceptional, are an everyday consequence of the chronic shortages of a redistributively managed economy (Kornai 1979).

To cope with uncertainties of supply and changes in output targets, managers of socialist firms hoard labour as a flexible factor of production. If the capitalist firm tends to lay off or at least stop hiring workers as a response to uncertainties of demand, the socialist firm hires more workers to mitigate uncertainties of supplies. Whereas the 'reserve army of labour' stands unemployed outside the gates of the capitalist firm, the 'labour reserves' of state socialism are underemployed inside the enterprise.

The internal labour of the socialist firm can be mobilized during rush work at the end of planning periods or allocated to deal with 'forced substitutions'. On these latter (and frequent) occasions when the firm must produce with inputs that are available rather than those called for in technological prescriptions, labour reserves might be used to process raw materials in-house, modify production processes, and retool equipment to adjust to unstandardized flow through. Moreover, because capital goods are often kept in operation beyond the point of technical obsolescence (a low scrapping rate is the by-product of capital shortage) and equipment maintenance is postponed during storming periods, machines are prone to breakdowns and require workers with idiosyncratic knowledge. The attempt to manage an economy scientifically as if it were one factory prevents the scientific management of any given factory. External dependence on a redistributive bureaucracy produces internal dependence on a co-operative labour force. This dependence forms the basis for 'selective bargaining' (Stark 1986) by workers inside the firm and for the second economy outside it. To illuminate these processes fully, we must turn our attention from relations between enterprises and central ministries to those between enterprises and households.

Expenditures of labour

With the nationalization of banking and industry and the near-elimination of small private proprietors in agriculture and services, the modern redistributive economy, as noted above, represents an unprecedented concentration of ownership of productive assets. But there is one asset, vital to our understanding of the dynamics of state socialism, that has not been nationalized. For, with the exception of short and highly unstable periods, labour remains *de facto* and *de jure* the property of individuals and households. On the one side of the firm, the private character of labour means that managers face the problem of getting labour from labour power, that is to turn the wheels of nationalized industry they must find measures to stimulate the performance of 'private' owners of labour. On the side of the household because so few other assets are privately held, households have virtually no sources of income other than earnings from labour.

These needs and interests would appear congruent, and indeed they are – to a point. The firm's almost insatiable appetite for labour combines with households' search for wages to produce labour force participation rates much higher than those of Western Europe. But at the point that the household has pushed all its able bodies into active wage-earners, it can no longer improve its standard of living by an 'extensive' increase in the rate of participation but looks to more intensive utilization of labour at higher rates (and perhaps alternative forms) of remuneration. Similarly, enterprise managers have an interest in securing the largest possible wage fund in order for the firm to retain its (idiosyncratically skilled) labour force and stimulate their efforts. But this lobbying on behalf of the firm and its employees cannot yield boundless fruits: enterprises are competing for wage funds from that fixed proportion of national income that central planners allocate for labour.[6] Thus, a significant proportion of workers confront a gap between the level of effort that they are capable and willing to expend and the level of reward they are likely to receive.

Workers' response is conditioned by a situation in which households, in contrast to firms, face hard budget constraints. Because its expenses must be covered by income, the household is cost sensitive and attempts to economize its resources. As such, it seeks the best return on expenditures of labour, its sole income-generating resource. Some workers can improve the reward/efforts ratio through informal negotiations on the shop floor (Héthy and Makó 1972; Kalász and Köllö 1984). This process has been characterized as selective bargaining (Stark 1986) not only because of its *ad hoc* nature, but also because it is limited to those workers whose skills, idiosyncratic knowledge or strategic location at key points in the production process provide an exploitable dependence (Köllö 1984; Stark 1986; Ladó and Tóth 1988). Others can use turnover to yield short-term wage improvements. But the attraction of higher basic wages (as the only earnings indicator visible to an outsider) can make turnover a self-defeating strategy where longer-term wage gains accrue through bonuses and premiums not linked to the basic wage. Quitting too often for initially greener pastures can preclude building up the contacts and connections through which bonuses, premiums and easy over-time are channelled (Lukács 1986). Given the drawbacks of turnover and the limitations of selective bargaining, a rational strategy for the economizing household is to attempt to maintain the price of labour power while reducing the actual expenditure of labour. Thus, corresponding to the hoarding of a labour reserve by the firm as a hedge against bureaucratic uncertainties, we find workers withholding labour in production.

To the economizing household, labour withheld from the socialist firm is labour that can potentially be utilized elsewhere. The first outlets close at hand are self-provisioning activities such as home-building, repairs and gardening. But labour that the household is capable and willing to expend can also be employed in the off-hours, selling skills to other households where the socialist sector leaves vast unfulfilled demand in construction, repairs or personal services (sometimes with tools and materials 'borrowed' from the place of regular employment) or providing goods of higher quality than those available in the socialist sector. The growth of private construction in turn, stimulates private transport of construction materials, and the more intensive cultivation of small household plots not only increases demand for transport of agricultural products but also creates a market for the skills of designers and machinists to produce new technologies (small horsepower tilling equipment, heating pumps for plastic covered hothouses, etc.) appropriate for small-scale, intensive agriculture. More private vehicles and more private equipment, of course, generate more private jobs in repair. And as moonlighting jobs grow in number, so grow the opportunities for economizing households to compare earnings in the off-hours with those in the firm. Increased opportunities for exit yield, in turn, an increase in the number of workers who can participate in the selective bargaining over efforts and rewards. Managers, for their part, are often forced to tolerate this partial exit, even though it steadily erodes the incentive power of enterprise wages, for such may be the only option to retain the firm's employees. The operation of the modern redistributive economy thus gives rise to a second economy as an integral feature of state socialism.

Dimensions of the second economy

By 'second economy' we refer to a broad range of income-generating activity outside the boundaries of the redistributively co-ordinated and managed economy. Second economy units are privately owned, and like households and unlike socialist firms, face hard budget constraints. Their external relations are co-ordinated through markets or networks of reciprocity, and the management of their internal affairs (decisions about investments, operations, wages, etc.) is not governed by official policies and protocols. Some second economy activities are legal and some are illegal, but many second economy activities cannot be easily categorized within that dichotomy (Gábor 1991). Such is the case when taxation, credit and purchase and supply policies are written in such a way that even the most scrupulous private producer cannot be in consistent compliance with mutually contradictory regulations. Nor can the dynamics of the second economy – its expansion and contractions, or its qualitative transformation – be written simply as a history of the tightening or loosening of legal restrictions. On the one hand, legal prohibitions in themselves cannot curb a second economy where violations are the norm and enforcement the exception. On the other, legalization in itself cannot make a shadow economy into a legitimate private sector where a distrusting populace fears re-expropriation, and where even legal and formally registered activities have an official status as less than fully legitimate.

For these reasons we refer, as do the Hungarians, to a large part of the second economy as existing within a zone better captured by the terms 'alegal', not 'illegal', or 'tolerated'. Above all it should be understood that this tolerated zone is not fixed by legislative initiative or the beneficence of officialdom. In the late 1960s and throughout the 1970s, Hungarian peasants and workers did not sit on their hands waiting patiently for the government to pass new legal measures. They ventured into the second economy and forced the state, in one field after another, to tolerate activities that were once illegal but were not yet legalized, and to institutionalize forms that were legal but were not yet legitimate. The boundaries of the second economy and the relative proportions of its legal, illegal and alegal parts are products of contestation between state and society – a continuously changing outcome of a struggle in which society attempts to create and maintain a sphere of activity relatively autonomous from the state.

We may speak of the relative autonomy of the second economy to the extent that its organizing principles are different from those of the redistributive state and its processes are insulated from control by state elites. This does not, of course, imply that the systemic reproduction of the second economy is isolated from the socialist economy or that its participants have severed their ties with the socialist sector. In fact, because participation in the second economy is seldom undertaken on a full-time basis, most second economy producers continue some kind of employment in socialist firms. This strategy is motivated in part by the goal of maintaining security of employment and access to health insurance, housing credits and other benefits that are conditional upon holding a job in a socialist enterprise.

The decision not to invest all of one's financial and human resources in full-time private pursuits is also shaped by the state's contradictory policy toward the second economy with an ambivalence not entirely unlike the posture of some capitalists toward the welfare state in our own societies. On the one hand, politicians are conscious of the compensatory effects of the second economy (as a safety net for some families, auxiliary supplier for some industries, and an alternative means to raise the standard of living for the majority of households), and on that account, support policies that tolerate its existence. On the other hand, state elites fear that the second economy threatens the dominant ideology and weakens the incentive power of wages in the socialist economy. For this reason, they adopt policies that constrain its expansion, lead to its distorted reproduction, and discourage full-time participation. These policies include capricious taxation measures that make it difficult to predict future tax liabilities; severe limitations on the availability of legal credit; and practices that put second economy producers at the end of the queue when having their purchase orders filled by socialist suppliers and last on the waiting lists to be paid when they do business for firms in the state sector (Galasi and Gábor 1985).

These and similar policies have the (not entirely unintended) consequences that small-scale producers must resort to under-the-table dealings such as systematically underreporting income, offering bribes and kickbacks to acquire materials and contracts, and obtaining illegal credit at often usurious rates.[7] Technical violations of legal restrictions prompt renewed charges of blanket illegality and corruption in the second economy, and fuel efforts to restrict its expansion that, in turn, heighten the perceived threat of expropriation and discourage further investment in productive assets. Shortage conditions, moreover, can produce windfall profits even for private producers who have conscientiously avoided any corruption, and who, in the absence of legal avenues for productive investments, spend these on large houses and big cars. The visibility of this consumption increases the likelihood of public complaints against 'unearned incomes', and this condemnation engenders more fear among small-scale producers, which further discourages the would-be full-time entrant.

The end result is the low propensity to invest legally in the second economy, the tendency for such investment as does take place to be directed toward immediate and short-term gain, and the decision not to opt out of employment in the socialist sector. The shortage nature of the socialist economy perpetuates a situation in which only a minority of households live solely from first economy earnings; the policy preferences of state elites reproduce a pattern in which only a marginal proportion live solely from second economy incomes. The majority of households derive incomes from both. As István Gábor (1991) argues, 'household strategies of parallel and simultaneous participation in both economies become the norm'.

For some analysts (Kemény 1982, Sampson 1986), income supplements from this dual participation reduce conflicts and tensions that would otherwise build up in the socialist sector. The second economy, in this view, is a kind of safety valve serving ultimately to maintain the system. Although the second economy is an important factor in the overall reproduction of state socialism, recent statistics suggest that the safety valve metaphor understates the extent of second economy activity and thereby fails to capture the contradictory dynamic of state sector/second economy relations. In 1987, for example, small-scale agriculturalists accounted for only 11 per cent of arable land in Hungary but produced over 36 per cent of agricultural production (KSH) 1987: 34), including 74.0 per cent of the vegetables, 60.8 per cent of the fruit, and 53.5 per cent of the pigs raised in that year (KSH 1987: 190). Turning to more urban occupations (with statistics confined to legally registered participants) the number of private retail tradesmen is still small but has risen from 10,229 in 1975 to 31,827 in 1987, and accounts for about 32 per cent of commercial shops, restaurants and bars (with an additional 12 per cent of all retail and catering units leased to private management; KSH 1987: 261–3). Similarly, the number of registered self-employed industrial producers rose from 103,412 in 1980 to 154,611 in 1987 (KSH 1987: 407). Hungarian consumers turn to the second economy to buy everything from bread for their kitchen tables to software for their personal computers. For example 42 per cent of housing construction (Gábor 1988; see also Sik 1988), and by a conservative estimate, almost 85 per cent of building repairs (Markó 1986: 30) are undertaken by second economy producers. According to estimates from survey data, nearly three-quarters of all households derive some income from the second economy (Kolosi 1980: 41; see Rona-Tas 1989 for an analysis of the distribution of second economy earnings and their consequences for inequality). A recent study by Hungarian economists (using nation-wide time budget micro-surveys conducted by the Hungarian Central Statistical Office) estimates that 33 per cent of all active labour time in 1984 (excluding housework) was spent in the second economy (Timar 1985).

The image of a safety valve venting pressure to prevent an emergency seems a particularly inapt metaphor when one out of every three hours worked for income in Hungary occurred in the second economy. Rather than a mere valve, the second economy has become an alternative engine linked, no doubt, through a complex circulation system to the energy of the first economy, but increasingly powered by its own energy drawn from sources that were not tapped by the socialist sector.

Pressures for change

The more marginal in size and the more illegal in character, the more the second economy is conservatizing in its systematic effects. But with its expansion, the second economy reaches a point where it becomes a source of increasing pressure for change in the first economy. Most important for purposes of our comparison are the changes in the employment relation in the socialist sector brought about by the growth and qualitative transformation of the second economy.

More significant than increasing consumer choice in the quality and availability of products, the expansion of the second economy increases *producer* choice: from no choice but wage labour in the socialist firm, an expanding second economy now provides alternative forms to invest productive activity including such options as self-employment, small partnerships, franchise arrangements, membership in small co-operatives, and waged employment for second economy entrepreneurs. By increasing the opportunities for even partial exit, the second economy expands the room of manoeuvre for workers inside the socialist firm and increases the likelihood that the terms of employment (wages and conditions of work) will be negotiated through transactive bargaining between workers and managers rather than being administratively imposed. We should not expect that this bargaining will immediately take the form of unionized collective bargaining familiar to us in the West. But to the extent that the second economy increases pressure for change, we would expect that more workers should be brought into the selective bargaining on the shop-floor, that the range of negotiable issues should expand, and that this selective bargaining should be increasingly brought out of the shadows to receive official recognition in more institutionalized (but not more bureaucratized) forms.

Evidence that such changes are taking place can be seen in a recent organizational innovation in which groups of workers inside Hungarian factories received the right to form semi-autonomous subcontracting units, known as 'work partnerships' (*Vállalati gazdasági munkakközösséggek*, hereafter VGMs) producing goods or services in their off-hours using equipment of socialist enterprise. The terms of these subcontracting agreements are bargained between unit managers and representatives elected by each partnership (rather than by trade union officials accountable to management), and the undisguised nature of this bargaining is an official recognition of the selective bargaining that formerly took place only in the shadow negotiations of the shop-floor. (See Stark 1989 for details of the operations of these partnerships.)

For the purposes of this chapter, two points must be emphasized.

First, the establishment of the partnership form was directly linked to the expansion of the second economy (Stark 1989). Second, through the higher rates of earnings and the increased opportunities for representation, the VGMs provide a means to differentially reward strategic workers, tie their interests to those of the firm, reduce turnover, and improve the likelihood of their co-operation within the production process. As such, it performs functions not dissimilar to those of the 'internal labour markets' of the large capitalist firm (Stark 1986). The difference is that in market economies these mechanisms take the form of internal bureaucratic rules while in bureaucratic economies they take the form of internal market transactions.

The central point that these organizational innovations demonstrate is that, whereas workers in capitalist economies differ in the extent to which they are protected from the market, workers in the socialist economy differ according to the extent to which they can participate in the market. In capitalism, informal economy workers tend to fare worse relative to employees in the regulated economy, and subcontracting and outcontracting are typically associated with fewer protections, lower benefits, and an absence of union representation. In socialism, by contrast, rates of earnings are often higher in the second economy and workers who can participate in subcontracting schemes are among the most highly rewarded, with access not only to higher earnings but also to alternative means of interest representation.

A COMPARATIVE MODEL OF MIRRORED OPPOSITION

In examining the relations between regulatory bureaucratization and the informal economy and between redistributive bureaucratization and the second economy, we have argued that the distinctive patterns of each system could be revealed through their mutual contrast. That is, a comprehensive account of systemic differences requires a multi-sided comparison in which we simultaneously (1) compare economic institutions across sectors within systems and (2) compare the relations between sectors across systems. Pursued systematically, the specificity of any given institution in the resulting model is grasped not through some essential traits but only in relation to the broader configuration within and across systems.

Figure 2.1 presents in graphic form the model of such a multi-sided comparison of the dynamics of bureaucratization and informalization under capitalism and socialism. Its elements are taken from the analysis above. For each system we present (1) the co-ordinating mechanism through which the enterprise is linked to other units in the economic environment, (2) the characteristic feature of internal labour markets, (3) the forces in tension with the dominant system co-ordinating mechanism that stimulate the development of these forms inside enterprises, and (4) the informal/second economy.

Most generally, the overall logic of the configuration shows the features of capitalism and socialism as mirrored opposites. Take, for example, the relationship between external co-ordinating mechanisms and internal labour markets: whereas in capitalism we find internal bureaucratic rules in a predominantly market environment, in socialism we see internal market transactions in a predominantly bureaucratic environment. Figure 2.1 also shows the distinctive patterns of bureaucratization in the two systems. As the dominant co-ordinating mechanism in socialism, bureaucratization is redistributive. Capitalism's regulatory bureaucratization, by contrast, is juxtaposed to the dominant logic of the market and as a coexisting and opposing principle, stimulates changes in the system – not least of which are internal to the capitalist enterprise.

The configuration becomes more complex when we turn to the systemic 'locations' of the informal economy and the second economy. Where should they be situated when a direct comparison of their patterns of ownership, budget constraints, economic co-ordination and internal governance yields marked similarities? Both are characterized by private ownership, hard budget constraints, and market co-ordination. And in both cases internal governance is not regulated by bureaucratic procedures (the employment relation, for example, is not regulated by bureaucratic rules governing hiring, firing, promotions, etc.). If our analysis remained at the level of relations internal to each informal economy (whose similarity is captured in Figure 2.1 by representing each in the same circular form), we might conclude that processes of informalization are essentially the same in two social systems.

Not confined to comparing internal features of the respective informal economies, our analysis proceeded to examine how the processes of informalization articulate with the broader institutional matrix of capitalism and socialism. Comparing across sectors, we argued that the governance of the employment relation in

MARKET CO-ORDINATION

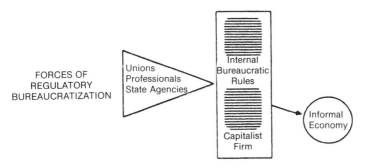

REDISTRIBUTIVE BUREAUCRATIC CO-ORDINATION

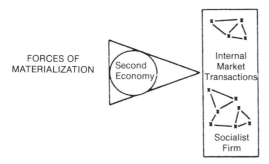

Figure 2.1 Bureaucratization and informalization of employment in
capitalism and socialism

capitalism's informal economy differs from the regulated labour
relations of the formal sector. But if the informal economy escapes
regulatory bureaucratization, it does so on the basis of market co-
ordination and private ownership congruent with those of the
dominant mode. In the socialist case, these same features are opposed
to, rather than congruent with, the dominant mode. Moreover, by this
difference, the non-bureaucratic governance of the informal economy
stimulates the institutionalization of transactive bargaining inside the
firm. We have seen this pattern once before – where an opposed but
subordinate logic is a force for change – in the bureaucratization of the
employment relation that remade the economic institutions of
capitalism. To capture this comparison, the second economy is also
pictured in Figure 2.1 in a triangular form representing a force of
systemic change remaking the economic institutions of socialism. As

the counterpart to the trade unions, state agencies and professional associations that promoted bureaucratization in capitalist market economies, the second economy (in a systemic mirrored opposition) is a force of marketization in socialist redistributive economies. Unanticipated at the outset, pursuit of a multi-sided comparison leads us from the surface resemblances of economic informality across social systems to uncover structural similarities between the second economy under socialism and trade unions under capitalism.

If trade unions and the second economy play analogous systemic roles stimulating changes that improve the bargaining power of workers, they do so, of course, through different means. In both cases economic institutions (for example, the internal governance of the employment relation) are reshaped by interest-directed action. But the internal rationalizations of employment under capitalism was spearheaded by formal organizations (unions, state agencies, professional associations) whereas the expansion of transactive bargaining under socialism is a product of social organization (unorchestrated actions by individuals and households in their everyday participation in the markets and networks of the second economy). Similarly, if the classificatory rules of bureaucratized employment providing some protection from the market were borrowed from forms developed outside the firm and if the affiliative forms of institutionalized bargaining providing some participation in the market were borrowed from the second economy, in both cases these borrowings were accompanied by an *extension of rights*. But whereas workers' protection under capitalism comes about by an extension of citizenship rights (due process, freedom of association, non-discrimination, etc.) into the economy, under socialism market participation comes about by extending property rights (rights to make contracts, to enter into economic partnerships, etc.) into statist organizations.

EPILOGUE INTO THE FUTURE: FROM SECOND ECONOMY TO LEGITIMATE PRIVATE SECTOR

The question of whether these property rights might expand to create a legitimate private sector heads the political agenda in contemporary Hungary. Such a development would signal the emergence of a socialist mixed economy (Stark 1989; Szelenyi 1989) rather than state socialism with a second economy. It would reflect a qualitative transformation rather than a mere expansion of the second economy: whereas producers in the second economy supplement incomes, in a fully legitimate private sector they would be free to accumulate capital. Recent measures indicate that the Hungarian leadership is taking such steps. With the economy floundering, new legislation and administrative directives establish the right to form limited liability companies, provide for majority ownership of firms by foreign capital, and allow private Hungarian firms to employ up to 500 workers (raised from the former limit of 15) in hopes that an expanded private sector will improve performance and promote economic growth.

It is still too early to assess the consequences of these new measures (although preliminary indications are that they have probably not gone far enough to achieve the desired effects). Here I briefly indicate the problems and prospects in terms already develped above. As we look into the 1990s it would be a mistake to assume that the obstacles blocking the creation of a dynamic private sector can be removed by reversing the legal principle according to which 'Everything is prohibited that is not explicitly allowed' to a new principle in which 'Everything is allowed that is not explicitly prohibited'. The switch to the new principle is required, but is not sufficient. That is, the development of a legitimate private sector requires not only lifting restrictions but also establishing new regulations (Nee 1989). In terms of the analysis above, the limited and distorted markets of the second economy can exist in the interstices of a redistributive bureaucracy, but a dynamic private sector will require some degree of regulatory bureaucracy. The switch to new legal principles will entail making explicit more detailed prohibitions in place of the earlier global one. Moreover, private investors are likely to be more confident (or at least less fearful of state intrusions) where prohibitions (if not too great in number) are clearly spelled out rather than unstated. For these reasons, and because dynamic markets require a stable legal infrastructure to facilitate complex exchanges, a socialist mixed economy, in contrast to its state socialist predecessor, will have fewer restrictions but more (precise, formalized and delimited) regulations.[8]

Despite the qualitative difference between legal-rational regulations and redistributive directives, the two types of administrative practices can be all too easily confused in the transition to a socialist mixed economy. On the one hand, bureaucrats accustomed to the redistributive mode might learn new routines when affairs are running smoothly; but when political or economic problems arise, they are likely to slip back into the familiar redistributive patterns –

and the proliferation of rules regulating the market may provide the ready pretext to do so. Entrepreneurs, for their part, are quite likely to confuse the more detailed regulations as signs of a hostile investment climate even where they are meant to foster investor confidence. And if they slip into familiar patterns of less-than-legal second economy dealings this is likely to trigger a shift from the benignly regulatory to aggressively restrictive state interventions. Decades of mutual suspicion thus create the circumstances for two-sided, self-fulfilling prophecies. The most likely outcome then, will be a cyclical pattern of alternating periods of over – and under-regulation.

The development of a socialist mixed economy will also create possibilities for new class alignments. If present trends continue, in the 1990s we shall see the emergence of a new class in Eastern Europe – not Djilas' New Class of party elite but a new class of entrepreneurs accumulating captial. With what social groups might it ally? Will it be with workers to increase the scope of transactive bargaining and open more avenues of exit from the socialist sector? If so, perhaps an expanded and officially recognized private sector will form an embryonic civil society resulting in not only an expansion of property rights but also an expansion of citizenship rights. Alternatively, an alliance of new entrepreneurs and the old state socialist elite may take place. If so, democratization and the growth of private economic activity may have a curvilinear rather than linear relationship in the socialist context with the corruption typical of black markets at one end and with class collaboration to repress workers at the other. Because both these scenarios of alignment are possible, the outcome will be determined by how interests come to be shaped in the clash and pull of transformative politics. In either case, the period of transition from second economy to recognized private sector will be a critical one as alliances forged or broken then will shape the socialism of the coming century.

ACKNOWLEDGEMENTS

Research for this chapter was supported by grants from the International Research and Exchanges Board (IREX) and the Graduate School of the University of Wisconsin. An earlier version was presented at the annual meetings of the American Sociological Association, Chicago, August 1987. I would like to thank Stephen Bunker, Paul DiMaggio, Lauren Edelman, István Gábor, János Lukács, Kay Mohlman, Victor Nee, Stephen Petterson, Ivan Szelenyi and

especially Monique Djokic, for their helpful comments and suggestions on an earlier draft.

NOTES

1 This chapter previously appeared in *Sociological Forum* (1989) 4 (4):
637–63.
2 In its initial stage (e.g. Hart 1973; Weeks 1975) research on the informal
sector examined patterns of self-employment in the informal service
sector of developing economies as a means for urban poor to cope with
the disruptions of migration and wage labour. The second decade of
informal sector research in the Third World has changed the unit of
analysis from the survival strategies of households to the employment
strategies of firms (Portes and Benton 1984; Benería and Roldán 1987;
Roberts 1989).
3 As in the Third World, efforts by sociologists to understand the informal
economy in advanced capitalist societies focused initially on the strategies
of households in such activities as 'self provisioning' (Mingione 1983)
and 'work outside employment' (Gershuny and Pahl 1982). More recent
studies examine the employment strategies of firms (OECD 1986;
Fernández Kelly and Garcia 1988; 1990).
4 Although actors can be pressed to provide a posteriori rationalizations
(the 'rationale') for unstated cultural taken-for-granteds, bureaucratic
conventions are rationalized in advance. 'Rationalized' here does not, of
course, imply that bureaucratic conventions carry a universally superior
rationality. On codification and formalization, see especially Bourdieu
(1986).
5 The concept of redistribution thus differs from familiar notions of income
redistribution through 'transfer payments' since, in state socialism,
redistribution is not an auxiliary principle modifying market outcomes
(through taxation of incomes generated on the market) but assumes the
dominant role as the co-ordinating mechanism of productive activity
itself. For a path-breaking analysis of modern redistributive systems
drawing on Polanyi's (1957) distinction between markets, redistribution,
and reciprocity as 'modes of economic co-ordination', see Konrad and
Szelenyi (1979).
6 Gábor and Kövári (1985), in fact, demonstrate that recent changes in the
distribution of wage funds penalize firms that utilized labour more
efficiently in the previous round.
7 Forced to engage in such petty corruption, second economy entrepreneurs
thereby expose themselves to nefarious means of social control such as
official blackmail. For a contrast of forms of control of the informal and
second economies see Gábor (1988).
8 The distinction between the two types of bureaucratization is crucial here.
State socialist economies, of course, abound with administrative measures
known as 'regulations'. The point is that many of them are not regulatory
in the sense we use it here: regulatory behaviour assumes otherwise free
scope for autonomous activity.

REFERENCES

Baron, J. and Bielby, W. (1986) 'The proliferation of job titles in organizations', *Administrative Science Quarterly* 31: 561–86.

Baron, J, Dobbin, F. and Devereaux Jennings, P. (1986) 'War and peace: the evolution of modern personnel administration in U.S. industry', *American Journal of Sociology* 92: 350–83.

Benería, L. and Roldán, M. (1987) *The Crossroads of Class and Gender: Industrial Homework, Subcontracting and Household Dynamics in Mexico City*. Chicago: University of Chicago Press.

Benton, L. (1989) 'Industrial subcontracting and the informal sector: the politics of restructuring in the Madrid electronics industry', in A. Portes, M. Castells and L. Benton (eds) *The Informal Economy: Studies in Advanced and Less Developed Countries*, Baltimore, Md: Johns Hopkins University Press.

Block, F. (1987) *Revising State Theory: Essays on Politics and Post Industrialism*, Philadelphia, Pa: Temple University Press.

Bourdieu, P. (1986) 'Habitus, code et codification', *Actes de la Recherche en Sciences Sociales* 64 (September): 40–4.

Bourdieu, P. and Boltanski, L. (1986) 'The educational system and the economy: titles and jobs', in C. C. Lemert (ed.) *French Sociology: Rupture and Renewal since 1986*, New York: Columbia University Press.

Bravermann, H. (1974) *Labor and Monopoly Capital*, New York: Monthly Review Press.

Capecchi, V. (1989) 'Industrial reconstruction and informality in the red-belt', in A. Portes, M. Castells and L. Benton (eds) *The Informal Economy: Studies in Advanced and Less Developed Countries*, Baltimore, Md: Johns Hopkins University Press.

Castells, M. and Portes, A. (1989) 'World underneath: the origins, dynamics, and effects of the informal economy', in A. Portes, M. Castells and L. Benton (eds) *The Informal Economy: Studies in Advanced and Less Developed Countries*, Baltimore, Md: Johns Hopkins University Press.

Conk, M. (1979) *The United States Census and Labor Force Change: A History of Occupational Statistics*, Ann Arbor, Mich: UMI Research Press.

Doeringer, P. and Piore, M. J. (1971) *Internal Labor Markets and Manpower Analysis*. Lexington, Mass: D. C. Heath.

Edwards, R. (1979) *Contested Terrain*, New York: Basic Books.

Fernández Kelly, M. P. and Garcia, A. M. (1988) 'Invisible amidst the glitter: Hispanic women in the southern California electronics industry', in A. Statham, E. Miller and H. Mauksch (eds) *The Worth of Women's Work: A Qualitative Synthesis*. Albany, NY: State University of New York Press.

—— (1989) 'Informalization at the core: Hispanic women, home work and the advanced capitalist state', in A. Portes, M. Castells and L. Benton (eds) *The Informal Economy: Studies in Advanced and Less Developed Countries*, Baltimore, Md: Johns Hopkins University Press.

—— (1990) 'Power surrendered, power restored: the politics of home and work among Hispanic women in southern California and southern Florida', in L. Tilly (eds.) *Women, Politics, and Change*, New York: Russell Sage Foundation.

Gábor, I. R. (1988) 'Second economy and socialism: the Hungarian experience', in E. L. Feige (ed.) *The Underground Economies*, Cambridge, Mass: Cambridge University Press.
—— (1991) 'Second economy: lessons from the Hungarian 1980's' in M. Tardos and P. G. Hare (eds) *The Hungarian Economy: Theoretical and Empirical Analysis*, London: Routledge & Kegan Paul.
Gábor, I. R. and Kövári, G. (1985) 'Keresetszabályozás és munkahelyi osztonzes' (Wage regulations and work-place incentives), *Közgazdasági Szemle* 32 (6): 724–42.1.
Galasi, P. and Gábor, I. R. (1985) 'Második gazdaság: Léhetöségek és korlátok (Second economy: possibilities and limits)', *Mozgó Világ* 1: 10–15.
Gershuny, J. I. and Pahl, R. E. (1982) 'Work outside employment: some preliminary speculations', in S. Henry (ed.) *Informal Institutions*, New York: St Martin's Press.
Grossman, G. (1977) 'The second economy of the USSR', *Problems of Communism* September – October: 25–40.
Hansson, I. (1989) 'The underground economy in Sweden', in E. L. Feige (ed.) *The Underground Economies*, New York: Cambridge University Press.
Hart, K. (1973) 'Informal income opportunities and urban employment in Ghana', *Journal of Modern African Studies* 11: 61–89.
Hartmann, H. (ed.) (1985) *Comparable Worth: New Directions for Research*, Washington, DC: National Academy Press.
Héthy, L. and Makó, C. (1972) 'Work performance, interests, powers and environment: the case of cyclical slowdowns in a Hungarian factory', *Hungarian Sociological Studies, Sociological Review Series* 17: 123–50.
Hinton, J. (1973) *The First Shop Steward's Movement*, London: George Allen & Unwin.
Jacoby, S. (1985) *Employing Bureaucracy: Managers, Unions and the Transformation of Work in American Industry, 1900-1945*, New York: Columbia University Press.
Kalász, I. and Köllö, J. (1984) 'Work, power and wages in a plastic rolling mill', *Wage Bargaining in Hungarian Firms, Volume 1*, Studies of the Institute of Economics of the Hungarian Academy of Sciences, no. 23: 89–107.
Katz, H. C. (1985) *Shifting Gears: Changing Labor Relations in the U.S. Automobile Industry*. Cambridge, Mass: MIT Press.
Kemény, I. (1982) 'The unregistered economy in Hungary', *Soviet Studies* 34: 349–66.
Köllö, J. (1984) 'Labour shortage, manpower allocation and wage payment in a cotton weaving mill', *Wage Bargaining in Hungarian Firms, Volume II*, Studies of the Institute of Economics of the Hungarian Academy of Sciences, no. 24: 7–68.
Kolosi, T. (1980) 'Uj tendenciak a társadalmi szerkezet fejlödéseben' (New tendencies in the development of social structure), *Valóság* no. 3.
Konrad, G. and Szelenyi, I. (1979) *Intellectuals on the Road to Class Power*, New York: Harcourt, Brace, Jovanovich.
Kornai, J. (1979) 'Resource-constrained versus demand-constrained systems', *Econometrica* 47: 801–19.

—— (1986) *Contradictions and Dilemmas: Studies on the Socialist Economy and Society*: Cambridge, Mass: MIT Press.

Kornai, J. and Matita, A. (1987) *A vállalatok nyereségének bürokratikus újraelosztása (Bureacratic redistribution of enterprise profits)*, Budapest: Közgazdasági és Jogi Jönyvkiadó.

KSH (Központi Statisztikai Hivatal-Hungarian Central Statistical Office) (1987) *Statistical Yearbook, 1987*, Budapest: Központi Statisztikai Hivatal.

Ladó, M. and Tóth, F. (1988) 'In the shadow of formal rules', *Economic and Industrial Democracy* 9: 523–33.

Lenin, V. (1918/1970) 'Left wing childishness and the petty-bourgeois mentality', *Selected Works*, Volume 2, Moscow: Progress Publishers.

Lozano, B. (1989) *The Invisible Force: Transforming American Business with Outside and Home-Based Workers*, New York: Free Press.

Lukács, J. (1986) 'Organizational flexibility, internal labour market and internal subcontracting – Hungarian style', in R. Andorka and L. Bertalan (eds) *Economy and Society in Hungary*, Budapest: Karl Marx University of Economics.

Markó I. (1986) *A kisgazdaságok hasánkban (The small economies in Hungary*, Budapest: Kossuth.

Marx, K. (1847/1963) *The Poverty of Philosphy*, New York: International Publishers.

Merkle, J. (1980) *Management and Ideology: The Legacy of the International Scientific Management Movement*, Berkeley, Calif: University of California Press.

Mingione, E. (1983) 'Informalization, restructuring and the survival strategies of the working class', *International Journal of Urban and Regional Research* 7: 311–39.

Moser, C. O. N. (1978) 'Informal sector or petty commodity production: dualism or dependence in urban development?', *World Development* 6 (9/10).

Nee, V. (1989) 'Entrepreneurship and the politics of regulation in rural China', in V. Nee and D. Stark (eds) *Remaking the Economic Institutions of Socialism: China and Eastern Europe*, Stanford, Calif: Stanford University Press.

Nelson, D, (1975) *Managers and Workers: Origins of the New Factory System in the United States, 1880-1920*, Madison, Wis: University of Wisconsin Press.

OECD (Organization for Economic Cooperation and Development). (1986) *Flexibility in the Labour Market*, Paris: OECD.

Osterman, P. (ed.) (1984) *Internal Labor Markets*, Cambridge, Mass: MIT Press.

Peattie, L. R. (1982) 'What is to be done with the informal sector? A case study of shoe manufacturers in Colombia', in H. Safa (ed.)a *Towards a Political Economy of Urbanization in Third World Countries*, Delhi: Oxford University Press.

Pestieau, P. (1985) 'Belgium's irregular economy', in W. Gaertner and A. Wenig (eds) *The Economics of the Shadow Economy*, Berlin: Springer-Verlag.

Pfeffer, J. and Baron, J. N. (1988) 'Taking the workers back out: recent trends in the structuring of employment', in B. M. Staw and L. L. Cummings (eds) *Research in Organizational Behaviour*, Greenwich, Conn: JAI Press.

Polanyi K. (1957) 'The economy as instituted process', in K. Polanyi, C. Arensberg and H. Pearson (eds) *Trade and Market in the Early Empires*, New York: Free Press.

Portes, A. (1983) 'The informal sector: definition, controversy, and relation to national development', *Review* 7: 151–74.

Portes, A. and Benton, L. (1984) 'Industrial development and labor absorption: a reinterpretation', *Population and Development Review* 10: 589–611.

Portes, A. and Sassen-Koob, S. (1987) 'Making it underground: comparative material on the informal sector in Western market economies', *American Journal of Sociology* 93: 30–61.

Renooy, P. H. (1984) 'Twilight economy: a survey of the informal economy in the Netherlands', *Research Report*, Faculty of Economic Sciences, University of Amsterdam.

Roberts, B. (1989) 'Employment structure, life cycle and life chances: formal and informal sectors in Guadalajara', in A. Portes, M. Castells, and L. Benton (eds) *The Informal Economy: Studies in Advanced and Less Developed Countries*, Baltimore Md: Johns Hopkins University Press.

Rogerson, C. M. (1985) 'The first decade of informal sector studies: review and synthesis'. *Report*, University of Witwatersrand, Johannesburg.

Rona-Tas, A. (1989) 'The second economy in Hungary until 1982', unpublished PhD dissertation, Department of Sociology, University of Michigan.

Sampson, S. (1986) 'The informal sector in Eastern Europe', *Telos* 66: 44–66.

Schor, Z. (1981) 'Soviet Taylorism revisited', *Soviet Studies* 33: 246–64.

Sik, E. (1988) 'Reciprocal exchange of labour in Hungary', in R. E. Pahl (ed.) *On Work: Historical, Comparative and Theoretical Approaches*, Oxford: Basil Blackwell.

Stark, D. (1980) 'Class struggle and the transformation of the labor process: a relational approach', *Theory and Society* 9: 89–130.

—— (1986) 'Rethinking internal labor markets: new insights from a comparative perspective', *American Sociological Review* 51: 492–504.

—— (1989) 'Coexisting organizational forms in Hungary's emerging mixed economy', in V. Nee and D. Stark (eds) *Remaking the Economic Institutions of Socialism: China and Eastern Europe*, Stanford, Calif: Stanford University Press.

—— (1990) 'Work, worth and justice in a socialist mixed economy', Working Papers on Central and Eastern Europe, *Centre for European Studies*, Harvard University 1990, No. 50.

Szelenyi, I. (1989) 'Eastern Europe in an epoch of transition: toward a socialist mixed economy?' in V. Nee and D. Stark (eds) *Remaking the Economic Institutions of Socialism: China and Eastern Europe*, Stanford, Calif: Stanford University Press.

Thévenot, L. (1983) 'L'économie du codage social', *Critiques de l'Economie Politique* 23–4: 188–222.

—— (1984) 'Rules and implements: investment in forms', *Social Science*

Information 23: 1–45.

Timár, J. (1985) 'Idö és munkaidö' (Time and working time), *Közgazdasági Szemle* 32: 1299–313.1.

Waldinger, R. D. (1986) *Through the Eye of the Needle: Immigrants and Enterprise in New York's Garment Trades*, New York: New York University Press.

Weeks, J. (1975) 'Policies for expanding employment in the informal urban sector of developing economies', *International Labour Review* 111: 1–13.

Williamson, O. (1985) *The Economic Institutions of Capitalism: Firms, Markets, and Relational Contracting*, New York: Free Press.

Wright, E. (1978) *Class, Crisis and the State*, London: Verso.

3

INNOVATION AND THE DIVISION OF LABOUR IN STATE-SOCIALIST AND CAPITALIST ENTERPRISES

Otfried Mickler

INTRODUCTION

The fast political change in Eastern Europe is wakening our curiosity into power relations, social mechanisms and working conditions of the labour force in the socialist enterprises. The revolutionary process is changing the political institutions as well as the economical structures of socialist countries deeply. For that reason an international comparative investigation about 'conditions and consequences of the introduction of new technology at work', which was carried through from 1982 to 1987 in co-operation with several Eastern and Western social scientists at the Vienna Centre, can be seen as a starting-point for that dynamic process of societal transformation whose outcomes we can't yet forecast.

The investigation was designed as an international comparative project making use of case study reports provided by national research teams. Each team was responsible for the collection of national data and for making their own case studies – on average two enterprises per country. The case studies were undertaken at the level of the work-place, but also included information about the overall division of labour inside the enterprise. The teams applied the whole range of research techniques, ranging from intensive interviews with key persons, to observations, the study of documents and even limited surveys. The full research findings were published by Francis and Grootings (1989).

The investigation consisted of case studies of the process of implementing CNC (computerized numerical control) machine-tools in engineering enterprises of five Eastern (CSSR, East Germany, Hungary, USSR, Poland) and five Western countries (Belgium, Great Britain, Finland, the Netherlands, FRG). The level of investigation has both an enterprise and shop-floor focus. I select here a part of the investigation which deals with the social processes of introducing new technologies in socialist enterprises (CSSR, East Germany, Hungary and Poland) and enterprises in West Germany.

The central subject under investigation – the process of introducing new technologies – seems to be particularly useful for revealing the internal structures of power and decision-making in socialist enterprises. We know from a lot of empirical studies that the implementation of new technologies is accompanied by a decision-making process in which social actors use new technologies as a resource to solve socio-economic problems in the enterprise. The description of how management shapes new technology and the division of labour, which alternatives are taken into consideration and how the workers react, can give us insights into the conditions of management action, strategies and aims, as well as the situation and interests of workers.

International comparative research has shown that such innovation processes are closely interrelated with nationally specific historical and institutional developments at the enterprise and at national level (Maurice et al. 1982). The empirically proven 'societal approach' of the Aix Group could be helpful as a frame of reference to systematically interpret the substantial changes in technology and work at the enterprise level in relation to national peculiarities. This suggests that changes in a firm's work organization and use of staff in new technologies are connected with the nationally specific socialisation process. The comparison in **systemic** perspective (socialist-capitalist innovation process), however, makes it necessary to extend this approach on the macro-level by including some analysis of political-economic structure and of the economic dynamics of the particular countries. As the shaping of technology and work is dependent on economic conditions and given structures of enterprise organization, on the qualifications of the labour force and on the power relations in the enterprise, the outcome of the innovation process according to this approach may vary with differing national (and systemic) patterns of market and industrial structure, vocational training system and industrial relations.

Therefore we assume that the process of introducing new technologies in the enterprises of the East European socialist countries will be carried out according to their **systemic** and **nationally** specific patterns in a different way compared with a capitalist country like West Germany. The questions this raises are, how do socialist

74

enterprises cope with the challenge offered by the new technologies and how far does the shaping of technology and work differ from that in a typical capitalist enterprise?

New research about technology and work has shown that differing rationalization strategies at plant level have major consequences for working conditions on the shop-floor. In particular, new technologies (defined as programmable computerized machines) have a **flexible** potential and can extend the possibilities for shaping the division of labour and working conditions in a variety of ways. Under conditions of rationalized production typical of existing Taylorist work organization, the new possibilities of micro-electronic technology today basically offer two alternative concepts of rationalization. First, they can be used to increase the level of automation in enterprises which up till now could not be automated such as small batch production. This management strategy could be called **technocentric**. Second, however, the possibilities given by the new technologies of decentralizing and programming on the spot can also be applied in a **non-Taylorist** way, that is to say, making use of human intelligence to increase productivity. In this case, work organization and the use of personnel have to be comprehensively reorganized, which means a partial departure from the traditional Taylorist types of work organization.

In the special case of introducing CNC-machine-tools, there is considerable consensus in the social sciences that the organizational and personnel allocation of programming and maintenance competences determines whether the form of work organization will restrict the work situation of the machine operator. The **technocentric model**, by the strict centralization of programming in the office, threatens workers by downgrading their occupational qualifications, increasing their monotony, intensifying productivity requirements and enhancing substitutability. **Non-Taylorist** forms of work organization can, on the other hand, lead to an improved work content and new career opportunities through direct programming on the machine or through co-operation with the programmers. In this way operators' qualifications are extended by new technologies and new opportunities arise for the regulation of work-load, and the worker's status in the firm is strengthened.

What are the conditions and social forces which promote the implementation of technocentric or of non-Taylorist forms of work organization? And how are these alternative conceptions of the division of labour bound up with national and systemic characteristics? Using empirical research in this field, a hypothesis can be formulated that technocentric concepts of work organization in the area of new technologies will become established where management see them as primarily an opportunity for extending their power on the shopfloor, and/or where strongly segmented employee structures promote their establishment. In contrast, a non-Taylorist use of labour is to be expected in qualified homogeneous employee structures, above all where consensual relationships exist within the firm.

I think that the methodological problems of interpreting selected case studies are well known in social sciences. These problems are even more complex in an international comparative study (cf. Grootings 1986). In order better to control the different variables of this complex comparative analysis, some important conditions in the process of introducing new technologies have been held constant. First, I have restricted my study to mechanical engineering, which has special structures of production, that is enterprises produce complex investment goods by small batch production and therefore they use metal-cutting machine-tools and a qualified labour force in a flexible way. Second, I have studied only CNC-machine-tools thus holding constant the type of new technology introduced in all case studies. Third, I consider only large firms to exclude the specific organizational problems of small firms and because the formalized organization and industrial relations in large firms makes it easier to analyse the decision-making process. Finally, an attempt was made to select such engineering enterprises for case studies which have proved to be reasonably typical of the nationally specific trends of new technologies in production.

In the following sections I analyse the case studies from the point of view of the dynamics of the implementation process. Starting from a short description of the more familiar capitalist case in West Germany, I then present in greater detail the process of introducing new technologies in the socialist enterprises. After that, the shaping of the division of labour in the area of application of the new technologies will be compared according to the various systemic and nationally specific characteristics of capitalist and socialist enterprises. I then describe changes in the working conditions as they relate to qualifications, control of performance and internal power constellations.

THE DYNAMICS OF INTRODUCING NEW TECHNOLOGIES

West Germany as a capitalist country

West Germany has a highly organized long-standing industrial structure, where the large engineering enterprises in particular are firmly established in the world market. In West Germany engineering also has a supreme national economic importance. In engineering, large enterprises are those with from 800 to 2000 employees. In general these are independent, privately owned firms whose decisions on technological policy are taken in a decentralized way, by the manager of the firm personally, and are closely related to production needs.

For the large engineering firms an important economic upheaval was caused by the international economic crisis which developed from the mid-1970s, and which led to a reduced demand for capital goods, increased competition from products from low-wage countries, and international competition for sophisticated technologies (Figure 3.1.).

The leading engineering enterprises reoriented their production structure as a reaction to the above. The technologically sophisticated machine, hand-tailored for the client, increasingly replaced the cheaper series-produced machine. This profound change in the market and in production was the trigger to modernize their own manufacture by changing over to the flexibly automated manufacturing of quality products in very small batches.

In the large engineering firms of West Germany CNC machines have been introduced very quickly since the end of the 1970s, so that at present up to 50 per cent of production is made with them. The modern manufacturing sector has developed on the basis of CNC as a production-determining core, with the whole organization of the firm oriented towards it. With CNC machines the use of personnel in two or three shifts is the rule.

This massive modernization of production was made necessary by the increased competition on the world market which occurred from the mid-1970s. Accordingly, management cites, as the aims of CNC use: flexible automation in order to be able also to produce very small batches of high quality at favourable cost; the shortening of the throughput time in order to meet deadlines better, and the reduction in capital costs through shorter intermediate storage. Savings in staff have, in comparison, only secondary importance.

A sufficient labour supply of skilled workers was a favourable

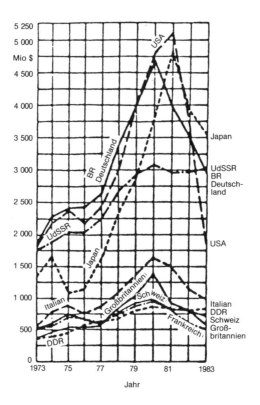

Figure 3.1 Turnover of machine-tools in dollars
Source: *American Machinist*, reproduced in *VDI-Nachrichten* of 23 March 1984

condition for the introduction of New Technology. The enterprises benefited from the high unemployment during the mid-1970s till the mid-1980s. Even young skilled workers had difficulty in getting a job appropriate to their talents in the stable employment segment of the industry. The external labour market is being increasingly shut out by the firms as they recruit their employees from their own vocational training schemes. In general, therefore, the firms have had since the early 1980s a sufficient reservoir (sometimes more than is needed) of qualified workers for use in technically complex areas of production and preparatory departments (design, planning, industrial engineering and maintenance).

However, in the various countries of the sample, 'qualified personnel' does not always mean the same thing, even if the classification into technical personnel, foremen, skilled and unskilled workers is applied in the same way everywhere. Very roughly, a distinction can be made between the system in most countries of general public education with a certain amount of vocational training in the secondary stage, and the system practised in the German-speaking countries of dual employer/state vocational training.

In this twin-track system of vocational training, which lasts three years, both practical qualifications (in the firm) and theoretical ones (in the vocational schools) are communicated, concluding with a national certificate as *Facharbeiter*. The large proportion of training which falls under this system in West Germany makes it the normal socialization pattern for workers, foremen and a large number of technicians, for whom it represents the basic qualification.

In engineering, in particular, a really shared homogeneous and fluid structure of employment exists on the basis of the craftsmen (mechanic, lathe operator, electrician) including the skilled workers and foremen in the workshop, and above that reaching into the technical staff of the planning departments. The hierarchy of production is therefore relatively weak; in production breakdowns or deficiencies there is, because of similar background experience, an easy point of contact for co-operation between technicians, foremen and workers.

The decision-making process for the choice of technology, its financial and its final implementation, took place against a background of about ten years' experience with NC machines. It was concentrated among a small group of top management. But because of the relatively small size of enterprises the preparation of the innovation process included consultation with the lower production management in the workshops. They formulated requirements from the point of view of the workshop and contributed their experiences with similar NC-machines. In general the works councils and employees supported this basic modernization of production, because in view of the threat from the crisis in market, they saw no other alternative if their enterprise was to survive.

In West Germany unions are organized according to the principle of the industrial association, not along party political lines, and they represent all the worker and employee groups of an enterprise (and branch) in the same union. While wage and general working conditions are regulated by negotiation in supra-regional tariff contracts, employees have a certain influence on the firms' innovation process, through 'co-determination' in the works councils, whose activity is regulated by law and must conform to the consensus of management. The works council cannot, as a rule, directly influence the innovation process of the enterprise, but can, nevertheless, steer it rather more indirectly by its influence over the use of personnel (e.g. through preferred recruiting of skilled employees), the vocational training of the firm and the particular terms of wage/performance agreements.

East Germany, Czechoslovakia, Hungary and Poland as socialist countries

The national economies of the socialist countries in the sample were guided by centralized state production and investment plans developed primarily in accordance with political aims. This implied the inclusion of individual firms in the national planning bureaucracy (central planning commission; branch ministers, e.g minister for mechanical engineering) for which the highest guidelines of action were not profitability or optimal adaptation to the market by the individual firm, but rather, the precise fulfilment of central production and investment plans.

Modernization projects, such as the introduction of the new technologies, were therefore usually initiated at the central-political level (party decisions were mostly the basis for modernization phases), conceived and developed with the aid of the higher planning authorities and the state research institutes. They were initially implemented in selected pilot firms, and later on in other firms according to set innovation plans.

This certainly somewhat simplified pattern of 'real socialist' economic activity has represented reality in East Germany and Czechoslovakia up to 1990. In Hungary and in Poland, modifications have been made, as a result of severe economic and political problems, in the direction of increasing freedom at the enterprise level. Thus firms possessed a certain margin for decision-making on sales policy and investment, and may, on their own responsibility, have used part of their earned profits for these activities. A Hungarian or Polish firm 'may' have gone bankrupt if it was badly managed, as happened in one of our cases, and may have dismissed staff if it is forced to reduce production. Yet from their permanent inclusion in central state production, investment and income planning there arise new specific contradictions for innovation decisions at the firm level (Nagy

1989: 89). Nevertheless, the margin for action of Hungarian and Polish managers was still much more like that of their Eastern colleagues than those of capitalist managers.

An important difference from capitalist firms in West Germany, which in engineering mainly are of small and medium-size, consists in the *combinat* organization, which is almost comparable to the structure of Western trusts. The *combinat* forms the organizational link between the state planning authorities and the manufacturing enterprise. The management of the *combinat* can be placed, as in a holding, over the manufacturing firms. However, in engineering especially, the management was usually integrated into the largest firm, where the essential decisions concerning business and technology of the member firms and the *combinat* as a whole are made.

The engineering *combinats* got resources for production such as raw materials, energy, labour and investment according to the central plan, but they could influence their budget allocation by bargaining with the state authorities. The bargaining power depends upon the size of the *combinat* and how it accommodates the main political priorities, such as developing heavy industries or promoting export industries to get Western currency. Because there was no market system and therefore real prices for supply and sales goods did not exist, the enterprises could not calculate the efficiency of production and of investment. The main guiding principle management had to orientate itself to was the precise fulfilment of state described plan quotas. The highly differentiated management hierarchy – from the branch minister at the top down to the plant managers – has functioned more in accordance to bureaucratic rules of executives in public administrations, than as managers orientated towards economic goals. Planning aside, the organizational reality in socialistic enterprises was even more complex, because Communist Party organization offered another layer of bureaucratic influence. The Party organization used to be deeply involved in the decision-making process of investment and the introduction of new technologies, and checked if the plan for the enterprise was precisely fulfilled. As a result of the ongoing political revolution in East Europe. which was undermining the monopolistic position of the Communist Party, this second branch of enterprise organization was abolished in 1991. The formerly strong links between state planning authority and enterprise are weakening too.

Very generally it is true that most socialist engineering firms have had no difficulty in selling their industrial goods. There was, on the contrary, because of the great need of the USSR and other Comecon states to catch up on industrialization, an insatiable demand for capital goods of all kinds. As the production graphs for engineering in the Comecon states show, even in the world-wide crisis since the mid-1970s and early 1980s, sales have not been impaired, so that here there still exists an economic basis for the standardized batch production of industrial goods (see Figure 3.1). However, in the course of increasing import–export connections between East and West, quality requirements for engineering products have risen in the socialist countries.

In general, in all the socialist countries there was a definite shortage of labour, which was hardly explicable in terms of the state guarantee of employment (socialist legitimation), but rather by certain deficiencies of the economic system. An important cause of this was, without doubt, the widespread and still very extensive method of production on out-of-date machines and with non-mechanized subsidiary processes, which produces a high demand for labour, especially unqualified labour. Also, for a number of reasons, the existing wage incentive systems contributed little to an increase in productivity (lack of wage differentiation, lack of consumer goods). But in addition, the frequently described policy of 'stockpiling' staff in the firms, played a considerable role in emptying the labour market. This accumulation of workers (who were badly paid and therefore only added a minimal burden on production costs), over and above actual need, secured for the firm's management a guarantee against unforeseen breaks in fulfilling plans caused by erratic or altered demands of the state planning bureaucracy. In Hungary in particular, labour market problems were increased by the extensive 'second economy' (discussed by Stark, Chapter 2), in this volume since work in this sector was far more attractive to qualified workers than that in the state enterprises.

The constant labour shortage provided workers with strong bargaining power which was used by experienced, qualified workers (permanent staff) to ease their performance or – as far as possible – to obtain higher pay. Unqualified workers had the opportunity of getting better working conditions and higher income by frequent changes of job.

But conflicts with management, damaging interests through changes in wage-performance, or the introduction of new technologies were hardly regulated by the union in the firm; they had to be individually dealt with or through unofficial action. The unions in the socialist countries undertook very different tasks from those in capitalist countries. According to the Leninistic definition of a union as a transmission chain from party aims to workers' consciousness, it had to fulfil several educational and social duties, and to strengthen motivation for good performance. In the case of introducing new technologies, the unions saw their task, above all, as the mobilization of employees for retraining measures.

The former socialist countries of the sample differ substantially with regard to the maturity of the development of industrial structures. So here the longer established industrial countries East Germany and Czechoslovakia, with their comparatively 'harmoniously' developed industries, confront the very one-sidedly industrialized, former agricultural countries of Poland and Hungary. As will be shown, these differences decisively influence the introduction of new technologies.

East Germany and Czechoslovakia

East Germany and Czechoslovakia, even before the Second World War, had thoroughly organized engineering production firms, a highly developed network of subcontractors and transport firms, and a disciplined and qualified work-force. In spite of many development problems in the post-war period (overemphasis on heavy industries, economic autarky, conflicts of political loyalty), both countries were able to develop their industry smoothly, so that modernization of manufacturing firms from the late 1970s could be achieved mainly under their own power.

Both countries, although they possessed intensive external trade links to capitalist countries, were relatively unaffected by the world-wide sales and debt crisis. Since there was no major backlog of catching up to be achieved in modern industrialization, their credit debts with Western financiers were small. They were therefore able to react to the crisis by introducing a policy of increased savings and rationalization without having to make basic changes in the functioning economic mechanism. This helped to promote the centralistic tendencies of economic bureaucracy.

East Germany and Czechoslovakia practise a kind of 'dual' vocational training like West Germany, continuing the traditional employer/state vocational training that existed before the second World War. Therefore a very homogeneous work-force which is formed on the basis of skilled workers and a common craft experience is found in engineering enterprises.

Hungary and Poland

Hungary and Poland were forcibly industrialized after the Second World War according to the Stalinistic economic model. This created great unevenness in the industrial structure, too much heavy industry, a lack of processing and subcontracting industries, and a labour market dominated by large masses of unskilled workers. From the early 1970s, both countries attempted a complementary industrialization strategy aimed at closing the worst gaps in basic industrialization and modernizing industrial production using Western credit financing for new technologies. The world-wide economic and debt crisis at the beginning of the 1980s hit both countries hard and forced them to make major political and economic changes in their modernization objectives.

Hungary reacted mainly according to a logic of independent economic policy. Financing difficulties in the early 1980s halted imports of new technologies from capitalistic countries and meant a departure from the path of industrial modernization. However, an attempt was made to approach these economic problems not by means of more centralization, but by a further liberalization of the economy. This included, in particular the extension the 'second economy' through the introduction of 'economic work communities' which could undertake production and service work within state enterprises on their own account (Nagy 1989).

In Poland economic reforms oriented towards the Hungarian model were introduced in enterprises in 1983 but with little success. Thus the new Polish government was making a serious attempt to introduce a market economy (Kulpinska and Skalmierski 1989).

As a consequence of one-sided basic industrialization there are, in Poland to a greater extent and in Hungary to a lesser extent, considerable imbalances both in the inner-industrial division of work (problems of amount and quality in the supply of pre-products, spare parts and services) and within the enterprise organization itself. Thus in the factories there are often highly mechanized islands of production working within a sea of obsolete technology. Since there is such a disproportion between the modernized core of production and the undeveloped subsidiary processes such as transport, maintenance and quality control, the highly efficient machines cannot be used to full capacity, and quality and productivity standards cannot be attained.

Although the large enterprises are strongly bureaucratized and formally organized on Tayloristic principles, all have industrial engineering departments, for example, they are functioning in reality

84

in a 'pre-Tayloristic' way, that is through permanent improvisation to overcome the various production problems. Hungarian social scientists call this a 'quasi-bureaucratic' way of production (Nagy 1989).

With regard to vocational training Poland and Hungary are orientated towards the system of general state education with certain supplementary vocational aspects. Vocational qualifications are mainly supplied as an addition to the general education system and in technical schools which usually have finely graded levels for their final diplomas. After completing their schooling, workers and technicians obtain their practical work experience in the firm, where they are given a more or less extended period of instructional training in the work-place. In addition, an educational overproduction of engineers can be observed, who therefore occupy positions right down to the lower managerial levels, like in an industrial engineering department. In Poland young engineers earn less money than experienced workers.

The employment structure in the Polish and Hungarian firms shows segmentation depending on privileges and influence in the firm. In addition to managers there is an influential group of qualified workers (central workers), and a considerable number of groups of unqualified workers (peripheral workers). In temporary coalitions of interest between the unions and the central workers, from which group the union functionaries are mainly recruited, the unions put the managers of the firms under pressure to retain the privileged wages of the permanent staff and thus prevent a shift in the firm's wage structure in the wake of new technologies.

Explaining the slower speed of introducing new technologies in socialist countries

In comparison with large capitalistic firms the socialist engineering industry has introduced CNC machine-tools at a much slower speed and is using them to a lesser extent. This applies even to the technologically advanced countries of East Germany and Czechoslovakia; however, the dynamic and economic use of new technologies here differs markedly from enterprises in Hungary and Poland.

East Germany and Czechoslovakia

By using its own financial resources and its own technologies the engineering industry pursued a policy of CNC modernization that saved foreign currency. As a consequence of insufficient capacity in the production of microprocessors, however, a significant number of CNC machine-tools were produced much later compared with West German CNC production. Whereas in 1981 more than 5,000 CNC machine-tools were produced in West Germany, East Germany manufactured only about 300 CNC machines (DIW 1984: 170). Furthermore the bureaucratic process of decision-making and implementation of new technologies through several hierarchical levels has proved to be extremely convoluted and open to error.

The most important aim in the use of new technology is the saving in staff through an increase in productivity, in order to make better use of the limited personnel resources. In addition the growing problems of selling investment goods on Western markets gave expected improvements of quality by CNC machine-processing a high priority too. While differences in numbers of CNC machines are significant, the few CNC machines currently in use are obviously well integrated into the production organization in the rationalized firms of East Germany and Czechoslovakia, because they are used by several shifts (two or three) everywhere (Assmann et al. 1989).

Hungary and Poland

At the end of the 1970s a relatively fast diffusion of new technologies entered Hungary and Poland through imports from the West. This was, however, abruptly stopped by the economic crisis of the two countries at the beginning of the 1980s. Since then the use of CNC machines has stagnated or grown very slowly within the framework of the countries' own limited technological and financial capabilities. A basic reason for the very slow growth in new technologies in the Hungarian and Polish engineering industry lies, however, in their lack of economic efficiency for production tasks in the enterprises.

Even more urgently, the most important aim attached to the introduction of new technologies was the saving of qualified labour it offered. In spite of high fluctuations and a lack of performance motivation among skilled workers, the aim was to better produce high-quality products and to maintain the continuity of the flow of production. For various reasons, however, these aims have not been achieved in the enterprises, so that the existing CNC machines often represent an additional burden for the firms rather than a way of easing their pressing production problems. They reinforce existing contradictions, rather than alleviate them.

Against the background of a more pre-Taylorist factory organization, the efficient integration of the expensive, highly efficient CNC machines into conventional engineering production, produces specific difficulties. Because of the lack of technological experience in handling new technologies, insufficient preparation for their introduction, and poor supportive processes (especially inefficient maintenance), an economically optimal use of CNC capacities has not been achieved. Moreover, since earning opportunities on CNC machines do not appear better to the workers than on conventional machines – in the Hungarian firms they are worse – the firms' managements have not been able to staff the capital-intensive CNC machines with enough personnel. Thus the CNC machines in the firms included in the sample were mainly used on one shift.

But there are also contradictions within the planning and implementation process of new technologies which hinder their dissemination in the firms. Because their introduction is initiated at the level of the *combinat* the top management frequently ignores the needs and organizational and personnel possibilities of the local units. Since in a situation of frequent production problems (caused by the 'shortage economy') the new technologies represent additional risks which are difficult to calculate, and local management has little enthusiasm in seeing them introduced. Management also fear resistance from workers in the firm's internal implementation of the new technologies. This is because any considerable firm reorganization places at risk the carefully balanced wage-performance hierarchy and threatens the privileges of permanent staff, on whose goodwill management is forced to depend for the improvised sorting out of constant bottlenecks. Local managers and permanent staff (including the firm's union representatives) therefore form a kind of conservative interest coalition against fundamental technical innovation. It is true that they cannot prevent them, but they can certainly affect their optimal functioning in the enterprise.

NEW TECHNOLOGIES AND THE DIVISION OF LABOUR

The smooth division of labour in West German engineering firms

The case studies (see Mickler 1989) and a representative investigation show that only a minority of engineering firms use CNC machines in **technocentric** forms (about one-third). The widespread application of non-Taylorist or **workshop-related** forms of programming is generally found. These range from programme-optimization by the machine operator on the basis of a pre-formulated CNC-office programme by the preparation department (the co-operative pattern, with a share of 40 per cent according to Rempp 1981); to completely independent programming on the machine by the tool-setter or operator, workshop programming has a proportion of 22 per cent).

From the point of view of work content, the inclusion of programming enriches the variety of work and for machine operators represents an enhancement to their skill and an extension of their own qualifications. Skilled workers can intervene in the programme sequence and programme minor sequence changes themselves at the machine. During the running-in of new programmes skilled workers must be able to control the algorithms of the programme drawing from their own practical experience. They must possess certain programming talents in order to undertake programme changes independently. The necessary optimizing procedure demands thinking of an abstract kind, and through their influence on programming, their responsibility for production achievement and product quality grows.

The programming work and the close co-operation with the programmers raise their social recognition, in particular, in relation to their superiors, some of whom cannot programme, and make the position of the skilled worker stronger in the firm, since the firm is particularly dependent upon these skills (Mickler 1989).

The relatively widespread application of workshop-related forms of CNC programming in West German engineering can be explained by the comparatively homogeneous employment structure based on skilled work, and the nationally specific pattern of industrial relations. The shared membership in the same occupational community by skilled workers, foremen and lower technicians offers very favourable preconditions for acquiring new theoretical qualifications in programming. It also makes co-operation easier between skilled workers and office programmers, because the latter as former skilled workers, can easily keep up professional contacts on the shop-floor.

Within management the more technocentric strategies, aimed at clear control of the workshop from above, mostly represent top management thinking, whereas production management as a rule, supports workshop-related forms of organization. The aim of the latter is, by means of the comprehensive use of professional qualifications and improved co-operation between the workshop and programming office, to optimally use the great production capacity of the CNC machines with a decreased use of personnel.

The workshop-related strategy of the management meets the interests of works council and employees since, although not preventing reductions in staff because of greater productivity, it does, however, mean that the skilled worker qualifications can be retained in the workshop on a new level. There can, of course, be individual conflicts of interest in the workshop between the technicians in the programme office and the programming workers at the machines, but these do not find any institutional foothold to grow, since both groups are organized within the same industrial union (IG Metall), and are represented by the same works council.

Technocentric forms of CNC machine use in East Germany and Czechoslovakia

CNC programmes here are produced by engineers, and the workers are not officially permitted to interfere in the programme. Work in the workshop is planned, co-ordinated in chronological order, and steered by trained engineers, known as technologists, in large planning and control offices who allocate tasks, materials, tools and subsidiary activities. The workers have, according to the official distribution of competence in the firms, responsibility only for the setting up and operating of the CNC/NC machines. Workshop programming (i.e. the exclusive programming of the CNC machines by worker or foreman) has not been very widespread. There appear to be several reasons why the engineering firms of East Germany and Czechoslovakia stick to the technocentric concept of CNC organization to a far greater measure than in engineering in West Germany, in spite of a similar qualified, homogeneous employment structure.

First, a technocentric concept of programming is entrenched in the logic of the strongly centralized decision-making and implementation process of new technologies in these two countries. It represents, so to speak, the final link in the long series of bureacratic layers which have to be gone through, and which do not want to give up control over the 'right' way, according to their philosophy, of efficiently using the expensive, highly productive CNC machines. A not inconsequential factor here may be distrust by the production management of the performance motivation of the workers. In addition the strong position of the planning office, with its educationally highly qualified personnel, probably supports technocentric tendencies. It appears appropriate that theoretically educated engineers should take over programming as a job which is both suited to their qualification and able to secure their competence and control over the workers on the workshop-floor.

However, the beginnings of a gradual loosening-up of the predominantly technocentric CNC organization concept were recognized in East Germany at the enterprise level. On the basis of their skilled worker qualifications many workers had already without officially organized courses, learned programming on their own initiative, the case study found 60 per cent of machine operators familiar with such skills. With informal approval from technologists, who see a practical contribution to smoother production in this process, the CNC workers use their knowledge to a greater or lesser extent for correction and optimization of the office programmes. This additional contribution of the workers is not recognized by a bonus in wages, although they certainly achieve solid advantages in performance regulation within the framework of prescribed times and thus gain time by it (Assmann et al. 1989).

In addition there was a discrepancy between qualified vocational training for almost all young people and their often underqualified employment in restrictive, high-stress fields of work. This was obviously growing, and with it, discontent, particularly on the part of young skilled workers. The creation of more qualified forms of work therefore appears to be an important contribution to the reduction of conflict and increase in motivation. The concept of workshop-related (CNC) programming in group form has been quoted in this context recently as an important contribution to the qualitative enrichment of work.

Informal practices of workshop-related programming in Hungary and Poland

The introduction of capital-intensive, 'potentially' highly productive CNC machines gave the basically pre-Tayloristic Hungarian and Polish engineering enterprises (where the workers themselves usually plan their work, fetch materials, and produce devices and tools) unfamiliar organizational demands. The requirement of more exact planning for CNC-appropriate work-pieces and sufficient equipment with CNC programmes was necessary in order to make efficent use of the CNC machines. But such a basic reorganization has not been undertaken even in a minimal form. It is true that central programming offices are being installed everywhere, because obviously there was a wish to catch up on the new technical demands of programming, but these contributed nothing essential either to increasing the efficiency of CNC production, or creating stricter control over workers. For without the active participation of the latter in CNC programming and planning nothing at all would function (Nagy 1989; Kulpinska and Skalmierski 1989).

The common character to CNC organization in the Hungarian and Polish enterprises, with its patchy centralism on the one hand and the self-confident worker autonomy on the other hand, has many reasons. The fact that a central programming office is established at all in a pre-Tayloristic factory must be explained by the hope of the firm's management that, in spite of all improvisation and daily trouble-shooting, it must be possible to achieve a minimum of control over the new expensive machines. The programming office was staffed by trained engineers, under the assumption that their 'weight' in the organization should maintain the boundaries of competence against the workers in the workshop. In daily practice, however, this **surface** technocentric strategy proved to be extraordinarily fragmentary. The programming technicians, who had absolutely no practical cutting experience, could neither secure a smooth flow of materials (because of lack of planning) nor deliver efficient programmes free of error. The CNC machines were therefore able to produce goods only because the workers, who have learned programming in courses or on their own initiative, used their practical knowledge of cutting techniques in the removal of errors and optimization of the programme.

The obviously consistent step of introducing a workshop-related organization of CNC programming in this situation, however, fails, not at least because of the lack of interest on the part of the qualified workers. For them there is, in the non-adapted organization of the firms, hardly any advantage and a number of disadvantages in CNC work. For instance, they were not placed in a higher wage group because they did not officially possess the qualifications necessary for programming. While in the Polish firms CNC workers on a set time-wage can at least get good time margins out of it, the piece-rate system of the Hungarian firm leads, in view of the frequent breakdowns and material bottlenecks, to a loss of income in comparison with conventional work. In Hungary, especially, unfavourable shift work on CNC machines is unattractive because it cuts the worker off from the lucrative earning possibilities contained in the 'second' economy. So in general, an officially workshop-related CNC organization, which would certainly require from the workers rather more career motivation and involvement than at present, would not be rewarding to the qualified permanent staff. In the medium term, little will be changed in the half-hearted inefficient organization of CNC use, which does, however, grant the workers considerable autonomy.

SUMMARY

The massive and relatively fast introduction of CNC machine-tools in West German engineering could be explained by the strong integration of the large firms within the capitalist world market and by comparatively good conditions of innovation, such as a co-operative decision-making process, a qualified labour force and consensual industrial relations. On the other hand, the initial relatively slow introduction of new technologies in the socialist countries is surprising, because there ought to have been, with the large unit complexes of firms and state subsidies, relatively favourable economic conditions for technological innovations. This difference can be explained, as the comparative analysis shows only through the combined effect of national and system specific structures and mechanisms. Bureaucratized decision-making processes, uneven industrial structures (particularly in Hungary and Poland) and a strongly defined manager–worker behavioural relationship caused by labour shortages, all decelerate or even block the use of the new technologies in the firm. The national and system specific influence on the enterprises' process of innovation expressed here confirms the general assumptions of the societal approach.

On the question of the form of the firms' division of labour and the use of personnel in the CNC system, the shaping of technology and work organization in the capitalist engineering enterpises of West Germany confirms the societal approach too. Thus the more workshop-related programming of CNC-machine-tools here can be explained by the specific national peculiarities of vocational training, a homogeneous employment structure and co-operative pattern of industrial relations.

In contrast, the shaping of organization in the socialist countries seems to run directly contrary to an interpretation according to the societal approach. For according to this, firms in East Germany and Czechoslovakia, on a homogeneous skilled labour force, ought to prefer workshop-related organizational forms, whereas in reality, they have, on the contrary, preferred overwhelmingly technocentric models up to now. On the other hand, the heterogeneous hierarchical employment structure of the Hungarian and Polish enterprises would imply a strict technocentric organization of CNC use, whereas, in reality, the workers have considerable planning autonomy and programming responsibility which very nearly corresponds to the workshop-related variant.

We were able to show that these contradictions could be plausibly explained through the different political and economic structures, the historical development of these countries and the related differentiated manager–worker behaviour pattern. In East Germany and Czechoslovakia on the basis of a developed industrial structure and rationalized firms, the socially dominating organization principle of bureaucratic centralism could be relatively successful. Against this, the mechanism of the 'shortage economy' in Hungary and Poland explains the parallelism of bureaucratic centralism as a goal and extensive worker autonomy as a reality in the enterprises.

It was a common factor in all the socialist enterprises of the sample that a large proportion of machine operators informally participate in the process of running in programmes and programme optimization. It was also noticeable that the exclusive staffing of programming offices with trained technicians does not, as one would expect from the organizational-sociological literature, undermine this participation, but in fact almost compels the contrary, because of the lack of practical work experience of the engineers. However, this constellation is not particularly favourable to co-operation between office programmers and CNC workers because there is not a genuine sharing of technical knowledge. Rather segmentation between workers and engineering staff was reinforced.

The hypothesis concerning the connection between bureaucratic control over the workshop and technocentric CNC organization is true within limits for the rationalized firms in East Germany and Czechoslovakia. In contrast, in the Hungarian and Polish firms, the 'quasi-bureaucratic' decision making structures form the background for a large measure of worker autonomy **in spite** of centralistic bureaucratic control claims made at the management level of the enterprises.

OUTLOOK: STATE-SOCIALIST INDUSTRY ON THE WAY TO CAPITALIST FORMS OF MODERNIZATION – THE CASE OF EAST GERMANY

Finally, against this background of specific economic and enterprise structures in socialist countries, we have to ask what modernization path the current process of social transformation could take and which socio-economic conditions have to be taken into account. It is true, that the introduction of a market economy, more efficiency of industrial production and more industrial democracy are widely shared political aims in East Germany. But how do these objectives fit the old economic and social structures? How far will new forces on the societal and the enterprise level change the bureaucratized structures and in what direction modernization will go is at present an open question?

First, I shall attempt some speculative answers to these important questions, restricting myself to the restructuring of East German industry because we can in West Germany observe this transformation process first hand and I can also use some empirical information from a sociological case study currently being conducted in an East German enterprise (Bluhm et al. 1990).

Most serious economists forecast that the process of capitalist transformation of the state-socialist industry in East Germany will take a highly dramatic course. They estimate that between half and two-thirds of the present enterprises will go bankrupt by 1994. Only one-third of the enterprises have a realistic chance of surviving if they are successful in modernizing their production. That is to say, capitalist restructuring of the East German industry will be carried through under conditions of a deep economic recession. Some of the present industries like chemistry, steel processing and metal mining will largely perish, other industries like cars and electronics must be considerably rebuilt, and yet others such as textiles and mechanical engineering will have a chance of surviving under market conditions only if they succeed in improving productivity by introducing new technology and by modernizing the enterprise organization. A high rate of unemployment is expected, perhaps 4 million, and therefore a very unfavourable labour market situation is likely during the early to mid-1990s. I shall concentrate my considerations on the small number of East German enterprises which have a real chance of surviving after undergoing a rigorous capitalist modernization of their produc-

94

tion. I shall deal with three central aspects of this subject: first, the future concepts and strategies of capitalist modernization to change the persisting structures of the state-socialist enterprises; second, the changing attitudes of the workers towards work; third, the rise of institutional forms of collective bargaining and of industrial democracy in the enterprises.

MODERNIZATION OF INDUSTRY AS A STRATEGY OF FORDISTIC RATIONALIZATION

As pointed out earlier, the politics of industrial development in East Germany since 1970 followed the concept of 'Fordism in one country'. The government tried to get efficient mass production by specializing the respective enterprises on few products and by merging these enterprises into huge *combinats*. The concept of Fordist production was stabilized by the core needs of the centrally guided economy. But in reality the Fordist model of production did not function very well in the East German enterprises because of many internal contradictions at the level of the state-controlled economy – shortages of equipment, labour and materials together with over-centralized investment politics – and because of falling work performance on the shop-floor, due to low motivation to work in an efficient and responsible way.

The managers of the enterprises now see, under the new conditions of decay of the state-socialist controlling mechanisms and weakening of their links to the *combinats*, the chance to finally carry through their old Fordist concept of production. Managers in East German enterprises are now seizing the favourable opportunity to strengthen the Tayloristic grip on the shop-floor. The application of the principles of market economy means for them, primarily a way of strengthening control from above, linking foremen to stronger hierarchical direction and thus enforcing work discipline. No effective resistance will be made to this Fordist strategy of capitalist modernization, because under the present conditions in East German enterprises the working class is weakened by unemployment and the introduction of market economy has a high degree of legitimation in the society. Thus we shall see the former East Germany in the 1990s the development and intensification of Fordism, and a more radical version than Western European countries experienced in the decades after the Second World War.

THE INTENSIFICATION OF LABOUR PERFORMANCE AND THE SHIFT TOWARDS AN INSTRUMENTAL ORIENTATION TO WORK

Workers' behaviour in East Germany, as in other state-socialist countries, used to have at least two faces, a socio-political one at the level of public appearane and the real one shown in life on the shop-floor (see Burawoy, Chapter 6 in this volume). On the one hand the enterprise and its political institutions (the Communist Party and trade unions) have exerted an important influence on the total life of workers and their families: from organizing cultural and political events, providing flats, kindergartens and holidays, to setting special shifts for political purposes. Thus the 'arm' of the socialist enterprise was reaching far into the private life of workers.

On the other hand, workers have taken pains to limit their effort and performance on the shop-floor to a minimum. Their position here reinforced the strong bargaining power which derived both from the permanent labour shortage in socialist enterprises, and the need for management to co-operate closely with workers in overcoming the permanent bottlenecks of the shortage economy. They orientated themselves towards achieving an unwritten agreement with the management, what we would call a 'negative class compromise'. That is to say, they refused to work efficiently in the enterprise because management was not able to give them a chance of considerably improving living standards. Consequently you could observe a broad retreat into private life by the workers quite in contrast to the high value of an engagement in socialized work which plays a central part in socialist ideology. Workers displayed only a small amount of 'passive strength', which could no doubt reduce attempts at worsening working conditions, but could not change the aims and content of industrial politics made by management and the party in the *combinat* and in the enterprise.

In the course of the ongoing decay of the formerly dominant socialist ideology of work, the relationship of the workers to their enterprise will surely be further depoliticized. We shall see develop real **wage-labour**, and an employment relationship without any ideological burden. First interviews with workers in East Germany show that they will prefer this kind of business-like working arrangement to the former ideologically burdened relationship. We can expect therefore the development of more instrumental orientation towards work as industrial sociologists have found among workers in capitalist enterprises. The enterprise will cease to be a place of great significance for the socio-cultural life of workers, instead it will be reduced in its meaning to a functional place where workers earn enough money to fulfil their consumer needs.

But the capitalist restructuring of the state socialist economy under the above described conditions of growing unemployment will very soon undermine the traditionally strong bargaining power of workers on the shop-floor. Management will now have the power to terminate the existing 'class compromise' and to enhance labour performance, work discipline and product quality. It is expected that workers, despite the obvious worsening of working conditions, will co-operate in a consensual way if they get sufficient income to improve their living standard gradually to the level of the working class in West Germany. But unemployment will naturally glut the labour market and depress wages, and therefore intensify the gap between the two Germanies.

The dramatic restructuring of the East German industry will produce a lot of conflicts between management and workers and between the workers on the shop-floor themselves. The various groups of blue-collar workers will be affected by capitalist modernization and dismissals in different ways; there will be as a consequence winners and losers. Workers in the comparatively overcrowded departments of office work and of maintenance work are likely to fall victim to the rationalization policies, but they won't give up without a fight because of their formerly strong position within the enterprise.

THE RISE OF INSTITUTIONAL FORMS OF INDUSTRIAL DEMOCRACY

The complete destruction of the potential of collective resistance may be seen as one of the worst effects of the Stalinistic forms of socialism that the working class in East Germany suffered. It resulted in a highly individualized labour force and in bureaucratized forms of conflict regulation which were dominated by the party organization. Hence after the decay of the Communist Party and the official party-orientated trade union, a renewal of independent institutions of industrial democracy cannot link up with the remnants of collective forms of worker resistance on the shop-floor. A first impression of the consciousness of the workers in East Germany shows not only uncertainty and helplessness to a high degree, but also the absence of the capacity to articulate their own interests in an appropriate way and to dispute them with management.

While it is true that new commissions of trade unions and works councils are at present being formed in most of the enterprises in East Germany, a close look at them, however, shows that they are mostly made up of the old trade union officials and dismissed managers, with only a few independent workers out of the democratic movement. Thus it is not very astonishing that this 'new' representation of interests is, on the whole, pursuing the same defensive politics of the old party-orientated trade union. It is reported that instead of representing workers' interests in an offensive way, they are refusing claims of the workers for an improvement of their working conditions. They now argue that with the prospective difficulties of the enterprise in maintaining a stable position in the market economy, immediate improvements in workers' conditions cannot be achieved.

Thus new institutional forms of industrial democracy will have a chance to grow in East German enterprises only if they develop alongside the course of conflicts with management as a result of the collective learning processes of the workers. At present it is quite difficult for us to find out whether or not such forms of real representation of interests could link up with the possibly hidden informal activities of groups of workers on the shop-floor. The trade unions of West Germany, which have just started to expand their organizational field into East German areas, will certainly play an influential role in this process. In spite of their bureaucratized organization they might initiate a lot of important impulses to further the process of industrial democracy within the enterprises. The role of the West German unions in this regard looks like the role the British trade union movement played in the late 1940s following the liberation from the Nazi regime, when they helped significantly to build up democratic institutions of trade unions in West Germany.

REFERENCES

Assmann, G. Nagel, D. and Stollberg, R. (1989) 'The introduction of new technology in industrial enterprises of the German Democratic Republic: two case studies', in A. Francis and P. Grootings (eds) *New Technologies and Work-Capitalist and Socialist Perspectives*, London: Routledge.

Bluhm, K. Kern, H. Naevecke, S. Voskamp, U. and Wittke, V. (1990) 'Zur Bedeutung des bisherigen DDR-Produktionsmodells fur Pfade industrieller Reorganisation – Ansatz und erste Erfahrungen aus der Feldarbeit im Kabelwerk Adlershof' (DDR), Gottingen, unpublished manuscript.

Deutsches Institut Fur Wirtschartsforschung (DIW) (1984) *Handbuch der DDR-Wirtschaft*, Reinbeck: Rowohlt.

Eyraud, F. and Rychener, F. (1986) 'A societal analysis of new technologies', in P. Grootings (ed.) *Technology and Work*, London: Croom Helm.

Francis, A. and Grootings, P. (eds) (1989) *New Technologies and Work-Capitalist and Socialist Perspectives*, London: Routledge.

Grootings, P. (1986) 'Technology and work: a topic for East – West comparison?, in P. Grootings (ed.) *Technology and Work*, London: Croom Helm.

Hoss, D. (1986) 'Technology and work in the two Germanies', in P. Grootings (ed.) *Technology and Work*, London: Croom Helm.

Kulpinska, J. and Skalmierski, S. (1989) 'The taming of new technology: a Polish case study on the introduction of a flexible manufacturing system', in A. Francis and P. Grootings (eds) *New Technologies and Work-Capitalist and Socialist Perspectives*, London: Routledge.

Maurice, M. Sellier, F. and Silvestre, J. J. (1982) *Politiques d'education et d'organisation industrielle*, Paris: PUF (Press Universitaire Français).

Mickler, O. (1989) 'The introduction and use of CNC in the Federal Republic of Germany', in A. Francis and P. Grootings (eds) *New Technologies and Work-Capitalist and Socialist Perspectives*, London: Routledge.

Nagy, K. (1989) 'New technology and work in Hungary: technological innovation without organizational adaptation', in A. Francis and P. Grootings (eds) *New Technologies and Work-Capitalist and Socialist Perspectives*, London: Routledge.

Rempp, H.U.A. (1987) *Wirtschaftliche und soziale Answirkungen des CNC-Werkteugmaschineneinsatzes*. RKW: Eschborn.

Part III

LABOUR PROCESS REFORM IN EASTERN EUROPE

INTRODUCTION

Perestroika and glasnost are now familiar terms in the West, symbolic slogans of reform, change and discontinuity in former Soviet-type societies. The chapters in this part of the book offer contrasting portraits of the nature of the reform programme as it affects the labour process within state socialism. They continue the comparative theme developed earlier, only here the contrasts are between the old regime and the nascent attitudes and structures which began to emerge in the late 1980s. The chapters are united by sharing a relatively optimistic view of the prospects for working-class interests and 'real' socialism arising from within the contradictions, and not the explicit objectives, of the current reform process. All three are interested in suggesting how work-place reforms can create new institutions for more open, collective forms of resistance and class struggle, and mechanisms of economic control generated from below, not imposed from above. As such, they share a focus on the politics of production and socialism at the level of the labour process that treats as relatively unproblematic some of the more critical issues of enterprise-state, plan-market relations within a future socialist society discussed in Chapter 1.

Chapters 4 and 5 examine the former Soviet Union, and complement each other by presenting general and personal accounts of the experience of past and current reform programmes. Both cast a sceptical eye over the prospects for fundamental change, cautious of the regime's resistance to ad hoc incremental reform. Chapter 6 explores the prospects for radical democracy and self-management in the recent Hungarian experience.

In Chapter 4 Don Filtzer rejects the characterization of the labour process in the former Soviet Union as socialist or planned. For him it is rather a particular class system, based on bureaucratic tutelage of state and party officials. Genuine planning and socialism requires democratic forms of organization for there to be correspondence between plans and results. The absence of democratic control and accountability in the current regime creates class divisions between planners and implementors, and sectional and individual challenges at every level of the system. Filtzer catalogues the inefficiencies, blocks on new investment, wastages and gaps between plan and practice that are part of this system. The organization of the labour process creates a forced dependence between workers and managers. Soviet workers exercise considerable discretion over their work speeds and scheduling because management are subject to their goodwill to fulfil plans in this erratic and uncertain environment. Shortages, substandard tools and materials make managers dependent on the skills and initiative of workers, who must constantly modify and rectify these anomolies to meet production targets. Cutting corners, fiddling, collusion and indulgency characterize the highly informal relations between workers and managers. This results not only in work-place autonomy for individual workers, but also in atomization for the working class as a whole, and the consequent disabling of collective protest and reform. The effects of this system on the ruling elite is their inability to modernize, rationalize and restructure the labour process to increase or improve production – atomization inhibiting collective reform. Long-term stagnation and crisis are inherent in the system, reform a constant requirement, but without fundamental political change and democratic control – which the party elite are unwilling to concede – it remains an elusive goal.

Filtzer charts the history of failed attempts at reform in order to prepare a backcloth to current developments. Sections of the ruling elite want to see unemployment, the traditional method of labour discipline in capitalism, used on Soviet workers, although the impact of this at the enterprise level is contradictory. The social ties, pension rights and seniority accumulated within the enterprise mean that workers have strong incentives to maintain employment, even if this means changes to their work. Managers are also reluctant to reduce labour surpluses because labour hoarding has been the traditional means of coping with the inherent uncertainties of production. While at state level unemployment is a proclaimed aim, its implementation at enterprise level is less clear cut. Where unemployment is having an impact is among women workers, who are concentrated in consumption goods sectors, which, due to their technological structure, gives them less autonomy and power to protect themselves. They suffer disproportionately compared with male workers in heavy goods industries, although, ironically, it is precisely these consumption goods industries that require expansion if reform is to occur.

Filtzer then examines changes in incentives schemes and moves towards group or collective working aimed at tackling the endemic individualism of labour process practices. Collective systems, such as the brigades, are forced to operate in ways which work against their widespread adoption. Group working, which increases productivity and improves quality, also leads to the raising of output targets, forcing rationalization and intensification within the brigades, but without a corresponding increase in wages. Workers are therefore penalized rather than rewarded for efforts at collective working. Similarly attempts to introduce work-place democracy – through Councils of the Labour Collectives (Russian acronym STK) – to allow workers to influence management decision-making, and make them, according to official terminology, 'masters of the enterprise' have been undermined by the weight of existing practices – blocked by existing trade unions and management fearful for their power. This corporatist strategy was instituted by the reform wing of the ruling elites to make workers responsible to their enterprises, but has done little to challenge hierarchical decision-making structures monopolized by management. In fact those elected into STK were frequently managers. Far from reflecting the views of rank-and-file workers, these new structures have established another layer of bureaucracy. Filtzer quotes from workers at an ostensibly successful Skoda STK, where the new initiative was seen as 'just another routine campaign, similar to those they had seen all their working lives'.

Filtzer's conclusions are that the reform programme is slipping out of control, as the basic problems of the wastefulness, obsolescence and inefficiencies of Soviet industry have actually increased. Attempts to reduce the atomization of labour and the failure of reform promises will, however, reintroduce traditional collective forms of organization and class struggle, such as strikes, which are increasing. Filtzer believes these forms of *collective* protest offer the only chance for fundamental change, a way of breaking the impasse and contradictory nature of top-down reforms which reinforce rather than transform the old regime.

Chapter 5 by David Mandel is in the form of an interview with Kolya Naumov, a worker in a large car factory in Moscow. It is a personal statement of his experiences inside the factory as an assembly-line worker – fresh from the provinces, living in an over-crowded dormitory – to night-school autodidact, skilled machinist and eventual foreman of a small section off-the-line in the same company. It is a subjective and historical tale of one man's experience from young worker in 1970 to mature foreman in the late 1980s. The chapter describes 'life on the line', and the universal experience of car assembly, made familiar in the West through sociological accounts such as Beynon (1973) or insider experiences such as Linhart (1981) or Kamata (1983). The assembly-line is a 'cruel and horrible thing', a 'nauseous, soulless machine' that has to be fought; 'beating the machine', creating one's own time and mastering the routine are all familiar enough features of this type of work. However, the dormitory system, the recruitment of young workers from the provinces and the integration of workers into the enterprise, all go beyond the cash nexus, and parallel Kamata's description of the life of a seasonal worker in Toyota. Indeed the lack of escape or resistance, the collusive trade union system, regular and uncontrollable speed-ups are common ground between the Russian and Japanese experiences. But there the comparisons end, because the inefficiencies, breakdowns, individualism and informal favouritism of the Russian factory contrast to the team-working and efficiency of production in Japan.[1] Piece-working dominates to reinforce individualism. The brigade system, introduced to challenge individualism, increase productivity and workers' accountability, was also based on individual incentive systems and therefore did nothing to change existing practices. Kolya Naumov gives a vivid account of the way informality between management and workers undermines collective protest against labour intensification as 'every worker has some favour to ask and some way to earn a little extra, and every boss also has ways of earning extra . . . we are all linked together by these sins'.

Protest and resistance is difficult, each worker puts his or her own survival first, frightened of stepping out of line or unable to articulate collective interests. 'The tradition of struggle has been destroyed and there is no experience'. This is a wonderful account of the fallacy of classical Marxist assumptions that the forces of production **collectivize** labour. We have a factory of 30,000 workers all thinking about their private deals and interests, and unable, because of the pattern of **social relations**, to articulate a collective voice. However, this does not mean that protests do not occur. Naumov not only describes his own individual opposition to the system, but also the obstacles to sustaining collective resistance. Repression and managerial power are brought down on those labelled 'trouble-makers'. Threats to inform the KGB and the gradual erosion of support from

106

others, fearful to associate with those who question the system openly, help to isolate those who protest.

This account is also the story of one man's career progression to foreman, optimism of his power to change the system from within, and gradual realization that 'good men' can make no impact on the environment of state socialisms. The reforms of the 1980s are placed against the backcloth of the failure of previous change programmes and the systems' resistance to radical reform. The institutional changes introduced in the 1980s, and described in detail by Filtzer in Chapter 4, are seen here in practice in this car factory and considered largely tokenistic. There were consultation exercises, collective discussion between enterprise management and rank-and-file workers, but these had evoked such powerful attacks on the directorate that they were not repeated. Nevertheless Naumov is not a bitter man, he has not fallen into apathy, cynicism or escapism – conditions common under this system. The sheer resourcefulness of Russian workers, who manage, despite the enormous difficulties, to organize production, is a source of optimism for him. 'If this talent and energy could be put to positive use, it could make miracles'. But we are not clear what future this would be.

In Chapter 6 Michael Burawoy examines the changes in the Hungarian state socialist system and the prospects for democratic socialism. This is based on his own experiences as a yogurt-eating American professor turned furnaceman at the Lenin Steel Works in Miskoic, where Burawoy carried out participant observation on numerous occasions and has maintained regular contacts with fellow workmates since 1987. The opening section examines Lenin's view of the requirements for socialism, its need for an international dimension and an advanced capitalist base, and hence the distortions in Eastern Europe, where the democratic elements of Lenin's vision of communism have never been realized. State socialism has been a dictatorship *over* not *of* the working class. Having established the incomplete and distorted nature of the regime's socialist credentials, Burawoy examines the dynamics of the system, the shortage economy and its contradictions. However, his principal aim is not to catalogue these well-known features, but rather to explore the clash between the proclaimed and real nature of the regime, the ritual and the reality, and how this affects the *consciousness* of those at the top and bottom of the system. This he achieves by drawing on an incident at the Lenin Steel Works, when, in preparation for a visit by the Prime Minister, the place was ritually repainted and cleaned. This front was necessary in order for enterprise management to maintain the outward appearance of organization as an aid to political support for investment income and in conformity with state socialist ideals. Burawoy uses the metaphor of 'painting' rather than 'building' socialism to explore the contradictory face of state socialism. Reform in the 1980s, he suggests, occurred because the ruling elite lost faith with this sham socialism, and its own rituals of legitimation. State socialism collapsed from above.

The remainder of Chapter 6 discusses the outcomes of this collapse in Hungary, including the emergence of new classes and ownership forms. Burawoy notes that foreign investment remained comparatively small – 10 per cent in June 1990 – and it was the old managerial class which had begun to turn its political capital into economic capital. Significantly the consequences of foreign investment have been the breakup of integrated state enterprises into smaller joint-stock companies, something which increased managerial hierarchies and wages, and reinforced existing competitive pressures between different sections of the Steel Works, thereby exacerbating problems of the old regime rather than increasing efficiency. Burawoy examines the different privatization options, from joint ventures to employee share schemes, the latter growing in popularity because they retain Hungarian ownership and increase worker accountability more directly.

Accompanying privatization has been the appearance of new forms of work-place representation, workers' councils, established as genuine forums for worker grievances in opposition to the discredited trade unions of the old regime. These forms are rooted in production, and have not expressed, as yet, a wider political voice. They also differ from the workers' councils that sprang up during the political upheavals in 1956, especially with their positive attitude towards privatization and the extension of employee share ownership. Burawoy is optimistic about the potential of this form of representation becoming a new force for radical change for a genuine socialism capable of embracing those elements of rationality, democracy and justice that Burawoy believes Lenin's vision of socialism embodied.

NOTE

1   Jurgens (1989) discusses the competitive individualism of management practices in Japan, but this is strictly for workers who are fighting their way to the top of the firm. Individualism in the Russian car factory

operated at all levels, alongside older management practices, such as nepotism. For a discussion of the parallels and differences between 'Stalinist socialism' and 'bourgeois Stalinism' see Blackburn (1991).

REFERENCES

Beynon, H. (1973) *Working for Ford*, Harmondsworth: Penguin.

Blackburn, R. (1991) 'Fin de siècle: socialism after the crash', *New Left Review* 185: 5–67

Jurgens, U. (1989) 'The transfer of Japanese management concepts in the international automobile industry', in S. Wood (ed.) *The Transformation of Work*, London: Unwin Hyman.

Kamata, S. (1983) *Japan in the Passing Lane*, London: George Allen & Unwin.

Linhart, R. (1981) *The Assembly Line*, London: John Calder.

4

ECONOMIC REFORM AND PRODUCTION RELATIONS IN SOVIET INDUSTRY, 1986–90

Don Filtzer

THE LABOUR PROCESS IN SOVIET INDUSTRY AND THE 'HISTORICAL TASK' OF PERESTROIKA

It has become the accepted wisdom among Western specialists in Soviet affairs that Mikhail Gorbachev's initial reform programme, known as perestroika (reconstruction), came to an end with the abortive *Putsch* of August 1991. According to this interpretation, the Soviet (or post-Soviet) leadership's commitment to full-fledged market reform dates from this event. Such an analysis, in our view, reflects a deep misunderstanding of what had transpired in the Soviet Union for a full year before the *Putsch*. The decision to adopt the market dates back at least to the summer of 1990 when Gorbachev and his entourage began putting in place a number of the institutional preconditions of a market economy, including clearly defined rights of enterprise owners, the decentralization of wage-setting, and laws governing denationalization and the protection of private invest-ment.[1] For the historical mission of perestroika had been to attempt to reform the economic system – to streamline it, reduce its top-heavy bureaucratization, and make the process of surplus extraction more efficient – while keeping its basic class relations intact. Although Gorbachev and his various circles of advisers always envisioned the use of 'market mechanisms' to achieve these aims, they at all times had sought to control their impact, so as not to force any radical change in the basic property relations from which the Soviet elite derived its power. This task was doomed to failure from the start and was abandoned in very large part because its success hinged on the elite's ability to restructure the labour process. This, in turn, proved impossible within the bounds of these property relations. The complete marketization of the system, with the inevitable restoration

110

of capitalism to which this would lead, was then reluctantly accepted as the only way in which the elite could attempt to take the country out of the impasse created by over six decades of Stalinism and still hope to retain some vestige of power and privilege.

To understand the nature of perestroika and why it failed we must first look briefly at the system of production relations which has prevailed – and prevails still – within Soviet society. As under capitalism, the two functions of creating and appropriating society's surplus product have been carried out in the Soviet Union by two distinct groups (we may call them classes in a conditional sense of the term), but a more detailed analysis of the origins and reproduction of the Stalinist system reveals the essence of the system and the reproduction of its social relations to be historically unique. The Stalinist bureaucracy, which took shape under the market conditions and social inequalities of the New Economic Policy in the 1920s, could not use the market as the basis on which to consolidate its power, since the reintroduction of private property which this would have implied would have eliminated the very functions from which the bureaucracy derived its power. Nor was planning an alternative, since this would have meant an end to the bureacracy's privileges. This claim may seem odd to those used to considering the Soviet Union and similar societies as 'planned economies'. But genuine planning must presume a definite and more or less predictable correlation between plans and results, which can occur only when planning is democratic and those who construct the plan are the same as those who must carry it out. Otherwise, as in the Soviet case, results will vary wildly from what was anticipated, because the implementors at all levels, from management right down to the most unskilled labourer in industry, agriculture or the service sector, will circumvent and bend instructions to make them suit their individual needs.

What this has meant in the case of the Soviet Union is that the ruling elite, deprived of either market or plan, has had to try and regulate the economy through bureaucratic tutelage and administration of things and people. The vehicle through which it has had to try and exercise this regulation has been its political control over the state, through which it maintains its control over the means of production. This control over the state, however, was secured and maintained only through the extreme atomization of the whole of the rest of society, necessitated originally by the need, in the late 1920s and early 1930s, to cope with mass peasant resistance to collectivization and working-class opposition to the privations and hardships caused by forced industrialization. Where the proletariat was concerned, this meant breaking down the working class *as a class* and denying it any means of collective organization and struggle. In this situation workers responded as they have done in other societies where collective activity was denied them: they responded as isolated individuals, by attempting to exercise control over the immediate work situation, including over the labour process itself. Thus from the 1930s onward Soviet production has been characterized by high labour turnover and absenteeism, and by the significant degree of control which the individual worker imposes on work speeds, job organization and product quality.[2]

This control has been perpetuated by the system of informal bargaining between work-force and management, which again – although it displays some similarities with shop-floor bargaining in capitalist enterprises – grew out of the specific conditions of Stalinist industrialization. Scarcity, irregular supplies, frequent plan changes, poor quality materials and components, coupled with a severe and ongoing labour shortage, became the standard conditions in which enterprises have had to work. Managers guided not by the profit-and-loss criteria of the market, but by the need to guarantee stable plan fulfilment and overfulfilment, adapted to these criteria by distorting nominal instructions in order to meet them in practice. They almost always tried to retard the introduction of new technology, since output falls during settling-in periods which might jeopardize plan performance. By the same token, once new equipment and techniques were running smoothly, their potentially better performance would lead to higher plans in the future. Similarly, within the gross plan managers would alter the product mix and focus on producing those items easiest to manufacture or which showed the best indicators (heavy parts if the plan was in tons; large numbers of easy-to-make items if the plan was by number of pieces; expensive pieces at the expense of cheaper, though no less vital, ones if the plan was in roubles). Because supplies are always irregular and of poor quality, managers still regularly bypass established supply channels, even entering into informal black-market or swap arrangements with other enterprises. And finally, managers have continuously faced a pressing need to reach a *modus operandi* with their work-force in order to minimize the destabilizing effects of externally given problems, including those stemming from the workers' own behaviour.

For workers this system has confronted them with two basic problems. First, how to cope with the internal chaos of the workshop (lack of supplies and tools, poor quality materials and components), and second, how to ease the strains imposed by the central authorities and/or management. Sometimes the two aims are in conflict with each other: if the production programme falls too far behind it means overtime and storming (the breakneck attempt to clear out backlogs at the end of the month, quarter or year), which are unpopular but unavoidable. At other times they are mutually compatible or self-reinforcing. Where possible the worker tries to slow down the pace of work, largely by controlling aspects of work organization which, in a smoothly running system, would be the prerogative of management, but in the Soviet system only the worker can affect. This has been easiest in manual jobs, where the worker can simply work slowly. But even for workers on assembly lines or machine production the myriad of interruptions waiting for supplies or a crane, the need to leave the work-bench to hunt down tools or parts in the store-room, or taking advantage of the long queues in the dining-room to extend the dinner break, all allow workers to shorten the effective working day and place definite limits on the elite's ability to extract a surplus.

Because of the ongoing labour shortage it has been difficult for managers to break this system. Rather, they have had to adapt to it by ceding workers considerable control over the work process, because they need their co-operation not to make matters worse, to help rectify various disruptions to the work routine, or to agree to overtime and storming. If earnings suffer, either because of external circumstances or because workers simply have not produced enough to make their customary wage, managers have been generally willing to allow various fiddles so that pay packets do not shrink. If discipline is lax but the worker or workers involved are too important to dismiss, management will turn a blind eye. There therefore has evolved a sophisticated system of shop-floor bargaining between work-force and management over areas of control.

When he came to power in 1985, Gorbachev and the reform wing of the Soviet elite were quick to recognize the need to break down this system of shop-floor relations as a precondition of economic reform. They also understood, as had Khrushchev before them, that this could not be achieved simply by altering methods of economic administration or recasting the incentives system, however necessary these steps might be. On the contrary, they saw that no fundamental change in the economy would take place without an end to the work-force's political atomization. This strategy had two strands to it. First, the working class would not surrender its partial control over the labour process and its associated mechanisms of shop-floor defence without a higher standard of living: access to consumer goods, decent food supplies, and better housing and health care. Second, the elite needed to instil in the working population a feeling that it now had a stake in the system. In this sense the political task of the reforms was to create a Soviet equivalent to civil society and hegemonic ideology through which the working class would see the current organization of society as both 'natural' and desirable, but without leading to the restoration of capitalism from which genuine civil society, based on competing individual interests, historically emerged.

It is clear that at first the political reforms which this entailed were to be strictly limited in scope – not simply to placate the conservatives inside the elite, against whom Gorbachev and the reformers had to consolidate their position – but to avoid any explosion of popular unrest that might threaten the elite's rule. Restrictions on freedom of speech and the formation of independent political organizations were relaxed. There were cautious moves to a parliamentary democracy, although at first the Communist Party was intended to retain its domination over the new structures. Equally important, where the working class was concerned, were attempts to incorporate the work-force directly at the work-place through the creation of representative works councils (Councils of the Labour Collective: Russian acronym STK) and the election of managers. The other side of this policy was the use of economic levers: some, like the wage reform promulgated in 1986, were quite traditional to the Soviet system, others, such as the introduction of mass unemployment, were new and reflected the elite's desire to make use of 'market mechanisms' without a full-scale market.

As we shall see in the course of this chapter, this policy was to fail, as it had to fail in a system with no coherent economic regulator. In global terms, it proved impossible to introduce aspects of the market without the market itself. This merely undermined the tenuous co-ordination provided – inefficiently and wastefully – by the old command system without replacing it with the co-ordination provided by the law of value. Nor did the policy of political integration have the impact that was intended. The political opening up of society allowed workers to discover methods of collective struggle, but the introduction of work-place 'democracy' did not alter worker behaviour, not simply because the 'democratization' was half-hearted and gave workers no real say in enterprise affairs, but because the continued disintegration of the economy made worse the very

114

problems of production on which workers' control over the labour process is predicated. Shortages of supplies, tools and parts continued and were actually compounded by the shift of enterprises to so-called profit-and-loss accounting (*khozraschet*) and the uncoupling of enterprises from centrally planned supply arrangements with other factories. The wage reform came undone for similar reasons: growing uncertainties over production made it increasingly important for managers to protect workers' earnings, all the more so as inflation began sharply to cut into real wages and the expected rise of mass unemployment among *production workers* failed to materialize, leaving most enterprises faced throughout 1990 and 1991 with a severe labour shortage.

The manifest collapse of the original model of perestroika led the elite finally to abandon it as a strategy. Instead, the elite accepted the inevitability of the full-scale introduction of the market and restoration of capitalism, even though this would place the elite in a highly unstable position without any guarantee that its individual members would themselves enter the new capitalist class that eventually will be formed. In terms of labour policy, many of its initial components have had to be scrapped with the shift to the market: the Councils of Labour Collectives have been stripped of most of their powers and elections of managers halted. Similarly the wage reform has been virtually abandoned: from January 1991 wages were decentralized and enterprises given the freedom to set their own pay scales and output quotas (called norms in Russian), so long as they honoured national minimum rates. More revealing, throughout 1991 industrial ministries and enterprise directors began scrambling to put themselves in place to become the new class of capitalists, generally by converting the enterprises under their control into joint-stock companies with themselves holding the majority of shares.

In the rest of this chapter I shall examine the main areas of the economic reforms as they affected work relations and the labour process, and assess the difficulties that beset their implementation. I shall then attempt some general conclusions about the possible future shape of work-place struggles under the new market condtions now being introduced, and the problems they pose for a working class that is only in the early stages of its historical reconstitution and has not yet achieved the self-consciousness and organizational strength required to pose itself – and socialism – as an alternative to the elite's hold on power.

ATTEMPTS TO INTRODUCE UNEMPLOYMENT

Since the beginnings of the five-year plans Soviet industry has been characterized by a severe and reproducible labour shortage. Its causes are several: the need to hoard labour as a hedge against taut periods, usually at the end of the month or planning period (so-called 'storming'); the structural inability, combined with economic disincentives inherent in the Soviet planning system, to mechanize auxiliary operations within production[3]; the workers' partial control over work speeds and labour organization; and the general tendency towards waste within the system, which means that Soviet production consumes considerably more inputs of means of production and labour power per unit of finished output than modern capitalist economies.[4] The other side of the labour shortage has been virtual security of employment. Although since Khrushchev it has been legally very difficult to dismiss a worker, this job security has more to do with the persistence of the labour shortage than any legal guarantees, which both managers and workers have proved adept at circumventing in other areas of factory life. The labour shortage has, understandably, been a prime factor in reinforcing workers' control over the labour process by undermining the effectiveness of any potential sanctions. Managers are reluctant to dismiss workers for discipline violations unless they are perceived as distinct trouble-makers, while the effectivensss of internal penalties is weakened by the threat that the worker might quit. It is little surprise, then, that the introduction of labour mobility and the shedding of 'surplus' workers should have been a major feature of the economic reforms. The figure most commonly cited in the press was that 16 million employed persons – most of them industrial workers – should be made redundant by the year 2000.[5]

There were, in fact, two distinct, if not conflicting, strategies among reformers concerning unemployment. According to one strategy, workers were to be let go as a result of technical modernization and a general streamlining of production, enforced in turn by the need for enterprises to show a profit under the new conditions of financial management. Redundant workers would, however, be re-employed almost *in toto* in other areas of the economy. According to this scenario, then, work-force reductions would not lead to long-term unemployment, but would merely release workers currently unproductively employed for the expanded production of use values or the provision of services. The other strategy (championed by such strident marketeers as Popov and Shmelev) saw redundancies leading to genuine unemployment, which was to act as a disciplining vehicle and a means of coercing workers into surrendering shop-floor prerogatives, similar to the strategy pursued by the Conservative government in Britain after 1979.

Despite the considerable gulf between these two approaches (the first would do nothing to weaken workers' power, either individually or collectively on the shop-floor), both saw the erosion of legal and *de facto* protection of employment as essential to introducing labour mobility and undermining the practice of labour hoarding.

On paper, at least, the regime at the beginning of perestroika imposed strict conditions to defend the rights of workers made redundant, including two months' written notice, the offer of alternative work in the same trade and skill grade, and the protection of earnings for the first two to three months of unemployment.[6] In January 1991 the government passed a new employment law, which provided for the payment of an actual unemployment benefit for six months, but tied the size of benefit not to average earnings, but to the considerably lower basic wage. At the same time, the law granted those newly made redundant and the long-term unemployed the right to enter retraining schemes or join locally financed public works projects.[7]

There are still no precise figures for how many unemployed there currently are in the Soviet Union. In spring 1990 the State Committee for Labour and Social Questions (Goskomtrud) put the number at around 2 million, but even Goskomtrud's own officials conceded that this was no more than just a guess.[8] A later estimate by the State Committee for Statistics (Goskomstat) claimed 4 million people who were either seeking work but were unable to find it or were simply unwilling to work in the state sector.[9] If nothing else, both these figures ignore the huge black labour market estimated by one specialist to embrace 5 million formally unemployed people and another 15 million 'hidden unemployed'.[10] The issue is further clouded by the existence of long-term structural unemployment and underemployment in the Central Asian Republics which, no matter how serious its social and political impact in the areas concerned, is a separate problem from the use of redundancies to introduce labour mobility – and with it an assault on the existing pattern of shop-floor relations – in established industrial centres.

Even at the beginning of perestroika redundancies did not develop as originally intended. For the economy as a whole, between 1986 and

1988 some 3 million employed persons lost their jobs, of whom 1 million were directed to new posts within the same enterprise (filling out second or third shifts or staffing new production units) and 1.5 million went to other branches of the national economy, including services and co-operatives. In all, only 370,000 vacancies were eliminated for the economy at large. The cuts fell proportionally heaviest on specialists and white-collar employees rather than on ordinary workers, although in absolute numbers more workers were released from their jobs.[11] Where production workers were concerned, a study by the State Committee on Labour and Social Questions (Goskomtrud) covering the period 1986–7, found that some two-thirds of workers who lost their jobs were redeployed to cover labour shortages in the same enterprise. Often normal transfers were listed as 'redundancies', merely to show compliance with the official campaign. Conversely, many of those who had been made 'redundant' did not even know that they had been let go or moved to other jobs. On the other hand, management often took advantage of workers' desire to avoid leaving the enterprise in order to impose worse pay or working conditions. Thus during this early period lay-offs, or the threat of lay-offs, appeared to have some 'disciplining' effect on workers within production, but it did not produce greater mobility, a key aim of employment policy at this time.[12].

By 1990 even this mild disciplining function had been undermined, as industry was beset by a near-universal labour shortage. Unemployment eventually rose, but almost exclusively at the expense of factory technical personnel, rather than workers. Where the latter are concerned, unemployment policy was left in tatters as workers, both skilled and unskilled, abandoned production, leaving factories to cope with the bottlenecks caused by a rising number of unfilled vacancies. As early as January 1990 there were nearly 1 million empty workplaces in industry, and another 650,000 in construction.[13] The situation clearly worsened over the course of the year, since by the late 1990 the USSR's Deputy Minister of the Metallurgical Industry reported a shortage of over 500,000 people in that branch alone.[14] Factories with planned establishments of 10,000, 12,000 or 13,000 workers were routinely reporting shortages of 1,000–2,000 workers or even more.[15] It is probable that two tendencies were operating simultaneously to put a squeeze on the supply of labour power. First, as both the national press and factory newspapers have long reported, skilled workers have been leaving the state sector to take up jobs in co-operatives, where wages are higher and working conditions often better. This process has perhaps been most visible in the building trades,[16] but it has affected virtually all sections of industry.[17] Second, unskilled workers, primarily women, are leaving industry to go either into the private sector or simply back into the home.[18] The 1989 All-Union Census revealed that some half a million women had already left industry, transport and construction since 1979,[19] a process which almost certainly accelerated during 1990 and 1991. Most probably, high inflation has meant that the low pay of most female industrial jobs no longer offers an incentive to put up with the heavy and usually hazardous conditions in which most women work.

It is possible, if not even probablè, that the switch to the market economy will begin to reverse this situation, at least in those urban centres heavily dependent on the defence sector, which is now experiencing a sharp fall in demand for its output. This will bring in its wake new problems, in particular the regime's ability to make unemployment *politically* acceptable to the working class. Policy here is already likely to have been undermined by the low level of unemployment compensation provided for by the January 1991 employment law, especially in the context of high inflation. Another side of this is the regime's complete failure to construct an adequate system of job placement bureaux. Almost uniformly such bureaux (originally labelled Centres for Job Placement, Retraining, and Vocational Guidance, and part of the new State Employment Service) are underfinanced and have only weak ties with local enterprises. The latter inform the Centres only of the least prestigious jobs for which they are hiring, presumably because they have no difficulty filling the more skilled and interesting vacancies themselves. Conversely, factories often refuse to hire people referred by the Centres.[20] Workers, of course, were quick to recognize the reality of the situation: in mid-to late 1990 only 5–6 per cent of those losing their jobs actually turned to the Centres for assistance.[21] The reorganization of the Centres into the new State Employment Service, established by the employment law of January 1991, made little difference in their operation. As late as June 1991, just ten days before official registration of unemployed people was set to begin, Leningrad had only fifty to sixty workers to run its entire system, there were few computers, and the city's twenty-two district retraining centres were not yet operational.[22]

The introduction of *khozraschet* has itself acted to undermine this aspect of regime policy. In order to cut costs and maximize incomes, enterprises and their sub-units have sharply reduced funds for training young workers and for upgrading or retraining those who might need to acquire a new trade. Enterprises have found it cheaper simply to poach skilled workers from other factories. In addition to further eroding the already poor skill profile of the Soviet work-force, this – together with the growing reluctance of enterprises to hire young first-time entrants – is leading to the emergence of a clear, although as yet still small-scale, pattern of *structural* youth unemployment.[23]

LABOUR DISCIPLINE, THE USE OF WORK TIME, AND THE ORGANIZATION OF PRODUCTION

The advocates of economic reform well understood the legacy of atomization on workers' morale and productivity. This was supported by sociological surveys purporting (not surprisingly) to find that after four years of reforms most workers still evinced a low level of job motivation *which would not be overcome by the promise of higher wages.*[24] Another barometer of morale is the high labour turnover suffered by various sections of industry and construction, generally in response to poor housing and working conditions and low pay. The pressures caused by high turnover have always been a source of major industrial disruptions. In the Khrushchev period the inability to hold on to machine-tool operators in the engineering industry caused a major crisis in that sector. Under perestroika the growing labour shortage led to serious bottlenecks within most branches of industry, further compounding those which arose due to the general breakdown of the supply system.[25] In part this was due to the absence of workers to perform essential tasks, whether in production proper or auxiliary services. But it equally arose from the sharp deterioration in labour discipline that the labour shortage, especially in the more relaxed political climate of glasnost, permitted.

In 1989 it was estimated that throughout industry only 62 per cent of calendar time was actually worked.[26] Although this largely reflects the poor use of second and third shifts, it also indicates substantial losses among workers directly engaged in production. A sociological survey of output restriction among machine-tool operators at an engineering works in Gor'kii found that over half those surveyed deliberately held back output. In addition, the author cited All-Union surveys from 1986 and 1988 which claimed that over 80 per cent of workers admitted not to work at full capacity.[27] Some of the reasons adduced to explain this behaviour are similar to those described by

Western industrial sociologists like Roy and Lupton,[28] in particular the perception by workers that if they overfulfil their targets by too great a margin they will merely have their rates cut.[29] At the same time the curtailment of effort was seen as 'a concealed form of protest' against specifically Soviet problems of production.[30]

Virtually every enterprise about which we have been able to gather information, either through interviews or by reading their factory newspapers, has reported problems with discipline. Alcoholism, always a scourge of factory life in the Soviet Union, continues to be a major problem.[31] So, too, do theft and pilfering,[32] although with all three of these phenomena it is difficult to determine if they really became more severe under perestroika or were simply more freely reported. Factories also claimed that the labour shortage forced them to take on large numbers of temporary workers, many of them students, who had no commitment to their job and hence showed little inclination to follow orders or established operating procedures.[33] But skilled workers have equally taken advantage of the labour shortage to assert their independence, either by striking to win higher wages, or by simply refusing to take on jobs they deemed unprofitable because of their complexity or relatively low job price.[34]

Workers' ability to assert their independence on the shop-floor – whether through such depoliticized actions as drinking or theft, or more organized and self-conscious protests – is a function not simply of conjunctural factors like the labour shortage, but of the more permanent structural features of the Soviet production cycle. There has always been a strong reciprocal connection between the intrinsic dislocations of Soviet production and workers' control over the disposition of their time. Disruptions provide workers with countless opportunities to steal free time for themselves, while workers' greater control of the pace of work becomes a source of further disturbances. The fact is that the economic reforms had no impact on the primary distinguishing characteristics of Soviet production: storming and supply problems, use of obsolete equipment, hoarding of uninstalled equipment, and waste of resources. On the contrary, the main features of the shop-floor regime have remained essentially intact.

Factories continue to operate with outdated machinery which, instead of being scrapped, is left in service (with increasing repair costs) often alongside recently acquired modern equipment, which is then inefficiently utilized. At the Zil car plant in Moscow over 40 per cent of equipment in 1986 had been in service for over twenty years.[35]

The Siberian Heavy Engineering Production Association (Sibtyazhmash) lists nearly one-third of equipment as over twenty years old and a further quarter more than ten years old.[36] At the Moscow Soap-Boiling Factory the advanced age of equipment (some machinery is forty years old and the sewage system dates back to 1925) made it extremely difficult for the factory to expand output in response to the 1989 soap shortage[37] In theory the shift to *khozras-chet* should have put pressure on factories to scrap outdated equipment and replace it with more modern machinery, but progress so far has been slow, in part because the new financial arrangements have made managers wary of acquiring more expensive specialized machines that may not be fully utilized. In engineering, therefore, factories are actually buying and installing old-style universal lathes, since they know these will be more fully operated even if their productivity is lower.[38] Matters are not helped by the poor quality of Soviet specialized machine tools, in particular those with programmed controls, which are expensive, of limited efficiency, and have aroused considerable suspicion, if not hostility among workers.[39] The same is true of attempts to introduce robotization.[40] The end result is that indices of equipment utilization – always notoriously poor in Soviet industry – have failed to improve. Factories continue to acquire vast quantities of machinery which they often cannot even instal, much less use productively.[41]

Campaigns to encourage industry to expand second and third shifts have had slight impact, since managers find little economic sense in incurring the extra expense of running these shifts when equipment utilization on first shifts is still so poor. Even before the general supply crisis of late 1990–1, losses of machine-time due to non-delivery of supplies, shortages of spare parts and frequent breakdowns were running in some plants in the iron and steel and ore extraction industries as high as 40–60 per cent.[42] The emergence of strikes as a weapon of industrial struggle have over the years become another major source of bottlenecks. This was perhaps first evident with the blockade of fuel supplies to Armenian factories by Azeri militants. The problem took on more widespread dimensions with the miners' strike of summer 1989, especially in the iron and steel industry, where shortages of coking coal and coke by-products were still crippling production in March 1991, when the new miners' strike began.[43]

Similarly, the system is still characterized by inordinate wastefulness in the form of defective production, a swollen repair and maintenance sector, and a vast overconsumption of inputs of means of production and labour power. Soviet industry consumes three times as much metal and energy resources as does US industry in the manufacture of comparable products. This is partially due to the low level of production of alternative materials, such as plastics and ceramics,[44] but the main cause is in the nature of the system itself, with its emphasis on gross output and the indifference of workers towards the quality of the job they perform. The USSR produces more cement than any other country in the world, yet every fifth factory works merely to replace the losses incurred through careless handling by the railways and on building sites.[45]

The regime's inability fundamentally to affect this pattern of internal dislocations must inevitably undermine its attempts to use modernization as a means of disciplining the work-force and prompting workers to surrender traditional methods of shop-floor defence. More to the point, it can actually jeopardize attempts to introduce the market itself, for it is difficult to see how a capitalist industry can take hold, even in a deformed and undynamic state, unless the new class of owners can solve the problem of restructuring the labour process. Waste and inefficiency will counteract any measures designed to ease the pressures on line managers to hoard labour (including the need to maintain an ever-increasing repair and maintenance sector[46]) and will continue to provide workers with the basis for exercising individual control over the labour process. This is especially true of auxiliary shops, which continue to be badly undermechanized, giving workers there greater control over the pace and organization of their work.[47] The other side of this is the continuing demoralization of the work-force which the manifest futility of this system of production causes. It was summed up succinctly by two mine-workers following the strikes of 1989. According to N. Anokhin, a member of the Pro-kop'evsk City Workers' Committee in the Kuzbass:

> The miner moreover must see the use of his labour: that the coal went on heat, lighting or something else sensible. But what does the miner see? That the coal went to make poor-quality metal which rusts. That the coal was transformed into a mountain of machines which fall to pieces. That the coal has been stockpiled in warehouses where it simply piles up. And after all this they say to him, 'Dear comrade, let's have more productivity, extract still more!' It's logical to ask: why extract still more if the coal

that's been extracted isn't being used, but is being turned into smoke and ash?[48]

A similar argument was advanced by V. Golikov, an electrician at the Pervomaiskaya mine in Berezovskii (Sverdlovsk oblast'):

> This is an economic riddle, a paradox: the richest territory (*krai*), a developed industry, people who are in no way work-shy – and suddenly they are eternal debtors. Debtors to whom? Why? Who, for example, will say how much coal the country needs? Gosplan knows, you will answer. But how much is lost? No one would venture even an approximate answer to this question. Tens of millions of tons of fuel pile up in coal stores or in slag heaps – and there's nothing to cart them away in. Tens of millions more tons go literally up the chimney due to defects in energy plants. They demand more extraction from the miners, but the more we extract the more is lost, and we become ever poorer.[49]

The contradictions of perestroika have been mirrored in the contradictions within workers' political consciousness. Atomized workers, through their actions, have continued to be a major cause of economic crisis within the system, while the dislocations and waste which are its expression have acted to reinforce workers' demoralization. Yet perestroika and glasnost also saw workers begin to discover collective forms of struggle, and through them create the *potential* for a radical change in their outlook towards production. To date this has expressed itself primarily in pro-market sentiments among independent workers' organizations, the implications of which I take up again in the conclusions.

CHANGES IN INCENTIVES SYSTEMS

Since the early five-year plans the Soviet regime has consistently failed to develop its wages system into a coherent and effective system of incentives. It is noteworthy that complaints about the failures of the wages system at the start of perstroika differ little from those published in the 1930s and 1950s.[50] Managers have traditionally kept output quotas (known as norms in Russian) relatively low, allowing workers to earn substantial payments for overfulfilment. Bonuses for plan fulfilment or meeting various quality indicators are paid so routinely that they amount to no more than an automatic supplement to the basic wage. In a number of industries, most prevalently in construction, workers regularly receive payments for work they did not carry out (*pripiski*). Of all these problems, that of norm-setting has perhaps proved the most intractable. Managers have simply been unwilling to impose tighter, so-called 'technically based' norms[51] in the face of the perpetual uncertainties of Soviet production (non-arrival of supplies, unanticipated plan changes, poor quality components, etc.) which could make fulfilment impossible and thus lead to conflicts with the work-force.

The result, at least in the eyes of the regime, was to rupture the basic relationship between earnings and work effort and performance. This is summarized under the rubric of 'egalitarianism', or 'levelling' (*uravnilovka*), a grotesque misnomer whose usage dates back to the Stalinist policy of justifying the widening inequalities that accompanied the consolidation of the bureaucratic system. The Soviet wages system is indeed characterized by a myriad of anomalies, whereby workers in identical trades, with identical skills, and working under allegedly identical conditions will often have very different earnings, depending on locally determined norm-seting and bonus procedures.[52] Moreover, since Khrushchev the differentials between the highest and lowest paid have narrowed, as have those between technical personnel and manual workers.

The main aim of the 1986 wage reform was to widen these differentials, both among manual workers and between technical personnel and workers, in the belief that the prospect of higher rewards would encourage workers to exert greater effort and would ease the problems of recruiting specialists in key areas.

While there is general agreement among market-orientated economists about the need to expand differentials, concurrent plans to reform the pricing system (which would have led to sharp rises in the price of food and other consumer basics) had temporarily to be set aside because of the threat of popular unrest they would have provoked.

The main intentions of the reform were strikingly similar to those of the Khrushchev reform of 1956–62[53]:

1 To raise output quotas, together with basic wage rates, in the attempt to reduce the importance of overfulfilment payments, and thereby reduce the pressure on local managers to keep norms low.
2 To make more extensive use of quality and performance bonuses,

to prompt workers to pay greater attention to economizing on materials and adhering to operating procedures. In many enterprises bonuses for fulfilling plans and norms were to be paid only if all output were defect-free.

3 To carry out a substantial regrading of workers, with many workers being put into lower wage and skill grades (*razryady*) as an inducement to upgrade skills in line with the demands of technological modernization. At the same time differentials between the more highly skilled and less skilled were to be widened sharply.

4 There was to be greater use of collective, or so-called contract payments, whereby workers' earnings would be tied to the production results of their work team (brigade), shop or enterprise, and each worker's individual share would be calculated according to a Labour Input Coefficient (KTU – literally, 'coefficient of labour participation'). In theory this would lead to better co-ordination between different links in the production cycle, since workers would no longer be concerned solely with maximizing individual results, irrespective of whether or not this improved overall enterprise performance.

5 In line with the contract system, workers were encouraged not to *overfulfil* plan targets (which merely exacerbates problems of co-ordination), but to achieve given targets with smaller labour costs, primarily by reducing the size of work teams or shop establishments. Under this system – as with similar schemes promoted in the 1970s – the remaining workers were to share part of the saved wages as a bonus.

6 In an effort to control wage overspending, in August 1989 the regime imposed a 3 per cent ceiling on wage fund growth and a tax on wage spending above this limit. Light industry (Group B enterprises) was exempt from the tax.

A major difference with the past wage reforms, however, was the fact that these changes took place in the context of the transfer of enterprises to self-financing, where incentive funds were to be formed out of enterprise profits. During most of *perestroika* the bulk of enterprises operated on a system where basic wage rates were guaranteed, but bonuses were to come out of a material incentives fund, paid for out of profits. Eventually all enterprises were to move to a more radical set-up, where an enterprise had to earn its entire wage fund out of income, that is where even basic wages were to be tied brigade, shop or enterprise performance.[54] As we shall see, the transition to this second variant of *khozraschet* encountered a number of difficulties, arising mainly from the fact that performance – and hence wages – remained heavily dependent on factors outside an enterprise's control, and certainly outside the control of its workers.

By the end of 1987 some 29 million people in the non-agricultural productive sector had been made subject to the reform.[55] Two years later (1 January 1990) this figure had risen to 60 million, or 86 per cent (including 95 per cent in industry) of the total number due to shift to the reform.[56] Throughout this period the press was able to single out certain model factories where the reform had led to improved efficiency and higher earnings.[57] The reform also appeared successfully to have reversed the differential between workers' and specialists' pay. For many years specialists had seen their earnings fall behind those of skilled manual workers – a major source of resentment among the technical intelligentsia, who felt that what they see as their superior status in society should be rewarded in a more open and even-handed way than the old system of privileges, which depended on arbitrary networks of personal contacts. By 1989 wages of specialists were rising faster than those of workers, although in some branches of industry (engineering and non-ferrous metallurgy, for example) they still lagged behind in absolute terms.[58] In virtually all other areas, however, the progress of the reform was beset by considerable difficulties.

A major problem was the relatively weak response of Soviet workers to monetary incentives. This has been conditioned by a number of historical factors: the scarcity of goods on which to spend their wages; the long-standing network of concessions from shop-floor management designed to protect earnings from falling below tacitly agreed local minima; the manifest failure of past experiments aimed at modifying the wages system; and general political demoralization. Moreover, there is a strong tradition of egalitarianism among the Soviet population, and most workers feel that they do not at present receive a 'fair' wage for the amount of work they do or in relation to their material needs. All this led one group of economists to comment that 'one of the lessons of the reform is the fact that for a rather significant contingent of workers (*rabotniki*), the growth of earnings is not a primary motivation for labour activity'.[59] For those workers who might have responded to monetary incentives, the opening up of market relations, particularly the legalization of co-operatives, partially undermined the potential rewards that the wage reform might have offered: many workers were simply unwilling to invest the increased effort needed to achieve higher earnings when they could earn far more either in co-operatives or by working on the black economy.[60] Similarly, the rapid rise in inflation meant that what increases in nominal earnings the reform brought proved too insignificant to stimulate workers to improve their performance.[61]

On the whole, many enterprises found that the shift to *khozraschet* left them with inadequate incentive funds, both for bonuses and for social and technological improvements. This was particularly true in light industry, the special problems of which I shall discuss on pp. 134–7.

Other enterprises ran into problems because management was too quick to shift brigades (work teams), shops or whole enterprises to *khozraschet* without first ensuring that their production operations were financially viable. Workers suffered wage cuts, which in turn became a major cause of the strike wave that hit the USSR during 1989.[62] A governmental decision in December 1989 substantially to raise charges for freight transport, fuel and social insurance contributions left iron and steel mills unable to meet their wage bills, and threatened steel-workers with pay cuts of between 25 and 100 roubles a month. Moreover, enterprises found themselves stripped of funds needed to put up housing or provide child-care facilities. An all-out steel strike in the Ukraine was narrowly averted only when the government promised temporarily to guarantee workers' wages and to review the price rises.[63] By 1991 this had become a general phenomenon: enterprises found themselves unable to cope with the higher prices they now had to pay to suppliers for materials, tools and parts, which in many cases – especially once the deferred price increases came gradually into force – were rising far faster than they themselves were allowed to put up their own charges.[64]

The main lever of any reform of the wages system is norm-setting, for it has been through norms that the regime has tried to exert direct influence over work effort. Yet it is precisely on this issue that the failure of the reform was most transparent. Managers did not in all cases prove willing to raise norms as stipulated by the reform. Although some factories (for example the Zil car plant in Moscow) imposed tighter, so-called technically based norms, with resultant low levels of fulfilment,[65] in general managers resisted pressures in this direction. Some raised norms by less than the rise in basic wages, thus granting their workers a *de facto* wage rise.[66] Others increased them merely in line with the rise in the basic wage, keeping earnings more or less guaranteed without putting any pressure on workers for extra output.[67] The main problem, however, was enterprises' continued unwillingness to impose genuinely 'technically based' norms,[68] which they have always been reluctant to use because they tend to penalize workers for production difficulties outside their control. There was a clear tendency for managers to ignore norm revisions altogether as early as 1989,[69] a trend that almost certainly intensified during 1990. So long as the features of the production cycle remained fundamentally unchanged, such resistance was inevitable, especially as managers were increasingly threatened by the loss of skilled workers to co-operatives offering higher wages, and saw low norms as one of the best means by which to inflate earnings and cut turnover.[70] Again, *khozraschet* itself undermined attempts to tighten up norm-setting, since enterprises could now boost their incomes – and with it their wage funds – simply by raising prices, thus allowing them to 'finance' slack norms.[71]

Plans to introduce widespread regrading were also distorted, although initially in the other direction. Essentially, many managers, finding themselves under pressure to cut production costs and free up funds to pay for stipulated rises in basic wage rates arbitrarily shifted workers into lower wage and skill grades (*razryady*), irrespective of whether or not such changes were warranted by the new Unified Wage and Skill Handbook.[72]

The difficulties in which the reform became bogged down are reflected in the fact that in 1988 and 1989 wages began to rise substantially faster than productivity, reversing the trend in both 1986 and 1987.[73] This wages-output 'scissors' widened further during 1990 and 1991, as average money wages continued to grow while total industrial production actually fell. Significantly, the reform never enjoyed the confidence of either managers or workers. According to the massive All-Union Monitoring survey of industrial workers, managers and technical specialists, in 1988 no more than 15 per cent of those surveyed felt the reform had yielded positive results, a figure which declined to just under 12 per cent in 1990.[74]

In late summer 1990 the regime finally decided to abandon the wage reform altogether. From January 1991 wages and norm-setting were both decentralized and devolved completely on to enterprises themselves.[75] Although from the regime's point of view this step contained the real danger that enterprises would distort wages policy even further, it was a necessary move if the economy were to shift completely to a market, including a market for labour power.

COLLECTIVE FORMS OF LABOUR ORGANIZATION

A major part of the wage reform entailed the shift from remuneration for a worker's individual performance to collective payments according to the so-called contract system. Like similar experiments in coal-mining and construction in the 1960s, and in various branches of manufacturing industry in the 1970s, the system involved a work team taking responsibility for an extire complex of jobs, receiving payment for the total result. In the past such arrangements have failed because the ability of workers to fulfil their contracts depended on too many external factors which disrupted production schedules and thereby jeopardized workers' earnings.[76]

The rationale behind this system was to give workers a material incentive to cut establishments. However, this aspect of the reform, too, encountered major difficulties. As with their predecessors in the 1960s and 1970s, collectives found themselves unable to meet their contracted obligations because of production problems. Although managers nominally entered into a contract with work teams to provide necessary materials and tools, these commitments were not legally binding, and workers proved defenceless against managerial failure to uphold them.[77] Sections and enterprises on leasing found their work disrupted – and their incomes cut – by the unreliability of suppliers, which further reinforced the trend towards direct barter agreements between industrial managers anxious to exchange mutually needed goods.[78] Brigades also found themselves victims of the traditional Soviet practice of 'ratchet planning', where results achieved in one period were taken as the basis for setting norms and plans in the period following. Thus brigades, having cut their numbers and effected significant savings, then found their wage funds cut, leaving them no better off for the extra work they have expended.[79] There have been recent complaints that the extension of brigade work has not led to better productivity, partly because the brigades are given poor preparation for their new responsibilities, and partly because they remain subject to the same problems of supply shortages and poor co-ordination with other stages of production that confront workers working individually.[80]

Not surprisingly, in view of these difficulties, workers' attitudes towards the contract brigades became characterized by general passivity or even outright opposition.[81] Journal and press accounts objected that the brigades led to increased pressure on the work-force and to conflicts over the payment of bonuses. Workers also charged that planning authorities were using the savings they had achieved to subsidize the administrative apparatus.[82] The result was an extremely low take-up rate by workers, with only 5 per cent of brigades working on the contract system in early 1988.[83] This is actually well below the proportion of so-called cost-accounting brigades (organized on a similar basis) in the 1970s and early 1980s. The brigades equally encountered opposition from foremen, who saw the system as undermining their authority on the shop-floor.[84] Managers, too, proved reluctant to encourage contract work, for a variety of reasons. Some disbanded successful brigades, allegedly out of fear that if contract principles were extended to the factory administration, the latter would have to accept a cut in staff.[85] Such explanations must be treated with caution. In fact, managers were far more likely to fear the possible conflicts arising from the resentment of workers who might be laid off as a consequence of the contract system. Managers were also said to be wary of the limited leeway that contract work gave them to manipulate the overall wage bill of a shop or section to protect the earnings of workers whose performance suffered because of disruptions to production.[86] At a deeper structural level, brigades, especially in small and medium batch production in engineering, displayed a distinct life cycle: as soon as they exhausted the possibilities to improve performance through better organization they began to fall apart, since further economies and advances could be achieved only via new technology and organizational measures for which the brigades were simply not prepared.[87]

The wage reform and the shift to collective incentives and work organization were to be accompanied by a 'democratization' of enterprise management, and the investment of key decisions over approval of production plans, disposal of profits, and the use of social development funds in enterprise collectives. The most common phrase used in official pronouncements was that workers were to feel themselves 'masters of the enterprise'. According to the 1987 State Enterprise Law, the collective was the sovereign power in the enterprise. Between general meetings authority was to reside in Councils of the Labour Collectives (Russian acronym STK), set up at enterprise, shop and brigade level. Officially, the STK were not to interfere in day-to-day managerial prerogatives. In theory the STK was to act as the 'legislative' arm of the enterprise and management as its executive. But management's right to execute was not to be challenged. Enterprise collectives were also empowered to elect middle and enterprise managers, although this right was virtually rescinded at the end of 1989.[88]

As of mid-1988 there were some 140,000 STK – representing 4.5 million people – elected at enterprises in industry and the service sector, in construction organizations, and in institutions. Some 90 per cent of these had been set up in the course of 1988, which gives some indication of the rapidity with which they were created.[89] In the first elections the STK were overwhelmingly headed up by management, and there were charges in the press that elections of the Councils and Council chairpersons were undemocratic, if not rigged (election by lists; open rather than secret ballots; sometimes only a single candidate). Where the election of managers was concerned, most contests were for top management only; elections of middle-level or line management – i.e. of those closest to workers on the shop-floor – were rare events.[90] Managerial domination over the early STK was clearly becoming a political problem, for in February 1988 the State Committee on Labour and Social Questions (Goskomtrud) and the All-Union Central Council of Trade Unions (VTsSPS) issued a 'recommendation' to enterprises that enterprise directors should not serve as STK chairpersons. After this more workers and technical specialists were chosen as STK leaders, but this did not make the councils more representative of rank-and-file interests. The domination of the councils by enterprise directors merely gave way to domination by middle-level management, who acted as proxies for their superiors.[91]

The institution of enterprise 'democracy' was never more than an incorporationist strategy on the part of the reform wing of the elite, designed to make workers take responsibility for enterprise performance, to surrender their individualized defensive shop-floor practices, and to abjure collective defence of their interests through strikes. The STK never even achieved the degree of worker autonomy within the enteprise originally proclaimed as their objective. They had, for example, no legal means to enforce adherence to their decisions, by either management or ministries.[92] They played little or no role in working out production plans or influencing other major areas of enterprise life.[93] Indeed, both management and trade unions pushed on to the STK matters which they themselves should have been handling and which were not the responsibility of the councils: housing allocations, violations of labour discipline, issuing bonuses, compliance with safety regulations, and the organization of rest breaks.[94] A 1989 study of STK carried out by VTsSPS's Scientific Centre concluded:

> The processes of inertia have, unfortunately, been far from overcome. In practice labour collectives have, for the most part, still not assumed their proper place in the system of self-administration. Many of the production, economic, and social questions that are worrying people they neither investigate nor decide; on those questions which they do discuss, their decisions are merely recommendations, rather than binding. In other words, making the labour collective the legislative power within enterprises is a task which in large part still has to be solved.[95]

It is not surprising that managers should have proved reluctant to transfer their powers to labour collectives, and managerial hostility and distrust of worker-participation in decision-making is well documented.[96] The result was demoralizing for workers, too, and there is little evidence that the distrust and apathy which they first evinced towards the STK diminished over time. A study of Moscow workers showed that some 80 per cent felt that the STK did not express their views and had no clear knowledge of precisely which issues the councils dealt with.[97] A survey of workers in Perm oblast' found that only 2 per cent felt that perestroika was making progress in their enterprise. A worker and STK member at the Soda Factory in Berezniki – allegedly one of the most active councils in the oblast' – stated that not a single STK initiative had come from rank-and-file workers, who in turn did not see the STK as a vehicle for resolving their problems. Many felt that the creation of the STK was just another routine campaign, similar to those they had seen all their working lives.[98]

Despite the impotence of the STK, the regime saw them as incompatible with the introduction of the market. In June 1990 the 1987 State Enterprise Law was superseded by a new Law on Enterprises,[99] according to which enterprises – including state enterprises – were to have owners who alone had the right to select managers. STK are no longer mandatory institutions, but may be formed by general meetings of work collectives if they wish. The new bodies which have replaced them, Enterprise Councils, have far fewer nominal rights than did the STK, even though the latter rarely were able to use them. This move did not, however, pass without protest. In September 1990 representatives from the STK of forty-six large enterprises, including the country's most important car plants, held a conference demanding the restoration of the STK's legal status, with enhanced powers for labour collectives, including the right to take over enterprises from the state without compensaion.[100] This was followed in December by the founding congress of the Union of Councils of Labour Collectives, which decried the way in which privatization was bringing state enterprises into the possession of the former bureaucratic apparatus.[101] Unfortunately, following the loss of a major dispute over the privatization of the huge Volga Automobile Factory in Tol'yatti the movement slipped into near total obscurity.[102]

THE CONTRADICTORY ROLE OF FEMALE LABOUR

If the most essential feature of the labour process within Soviet industry is the worker's substantial partial control over that process, women workers constitute an important exception to this pattern. Women are by and large ghettoized into two types of industrial employment. First, they make up the overwhelming share – and in industries such as textiles almost 100 per cent – of workers in industries where, due to the nature of technology used, workers have far less control over the labour process and are less able to 'conceal reserves' and ease the intensity of their work. These industries include in the main light industry and sections of engineering industry based on assembly-line production. Second, women make up the majority of workers in unskilled or semi-skilled manual auxiliary operations, where, because it is manual labour, they can exercise greater control over the pace of their work, but conditions and pay are extremely bad. Elsewhere I have argued that there is a specific relationship between these two types of employment which together have granted the elite a certain leeway, or buffer, which allowed it better to tolerate the concessions it is forced to grant to (primarily male) workers in industries and trades which it deems more important.[103] The argument can be summarized in the following way.

In industries such as textiles, the garment industry, and assembly line production in light engineering (e.g. watch manufacture), women are subject to a higher intensity of labour and rate of exploitation. The working day in textiles, for example, is almost totally utilized with few stoppages, as opposed to the quite considerable breaks in the work routine characteristic of heavy industry.[104] The women work under constant strain, in uncomfortable positions, subject to high noise levels and temperatures which reach 37° – 40°C. They also have to cope with high dust levels and vibration. The nature of the work requires intense concentration and manual dexterity. Equipment is designed without any account of female physiology. In general, equipment manufactured by the engineering industry for light industry and the food industry is designed for the statistically average *male* at the peak of his powers. Work norms are set in the same fashion, and are based on the amount of equipment that must be tended, rather than on the size of the work-force. Thus, as equipment has been modernized women have found their work-loads increased.[105] Women also do more night shifts than men, despite the fact that night work for women is technically banned.[106]

The state uses the surplus product created in these branches to subsidize investment in heavy industry. It takes almost all of the profits (80–90 per cent) from enterprises in light industry for the state budget and puts back very little by way of new investment or increased wages. A 1989 newspaper article estimated that the state was then receiving 10 per cent of its accumulation fund from light industry, but giving it a mere 1 per cent of its capital investment.[107]

This pool of highly exploited labour needs constantly to be re-recruited, since turnover is high and few women can cope with the strain of working in textiles past the age of 40.[108] What makes the replenishment of this work-force possible is the lack of alternative areas of employment. Throughout industry – even in light industry where women predominate – women are by and large excluded from skilled manual jobs such as fitters, tool-setters, electricians and repair and maintenance workers; in industries and trades where they work alongside men, as machine-tool operators, for example, women are ghettoized into the lowest wage and skill grades (*razryady*) where they find it difficult to earn promotion. Their advancement is further hampered by the rigid division of labour within the home, which sees women saddled with almost all of the responsibilities for housework and child-care. This leaves women with little time to devote to upgrading their skills and qualifications – an important avenue of promotion in Soviet industry – and reinforces traditional male prejudices about the competence of women to carry out skilled work.[109] Many urban women have taken refuge in the growing service sector, where pay is generally low but conditions are better, but this sector is still too small to soak up all potential women workers. This leaves the huge army of unskilled or semi-skilled auxiliary workers, whose retention serves a number of vital functions. First, they are a pool of cheap labour, which relieves management of the need to invest in mechanizing these operations – a tendency which will be reinforced by the economic reforms, when enterprises must be more selective about where they invest.[110] Second, given the general pattern of wage and job discrimination, these women carry out jobs that male workers will not do.[111] Third, and perhaps most important, as the only 'alternative' to work in high-intensity industries they ensure a steady supply into the latter of women workers. Thus the existence of this reserve army of low-skilled manual workers is a precondition to the regime's ability to maintain the reproduction of labour power in high-intensity industries, which are in turn vital to its attempts to regain some of the control over the surplus product which it loses in other areas of production.

The specific role of women workers has enhanced the elite's control in one other, very important way. Male workers derive considerable privileges due to the greater exploitation of women both in the work-place and in the home. The concessions men receive at work are, according to our argument, to a significant degree made possible by the subordinate position of their female colleagues. In the home they enjoy a privileged status, as women continue to service their needs. Together, this latent conflict between men and women reinforces the atomization of the work-force which the elite requires to stay in power.

Policy towards women workers under perestroika has been beset by at least two fundamental contradictions. First, the prospect of mounting unemployment and the desire to reinforce more traditional family values led the regime to encourage women to leave work and move back into the home.[112] This policy was extremely badly thought out, since it should have been clear that many of the jobs women would leave were those which men simply refuse to do. Only high unemployment could perhaps encourage out-of-work males to take on these jobs, but as we have seen, the reality – at least up until the end of 1991 – was a deepening labour shortage, not just among relatively skilled male workers, but among unskilled and semi-skilled women workers as well. If anything, the shortage of women workers in unskilled jobs has acted to undermine the regulatory role which female labour has traditionally played. Second, the entire strategy of perestroika was predicated upon the possibility of improving the standard of living. Yet the working and financial conditions under which enterprises in light industry operate have acted to undermine this objective. In the main, these enterprises have been badly hit by the introduction of *khozraschet* and self-financing, since they are now responsible for their own investment, wages and incentive funds, but continue to see the major part of their revenues syphoned off into the state budget. The press has been full of recent examples of enterprises working with old, outmoded equipment, and suffering high turnover due to their poor working conditions, but which cannot afford to invest in modernization, especially in the face of rising costs for equipment. Some cannot afford to maintain their kindergartens, while investments in new housing (many women live in old, dilapidated dormitories) are out of the question.[113] The result is that light industry has remained a low-wage sector where morale is poor and technical modernization slow. The impact this has had on the fate of the economic reforms was aptly described by one commentator:

> The reform which is based on strengthening incentives to workers, has barely penetrated that branch of industry which has to turn out goods for the materialization of these incentives. The government then has to take measures to limit wage rises, trim back incentives, and in essence, trim back the reforms in every industry.
>
> The logic of things states that it is precisely those enterprises which turn out goods for popular consumption which should be the leaders in the fundamental reconstruction of economic activity, which should prepare the basis for the others. What we now see on the shelves is a consequence of violating the order in which the reform should proceed, of not knowing how precisely to define priorities.[114]

Thus the role of female labour, which has been vital to the elite's attempts to regulate the economy, came to pose a major obstacle to its plans for economic reform and recovery. It has presented itself, in fact, as one of the central contradictions of perestroika. The elite requires the ghettoization of women workers into the twin armies of high-intensity labour and low-skilled manual workers, and will continue to do so until it can break down the partial control over the labour process exercised by workers in the rest of industry, construction and transport. Yet a precondition of achieving this latter, more fundamental objective is the transformation of the role of female labour – but this would then deprive the elite of an important regulatory mechanism through which it partially compensates for its lack of control elsewhere. It is a vicious circle whose potential resolution lies not in the elite and its policies, but in the workers themselves in the course of their developing class struggle.

CONCLUSION: CLASS STRUGGLE AND THE CHANGING FACE OF SHOP-FLOOR RELATIONS

In terms of the development of the socialist movement the defeat of the October Revolution and the rise of Stalinism have meant the loss of an entire epoch in human history. Within the USSR, and later Eastern Europe, the socialist tradition was smothered and the working class atomized. Internationally the working-class movement underwent profound deformation, a process aided by the rise of fascism in Germany and the destruction of mass, revolutionary working-class parties it brought in its wake. The reforms of 1986–90 in the Soviet Union were the response by a section of the elite to their perception that the Stalinist system had reached a dead end, that it had exhausted its possibilities of development. Perestroika and glasnost were never a socialist project – they merely created the preconditions for the re-emergence of class struggle in Soviet society.

The reform wing of the elite recognized the need gradually to end the atomization of the population, but was unable to find an alternative mechanism of 'social control'. It is doubtful that the elite ever fully understood the potential consequences of the reforms,[115] which helps explain why the situation in the USSR progressively slipped out of its control. Divisions within the working population run deep, as evidenced by the intensification of racial and ethnic antagonisms and the officially orchestrated, but no less menacing rise of anti-Semitism. The divisions around gender are equally important. Men derive considerable privileges from the subordination of women, both in the work-place and in the home. The experience of the West suggests that this situation will not change until women themselves begin to organize, press their own demands, and through this force a change in the consciousness and behaviour of male workers.

At the moment the situation is extremely fluid, and the elite, despite the ascendancy of its rabid pro-market wing, has no coherent strategy for how to deal with it. Most of the old industrial system, with its underlying social relations of production has remained intact, which limits the extent to which managers can free themselves from their reliance on workers' co-operation. If supplies do not arrive, if tools and parts are missing, managers still depend on the willingness and know-how of the worker to track down alternative materials and keep production going; if plans are changed or drawings and blue prints are incorrect, managers still rely on the worker's readiness and ability to adapt, if not redesign the production process. Bargaining also continues to take place over storming and overtime. Yet within the integument of the old system new relationships show signs of forming. Workers, with their atomization within production and in society at large fast fading away, are gradually learning new forms of struggle involving collective action and the formation of their own independent organizations. The miners' strikes of 1989 and 1991, and the April 1991 Belorussian strikes over price rises showed both the potential and the limitations of these struggles so far, but we are in the early days of the working class's historical reconstitution. The fact is that strikes are now a daily occurrence in the USSR, despite legal restrictions and massive propaganda aimed at persuading workers of their harmfulness. Not just workers in heavy industry, but disabled home workers have struck to press their demands for better wages.[116] And despite the prolonged absence of any mass strikes following the 1989 miners' strike, during the first five months of 1990 the USSR lost one-third more person-days and 15 per cent more output due to strikes and 'ethnic conflict' than in the whole of 1989.[117]

Even before the recent decision to move to a wholesale introduction of the market, the logic of the economic reforms was such that they would eventually lead to the restoration of the law of value (and hence capitalism) in the Soviet Union. If the shift to the market succeeds – and the response of the working class will play a significant part in determining the outcome here – then relations between workers and management and the state will take on the more traditional, but no less crisis-ridden forms seen in the West. The current impasse must be seen as an unstable transitional phase, posing the alternative of either working class power and socialism or a capitalist restoration. The fact that the new mass organizations, which grew largely out of the 1989 miners' strike (such as the Confederation of Labour based in Novokuznetsk and the League of Miners), are themselves in favour of the market does not blunt the truth of this statement. Workers will learn soon enough what the market means for them. Already these and other working-class organizations are demanding protection from what they see as the inevitable threat to jobs which the market must bring. All of this will take a long time to work itself out. In the mean time relations on the shop-floor will reflect the hybrid structure of the society as a whole.

ACKNOWLEDGEMENTS

This chapter is part of a larger research project on production relations in Soviet industry during the period of perestroika. The research is supported by a project grant from the Leverhulme Trust. Appreciation is also due to the Bundesinstitut für ostwissenschaftliche und internationale Studien in Köln, West Germany, for a Visiting Fellowship there during September–November 1989. Finally, I should like to thank Michael Burawoy for critical comments made on an earlier draft.

NOTES AND REFERENCES

1 For an analysis of these moves, and their consistency with the apparent rightward drift of Gorbachev's actual government during 1991, see D. A. Filtzer (1991) 'The contradictions of the marketless market: self-financing in the Soviet industrial enterprise, 1986-1990', *Soviet Studies* 43 (6): 989-1,009.

2 This process is described in detail in D. A. Filtzer (1986) *Soviet Workers and Stalinist Industrialization: The Formation of Modern Soviet Production Relations, 1928-1941*, London: Pluto. ch. 3.

3 In 1985 49 per cent of Moscow industrial workers were doing manual labour, a figure virtually unchanged since the 1950s: *Sotsiologicheskie issledovaniya* (1988) 1: 35 (I. S. Gudzovskaya and A. G. Kosaev).

4 According to E. M. Primakov, the national income of the Soviet Union in 1988 was 64 per cent of that of the United States, yet to achieve even this level of output the Soviet Union had to expend 80 per cent more fixed capital, 60 per cent more materials, twice as much energy, and make twice as many trans-shipments of goods: *Pravda* 8 August 1988.

5 *Ekonomika i zhizn'* (1990) 15: 12. Many of these people would be re-employed elsewhere in the economy. However, according to V. Kolosov, Head of the Administration of Labour Resources and Employment of the USSR State Committee on Labour and Social Questions (Goskomtrud), by 1995 5 million to 6 million people are expected not to be able to find alternative employment: *Izvestiya* 11 May 1990.

6 *Sotsialisticheskii trud* (1988) 9: 59-61.

7 'Osnovy zakonodatel'stva Soyuza SSR i respublik o zanyatosti naseleniya', 15 January 1991. Implemented by a decree of the USSR Supreme Soviet, 'O vvedenii v deistvie Osnov zakonodatel'stva Soyuza SSR i respublik o zanyatosti naseleniya', 15 January 1991: *Trud* 25 January 1991. Those made redundant due to the liquidation of their enterprises or because of establishment reductions will receive their average wage while seeking new work, up to a maximum of three months, provided that they register with the State Employment Service (*de facto* labour exchanges) as seeking work within ten days. If after three months the redundant worker has not been offered an appropriate job or refuses two such offers, he or she is deemed unemployed, and benefits are calculated

on the basis of their basic wage. Workers entitled to the higher three-month payments who also sign up for retraining will retain their average wage for the entire time of their training. For all others engaged on training schemes the size of benefits is sharply lower.

8 *Trud* 19 April 1990. On the unreliability of these estimates see the interview with V. Kolosov, head of Goskomtrud's Administration of Labour Resources and Employment of the Population, *Trud* 29 March 1990.

9 *Sotsialisticheskii trud* (1990) 10: 37 (I. Zaslavskii).

10 *Ekonomicheskie nauki* (1990) 8: 71 (O. Osipenko).

11 *Sotsialisticheskii trud* (1989) 8: 71 (V. Pavlov and V. Baryshev).

12 *Sotsiologicheskie issledovaniya* (1989) 1: 38–41 (I. E. Zaslavskii and M. V. Moskvina).

13 *Izvestiya* 29 January 1990.

14 *Rabochaya tribuna* 18 September 1990.

15 In February 1991 the Dneprospetsstal' works in Zaporezh'e with a normal establishment of 13,500 workers, had more than 2,000 vacancies: *Izvestiya* 11 February 1991 (V. Filippov). Similarly, in mid-1990, Leningrad's Skorokhod footwear production association was short by more than 2,000 workers out of a planned work-force of just over 11,000: *Skorokhodovskii rabochii* 17 August 1990. Our own interviews with a limited number of workers, low-level managers and technical personnel in Moscow and Leningrad, carried out during the summer of 1991, plus our review of factory newspapers from various branches of industry and regions of the country, indicate that these were typical and not isolated examples.

16 *Trud* 16 April 1991 (interview with G. D. Arzhanov, chairperson of the Central Committee of the Trade Union of Employees in Construction and the Building Materials Industry).

17 References, especially those from factory newspapers, are too numerous to list. Typical is the interview with Yu. Bokov, director of Leningrad's Severnaya verf' shipbuilding factory, reported in *Leningradskii rabochii*, 31 May 1991 (I am grateful to Anna Temkina for making the reference available to me). One enterprise paper claimed that as of early 1990 Leningrad industry as a whole had lost over 130,000 skilled workers to co-operatives since the time of the latter's legalization: *Kabel'shchik* (Sevkabel', Leningrad) 22 March 1990.

18 See, for example, the case of the fastenings shop at the Sverdlovsk Turbo-Motor Factory, which employs exclusively women on low wages and which in January 1991 had only 70 per cent of its normal complement of workers: *Znamya* (Sverdlovsk Turbo-Motor Factory) 25 January 1991.

19 *Vestnik statistiki* (1991) 2: 39.

20 *Sotsialisticheskii trud* (1989) 6: 54–8; (1989) 8: 57–8 (A. Arzamastsev); (1989) 8: 59–61 (V. Ishin and I. Lokhov). In the words of V. Skitev, Head of the Chief Administration on Labour and Social Questions of the Moscow City Soviet, 'We give little help to the people who come to us. And those coming to us are those with no protection, with no possibility to set themselves up through some patron. We lead them in a circle: go

here, go there, maybe they'll take you on. But we cannot really set someone up in a job': *Sotsialisticheskii trud* (1989) 6: 56.

21 *Sotsialisticheskii trud* (1990) 10: 41 (I Zaslavskii).

22 Interview with A. G. Golov, Leningrad City Council's Standing Committee on Questions of Self-Management, Work of Soviets, and State Organization, 21 June 1991.

23 *Ekonomika i zhizn'* (1990) 35: 16 (I. Kirillov); (1990) 36: 6 (V. Tomashkevich).

24 *Sotsiologicheskie issledovaniya* (1989) 3: 3–6 (I. F. Belyaeva).

25 On the disintegration of the supply network see Filtzer, 'The contradictions of the marketless market', pp. 995–8.

26 *Rabochaya tribuna* 28 July 1990.

27 *Sotsiologicheskie issledovaniya* (1990) 2: 50–5 (V. D. Kozlov).

28 D. Roy (1952) 'Quota restriction and goldbricking in a Machine Shop', *American Journal of Sociology* LVII (March): 427–42; D. Roy (1953) 'Work satisfaction and social reward in quota achievement: an analysis of piecework incentive', *American Sociological Review* 18 (October): 507–14; D. Roy (1954) 'Efficiency and the "Fix": informal intergroup relations in a piecework machine shop', *American Journal of Sociology* LX (November) 255–66. T. Lupton (1963) *On the Shop Floor*, Oxford.

29 *Sotsiologicheskie issledovaniya* (1990) 10: 8 (A. N. Komozin). We know from interview data that this is also the case in the Byelorussian garment industry.

30 *Sotsiologicheskie issledovaniya* (1990) 2: 55 (V. D. Kozlov). 'The basic causes of consciously limiting output remain worsening working conditions, an ineffective incentives system, an authoritarian style of management, the low competence of managers, abuse of position, the chronic disregard for workers' elementary needs, and finally, disappointed hopes for positive changes', ibid. p. 55.

31 *Mashinostroitel'* (Ivtekmash, Ivanovo) 21 January 1991; *Rezinshchik* (Sverdlovsk Rubber-Technical Goods Factory) 14 August 1990; Stankostroitel' (Machine Tool Manufacturing Production Association, Kuibyshev) 10 September 1990; 8 October 1990.

32 *Arsenal* (Arsenal Production Association, Leningrad), 26 November 1990; 7 January 1991; *Ritm* (Kharkov Tractor Parts Factory) 3 December 1990.

33 *Za stal'* (Kuibyshev Steel Foundry) 5 July 1990; 24 July 1990. In mid-1990 80 per cent of workers on automatic lines (but not the main car assembly conveyor) at Moscow's Lenin Komsomol Automobile Factory (Moskvich) were temporary, that is either students or recent, short-term recruitees. *Za sovetskuyu malolitrazhku* (Lenin Komsomol Automobile Factory, Moscow) 18 July 1990. The factory, which like most Moscow industrial enterprises has traditionally been dependent on migrant workers with limited residence permits (so-called *limitchiki*), also makes heavy use of contract workers, that is workers who sign an agreement to work at the factory for a specified period in exchange for the right to buy a Moskvich car: *Moskvich* 11 February 1991. This system has long been used in construction, where people from all professions and social groups will engage in building work in exchange for a flat.

34 *Za sovetskuyu malolitrazhku* 27 November 1989.
35 *Sotsiologicheskie issledovaniya* (1987) 3: 84 (V. S. Dunin and E. A. Zenkevich).
36 *Sotsialisticheskii trud* (1988) 3: 32.
37 *Trud* 19 September 1989.
38 *Sotsialisticheskaya industriya* 1 October 1989. The State Enterprise Law, which went into effect in January 1988, actually penalized factories for scrapping outdated equipment, by stipulating that the losses thus incurred had to come out of incentive funds: *Sotsialisticheskii trud* (1988) 7: 30 (Yu. Kalmykov).
39 *Sotsialisticheskii trud* (1988) 7: 30 (Yu. Kalmykov); (1988) 8: 40–1; (1989) 9: 54 (L. Sitnikova); (1990) 5: 35 (N. Khrulev and L. Salomatina).
40 *Sovetskaya Rossiya* 1 June 1988; *Za sovetskuyu malolitrazhku* 20 November 1989; 9 July 1990.
41 In January 1988 Soviet factories were carrying 12 billion roubles' worth of uninstalled domestic equipment. By January 1989 this had risen to 14 billion roubles. This excludes the large quantities of uninstalled imported machinery on which scarce hard currency has been expended: *Trud* 19 October 1989; 20 October 1989.
42 *EKO* (1989) 8: 87–8 (V. D. Roik). The Kalinin excavator factory estimated in 1988 that it was losing the equivalent of 2.5 months' production a year in stoppages because of late deliveries, and a further month because of the need to rectify defective goods and equipment from suppliers: *Sotsialisticheskaya industriya* 21 June 1988.
43 *Sotsialisticheskaya industriya* 8 September 1989; *Ekonomika i zhizn'*, (1990) 35: 2 (I. Donchenko); *Rabochaya gazeta* 5 January 1991; 28 February 1991.
44 *Sotsialisticheskaya industriya* 8 July 1988; 23 September 1989; *EKO* (1990) 7: 128 (E. G. Repin).
45 *Sotsialisticheskaya industriya* 5 October 1989. This, of course, is the other, deeper cause of the current cement shortage.
46 In the chemical industry expenditures on repair and maintenance come to nearly 80 per cent of the entire volume of capital investment. *Sotsialisticheskaya industriya* 13 October 1989. In the energy and power industry outlays on repair and maintenance have almost doubled from 1981 to 1991 and the repair sector accounts for one in every three of its employed personnel: *EKO* (1988) 6: 58–9 (Kh. A. Bekov and Ya. S. Ginzburg).
47 *Planovoe khozyaistvo* (1990) 2: 83–4 (Yu. Tushunov). According to Tushunov, whereas industry's total demand for equipment is met by 70 per cent, that for mechanization of warehousing is only 30–3 per cent fulfilled.
48 *Sotsialisticheskaya industriya* 9 September 1989.
49 *Sotsialisticheskaya industriya* 7 November 1989.
50 Filtzer, *Soviet Workers and Stalinist Industrialization*, ch. 8; D. A. Filtzer (1989) 'The Soviet wage reform of 1956-1962', *Soviet Studies* xli (1): 90–1.
51 'Technically based' norms are, at least theoretically, calculated on the basis of the optimal output that could be achieved using equipment at its

full technological capacity within a rational, problem-free organization of labour. Their opposite are so-called empirically based norms, which are calculated from time-and-motion studies of the working day as it is actually used, that is allowing for stoppages, breakdowns, problems with supplies, etc. In practice most 'technically based' norms are really empirical norms under the 'technically based' label.

52 These anomalies have been exacerbated even more in recent years through the proliferation of localized strike action.

53 The basic provisions of the reform were laid out in a 1986 decree of the Central Committee of the Communist Party of the Soviet Union, the Council of Ministers of the USSR, and the All-Union Central Council of Trade Unions, 'O sovershenstvovanii organizatsii zarabotnoi platy i vvedenii novykh tarifnykh stavok i dolzhnostnykh okladov rabotnikov proizvodstvennykh otraslei narodnogo khozyaistva', usually referred to now simply as Decree no. 1115. For details of the Khrushchev reform and its failures see Filtzer, 'The Soviet wage reform'.

54 At the end of 1989 8 per cent of industrial personnel (including clerical employees and technical staff) were on this second variant of *khozraschet* and another 3.3 per cent worked in enterprises on leasing. Together they accounted for just over 10 per cent of all industrial production and services: *Ekonomika i zhizn'* (1990) 31: 8 (A. Siginevich and I. Gurkov).

55 *Sotsialisticheskii trud* (1988) 6: 28 (Yu. Shatyrenko).

56 *Sotsialisticheskii trud* (1989) 8: 71 (V. Pavlov and V. Baryshev); *Izvestiya* 7 May 1990.

57 See for example the accounts of the Tasma Production Association (chemical industry, Kazan), *Sotsialisticheskii trud* (1989) 9: 65–8 (V. Spirkin); the Volgograd Silicate Building Materials Combine, *Sotsialisticheskii trud* (1989) 5: 28–30 (V. Tinyakov and L. Mironenko) and *Stroitel'naya gazeta* 17 September 1989; and the Bryansk Technological Equipment Factory, *Trud* 28 December 1989.

58 *Sotsialisticheskii trud* (1989) 8: 73 (V. Pavlov and V. Baryshev).

59 *Sovetskaya Estoniya* 15 March 1988 (Yu. Sillaste and D. Vanderflit), cited in *Sotsiologischeskie issledovaniya* (1989) 3: 4 (I. F. Belyaeva).

60 *EKO* (1988) 3: 95–6 (L. I. Gol'din).

61 See, for example, the comments by I. N. Gubaidullin, director of the Chusovoi iron and steel-works, *EKO* (1990) 6: 96.

62 *Sotsialisticheskii trud* (1989) 10: 71–2 (E. Leont'eva). 'Not letting the "lower ranks" in on the algebra of incomes and expenditures, enterprise heads and specialists ultimately find themselves, to put it delicately, in a tricky situation. Receiving *"khozraschet"* wages which contain less than the usual number of bank notes, the outraged workers refuse to take up their place at their machines, to go down the pit, or to sit behind the wheel of the bus. Poor working conditions, undemocratic methods of electing managers, and inattentiveness by local authorities towards the social conditions of workers' lives are all pregnant with explosion': ibid., p. 72.

63 *Trud* 9 January 1990; 24 January 1990; 31 January 1990. The measure affected all industry, but the Ukranian iron and steel-workers were apparently the first to react with a militant response. It is noteworthy

that the trade unions, wary of the unpopularity that they incurred during the miners' strike of summer 1989, were quick to intervene and champion the workers' case, no doubt in an effort to co-opt the issue and avert a strike. The price increases were eventually introduced later in 1990 and 1991.

64 For an early example of this, see the example of the Kursk Ball Bearing Factory, *Trud* 14 January 1990.

65 *Sotsialisticheskii trud* (1988) 5: 39.

66 *Sotsialisticheskii trud* (1988) 6: 29 (Yu. Shatyrenko); (1990) 10: 14.

67 *Sotsialisticheskii trud* (1989) 8: 72 (V. Pavlov and V. Baryshev).

68 *Sotsialisticheskii trud* (1989) 6: 32-3 (E. Antosenkov, N. Kovaleva, A. Makhmutova and Ya. Shagalov).

69 *Sotsialisticheskii trud* (1990) 10: 14.

70 ibid., p. 14

71 *Sotsialisticheskii trud* (1990) 8: 89 (V. Pavlov and L. Yurchikova).

72 *Sotsialisticheskii trud* (1988) 6: 38-9 (S. Petrova); (1989) 6: 29 (Yu. Shatyrenko); (1989) 6: 61-3 (V. Alimova); *Moskovskaya pravda* 12 September 1989; *Rabochaya tribuna* 13 May 1990; *Sotsialisticheskii trud* (1990) 8; 89 (V. Pavlov and L. Yurchikova).

73 *Sotsialisticheskii trud* (1989) 7: 113; (1989) 8: 72 (V. Pavlov and V. Baryshev); *Sotsialisticheskaya industriya* 23 November 1989 (P. Myagkov). In 1989 throughout the economy wages rose twice as fast as productivity: *Izvestiya* 7 May 1990. In industry wages rose three times as fast as productivity and nearly six times faster than total output: *Ekonomika i zhizn'* (1990) 9: 6 (I. Manykina); (1990) 12: 13 (Yu. Yakutin).

74 *Materialy vsesoyuznogo monitoringa po voprosam sotsial'no-ekonomi- cheskogo razvitiya promyshlennykh predpriyatii* (Moscow 1990), p. 10. For smaller local surveys showing the same trends, see *Moskovskaya pravda* 12 September 1989 (N. Volgin) and *EKO* (1989) 3: 14 (V. E. Boikov).

75 *Izvestiya* 8 August 1990; 27 October 1990.

76 On earlier forms of brigade organization see D. Slider (1987) 'The brigade system in Soviet industry: an effort to restructure the labour force', *Soviet Studies* July: 388-405; D. A. Filtzer (1987) 'The Soviet wage reform of 1956-1962', unpublished paper, Soviet Industrialization Project Seminar, Centre for Russian and East European Studies, University of Birmingham, October 1987, Appendix A; B. Arnot (1988) *Controlling Soviet Labour: Experimental Change from Brezhnev to Gorbachev*, London: Macmillan, ch. 9.

77 *Sotsialisticheskii trud* (1988) 3: 95-7 (G. Khnykin); (1988) 7: 46 (P. Petrochenko); (1988) 9: 30 (V. Kolosov).

78 *Sotsialisticheskii trud* (1990) 8: 44 (V. Korolev).

79 *Sotsialisticheskii trud* (1988) 3: 96 (G. Khnykin).

80 *Sotsialisticheskii trud* (1988) 7: 46-7 (P. Petrochenko); (1989) 6: 32 (E. Antosenkov, N. Kovaleva, A. Makhmutova and Ya. Shagalov).

81 *EKO* (1988) 4: 125-7 (A. A. Prokhrov).

82 *Trud* 3 Janaury 1990 (Murmanskmelioratisiya Association).

83 *Sotsialisticheskii trud* (1988) 4: 60 (V. Kolosov); (1989) 5: 36 (V. Korolev).
84 *EKO* (1989) 6: 207 (R. B. Gitel'makher).
85 *Sotsialisticheskaya industriya* 11 October 1989.
86 *Trud* 3 January 1990 (Solombal'skii Cellulose and Paper Combine).
87 *Sotsialisticheskii trud* (1990) 1: 50 (A. Rogov). During 1990 and 1991 emphasis shifted away from brigade work towards encouraging work units to enter into leasing arrangements with the parent enterprise or ministry. On the whole, lease or lease-contract collectives have come up against the same problems as the brigades: inability to cope with externally caused disruptions and limited accountability towards them on the part of management. For a more detailed discussion see Filtzer, 'The contradictions of the marketless market', pp. 991–5.
88 Ryzhkov, as part of his speech to the Second Congress of People's Deputies, said that election of managers would henceforth be confined to non-state enterprises (i.e. co-operatives and private firms): *Trud* 14 December 1989. This was merely a prelude to the almost total denaturing of the STK embodied in the Law on Enterprises of June 1990, discussed further on pp. 133–4.
89 *Sotsialisticheskii trud* (1989) 2: 80.
90 *Sotsialisticheskaya industriya* 8 July 1988; *Argumenty i fakty* (1988) 41: 7.
91 *Sotsialisticheskii trud* (1989) 12: 46–7 (A. Buzgalin and A. Kolganov); (1990) 2: 34–5 (A. Simakov). In some areas the fall in the proportion of directors leading STK was quite dramatic; in Perm oblast', for example, following the the Goskomtrud-VTsSPS intervention the percentage of managers heading up STK fell from 80 per cent to 15 per cent: *Sotsiologicheskie issledovaniya* (1989) 5: 70 (A. G. Aptip'ev). At All-Union level, however, as of 1989 only 30 per cent of STK were chaired by rank-and-file workers; the rest were headed by enterprise directors, their direct representatives, or subdivision managers: *Sotsialisticheskii trud* (1990) 2: 35 (A. Simakov).
92 *Sotsialisticheskii trud* (1989) 8: 52–3; (1990) 4: 45 (N. Bolotina).
93 *Sotsialisticheskii trud* (1989) 2: 83; (1989) 6: 36.
94 *Trud* 13 September 1988; *Sotsiologicheskie issledovaniya* (1989) 5: 72 (A. G. Aptip'ev).
95 *Sotsialisticheskii trud* (1989) 6: 36.
96 *Sotsiologicheskie issledovaniya* (1988) 5: 74–5; (1989) 2: 30–2 (P. P. Reznikov); *EKO* (1989) 3: 11–13 (V. E. Boikov).
97 *Trud* 13 September 1988.
98 *Sotsiologicheskie issledovaniya* (1989) 5: 71–3 (A. G. Aptip'ev). Similar results were obtained in a 1987 survey carried out by VTsSPS's Scientific Centre, reported in *Sotsiologicheskie issledovaniya* (1989) 4: 78 (A. N. Komozin).
99 Law of the USSR, 'O predpriyatiyakh v SSSR', 4 June 1990; implemented by the decree of the USSR Supreme Soviet, 'O poryadke vvedeniya v deistvie Zakona SSSR "O predpriyatiyakh v SSSR": *Ekonomika i zhizn'* (1990) 25: 19–20. Procedures for hiring managers in state enterprises

were laid down in a decree of the USSR Council of Ministers, 23 October 1990, no. 1073, 'O poryadke naima i osvobozhdeniya rukovoditelya gosudarstvennogo soyuznogo predpriyatiya', *Ekonomika i zhizn'* (1990) 45: 19.

100 *Trud* 30 August 1990; *Rabochaya tribuna* 9 September 1990.

101 *Rabochaya tribuna* 9 December 1990; 12 December 1990 (L. Biryukova and E. Mokhorov); *Izvestiya* 11 December 1990 (I. Demchenko). The Congress Resolution was published in full in *Rabochaya tribuna* 23 January 1991.

102 This was reported extensively in the press. For the most complete accounts, see *Ekonomika i zhizn'* (1991) 2: 12 (V. Ul'yanov) and *Izvestiya* 13 February 1991 (S. Zhigalov).

103 D. A. Filtzer (1992). *Soviet Workers and De-Stalinization: The Formation of the Modern System of Soviet Production Relations, 1953-1964*, Cambridge: Cambridge University Press, ch. 7.

104 *Sotsialisticheskaya industriya* 22 January 1988 (Lyudmila Telen'). Since early 1991 literally hundreds of thousands of women textile workers have been working short-time because of the deepening supplies crisis. This does not alter the basic nature of production in this industry.

105 *Trud* 14 September 1988 (T. Lozhnikova); *Sotsialisticheskaya industriya* 22 January 1988 (Lyudmila Telen'); *EKO* (1988) 8: 139 (Tat'yana Boldyreva); *Rabotnitsa* (1990) 1: 15-17 (Ada Levina).

106 *Sotsialisticheskii trud* (1989) 8: 63 (L. Shineleva). Industries have 'plans' for the elimination of night shifts for women workers, but the speed of implementation is so slow that, at current rates, it will take 74 years to end night work in light industry, 90 years in the chemical industry (where women are a majority of workers), 144 years in iron and steel, and 322 years in the petroleum industry: *Sotsialisticheskii trud* (1989) 4: 70 (A. Abramova).

107 *Sotsialisticheskaya industriya* 18 October 1989 (O. Berezhnaya).

108 *EKO* (1988) 8: 139-40 (Tat'yana Boldyreva). The average length of continuous service among textile workers has been falling steadily since the early 1970s and the industry now relies increasingly on migrant workers from the countryside. In the words of the manager of the 8 March Weaving Factory in Ivanovo, 'What mother who has experienced all the "delights" of a weaving or a spinning shop, is going to send her own daughter there?' *Trud* 14 September 1988 (T. Lozhnikova).

109 *EKO* (1988) 8: 130 (E. E. Novikova, O. L. Milova and E. V. Zalyubovskaya); (1988) 8: 144-5 (Tat'yana Boldyreva).

110 *EKO* (1988) 8: 149-50 (Tat'yana Boldyreva); *Rabochaya tribuna* 23 March 1990 (Moskabel').

111 ibid., p. 150. Since the mid-1960s women have been joined in these jobs by migrant workers of both sexes from the countryside or small towns (so-called *limitchiki*, or workers on limited residence permits). The offer of employment, even under bad conditions, gives them the opportunity to reside in a large city with the better access to supplies that comes with it. For recent discussions on *limitchiki* see *Sotsiologicheskie issledovaniya* (1987) 3: 80-5 (V. S. Dunin and E. A. Zenkevich); (1988) 4: 73-4 (E. Ya.

Butko and N. A. Denisov).

112 Decree of the USSR Supreme Soviet, 'O neotlozhnykh merakh po uluchsheniyu polozheniya zhenshchin, okhrane materinstva i detstva, ukrepleniyu sem'i', 10 April 1990: *Izvestiya* 13 April 1990.

113 *Sobesednik* (1988) 23: 4–5; *Sotsialisticheskii trud* (1989) 10: 14–15 (A. Shadrina, T. Tsvetkova and S. Kosyak); *Sotsialisticheskaya industriya* 18 October 1989 (O. Berezhnaya); 25 October 1989 (L. Biryukova); *Trud* 30 November 1989 (N. Nadezhdina). Enterprises in light industry were at one point being encouraged to raise money by issuing 'shares' to their workers. From the state's point of view this had the advantage of reducing the payment of credits from the state budget and soaking up the loose cash in workers' savings, which cannot be spent in the shops. The problem for light industry, however, was that the yield on these shares had to be paid back out of enterprises' material incentives funds, which were simply too small to support the share issues needed to mount new investment: *Sotsialisticheskaya industriya* 18 October 1989 (O. Berezhnaya).

114 *Sotsialisticheskaya industriya* 25 October 1989 (L. Biryukova).

115 The conservatives were, of course, an exception, but they had no viable alternative programme to offer that would not have led the country back to the dead end of stagnation and perpetual crisis.

116 *Trud* 25 November 1989; 13 April 1990.

117 *Ekonomika i zhizn'* (1990) 31: 15.

5

A VIEW FROM WITHIN
Interview with a Soviet auto worker
David Mandel

MOSCOW, JULY 1988

D. Kolya Naumov, How did you come to work in the auto factory?
S. I grew up in a provincial town. I liked to build things, read drafts
    and buy technical journals. My grades were very good, and I
    wanted to be an engineer. But after graduating from high school,
    when I went to the polyclinic for a medical certificate in order to
    apply to the institute, the eye doctor, who was a very nasty
    woman, saw that I couldn't read a single letter on the chart. She
    yelled, 'And you want to study at the institute?! With those eyes
    they won't take you anywhere!' I didn't know any better at the
    time, so I decided to enrol in professional-technical school. At the
    technical school they were surprised to see someone with my
    grades but they accepted me. I graduated with 'fives' in all
    subjects, except for a 'four' in military training. I studied to be a
    mechanic specializing in equipment repair.

    After a year of classes, we were sent for practical training at a
    factory. One day, out of the blue, we got a proposal: 'How about
    going to Moscow? There are great jobs waiting for you there, and
    you'll see the capital.' And we went, without the slightest inkling
    of what we would be doing. As it turned out, they had brought us
    to work on the assembly line. It was 1970, and there was a
    general shortage of workers. Of course, it was not at all what we
    had been trained for.

    I was 18. Some of us were 17. Those under 18 were supposed to
    be on a reduced work day, but there was nothing of the sort. The
    day I arrived, they handed me a pair of overalls and put me on
    the night shift. Being a conscientious lad, I tried to do everything
    as they told me. At first I could keep up, but at a certain point I

149

began to fall behind. I was running, running. Sometimes the line stopped, and I would try to catch up but I just couldn't. My back ached. I had to put a gasket on the pipe leading into the gas tank, attach some wires, smear black glue on the tank and stick on a piece of cardboard. Finally, I realized that I was totally exhausted. I felt like crying out, 'When will you finally stop?' The assembly line is a cruel, horrible thing.

Eventually, I got used to it. But later, I saw that healthy lads, just from their military service, refused to do that work. They insisted on starting with something easier and a training period. I hadn't known enough to do that.

D. Were there breaks?

S. Well, officially there was one. But usually there aren't any, because we don't always have parts, and we can't work. These idle periods become our breaks. But if there is a steady supply of parts, they can push us all day.

D. How often are these idle times?

S. One day is unlike the next. One week there may be few, and the next they can be very frequent, because you can never know which department won't come through. We live from day to day, because each day, in each shop, in each factory, in the entire country, people are running, running, and even so they don't meet schedules. Something isn't shipped on time something doesn't arrive, some shout, others make excuses. It's a mad running on the spot, with everyone shouting, 'Faster, faster', and the country is still in a constant mess. The parts that should have arrived at the start of the month are shipped only at the end.

Although I've been working for many years now, I still haven't developed the force or the nerves for it, because you can't plan anything. You want to buy a ticket to go home on Saturday, but you don't know – they might decide it's a workday. Of course, you can decide you won't work, but they'll remember and pay you back for it.

D. What happened to your studies at technical school?

S. We worked a half-year at the auto factory, and it came time for us to write our papers on repair mechanics. Of course, we didn't know a thing. So we got a textbook, copied from it and sent the papers home. We were assigned fourth grade as repair mechanics. Our teacher, who was quite a character, told us: 'If you parasites return home and I catch you, I'll thrash the daylights out of you. I've managed to get you fourth grade, but you don't know a damn thing about equipment repair. You'd better stay in

Moscow because you'll disgrace me here.' In Moscow they weren't opposed to our staying. They promised us residence permits and apartments after three years. So we stayed.

D.   What were your living conditions like?

S.   We lived in a dormitory for temporary workers. They came from all over the provinces. We were sixteen in a room and we worked in different shifts. The foreman would come in the morning and wake up those who were on the morning shift. But the second shift had come at 12 o'clock and was still sleeping and they would shout for us to be quiet. Of course, we weren't. And so every shift took its revenge on the next. We never got into real fights, but there was plenty of cursing and pillow throwing. The pillow fights were actually a lot of fun.

We ate in the factory cafeteria – coffee, a piece of salami. Sometimes we'd load up on loaves of white bread and cartons of milk. That was our food. No vitamins at all. That was probably when my gums began to go bad. Generally I lived for many years without vitamins. Milk, a piece of cheese, salami and bread. At the factory, you could get meat croquettes, sickening sour cabbage soup or milk soup. Most of the kids were from the countryside. Their organisms had developed under more normal conditions, and their health was better.

D.   Were there many Moscow natives among the workers?

S.   Not very many, though there were some. Now there seems to be a few more. Basically, these were kids who had come from the villages, people without connections in the city. There were few native Muscovites or people who had lived in the city a long time.

D.   And nationalities?

S.   The majority were Russians, Ukrainians and Armenians. More Armenians than Georgians. Also Azerbaijanians. There were few Uzbeks then, but now there are many because there aren't enough jobs at home. They are recruited for three years and then they return. This is especially true after the *limita*[1] was closed. Before you worked for three years as a *limiktchik* and then got a permanent residence permit. Now after three years – 'goodbye'. It's convenient for the factory, since it doesn't have to supply these people with apartments and day-care.

D.   Why do such people come then?

S.   They come because it's interesting to see Moscow. Some had got into trouble at home, spent time in jail and had trouble getting

151

work there. They are all kinds: honest and crooked. The latter are shirkers from day one.

D. How many workers are there at the factory and what proportion are Muscovites, in the sense of natives or long-time residents?

S. I'm not sure. Maybe 30,000. Of these, not more than one-third are natives or long-time residents. In other Moscow factories there are even fewer.

D. So you lived three years in the dormitory?

S. What three years! I lived there fourteen years. Of course, I spent only the first six months with sixteen in a room. We were young, and it was a good time. On Sunday, we would rest. We'd send messengers for wine, milk and loaves of white bread. We'd lie in our beds, and a mountain of empty packages would rise in the corner of the room. In the evening, we went to dances at one of the factory clubs. After six months, most of my school-friends went to the army for two years. I was exempted because of my eyes. I was moved to a different dorm. I was lucky to get a one-room apartment with four others. It had a kitchen, bathroom and hot water, unlike the old dorm.

D. What are washing conditions like at the factory?

S. In our department there's a large changing room for 500 people with lockers and a small shower room with about 14 stalls. But not everyone uses the showers. Some just wash at the sink.

D. Do you get work clothes?

S. Yes, that's free. At some factories they wash them for you, but not ours. When we first arrived, we would build up a layer of dirt that you could scrape off with a knife. I've noticed that young people don't take care of their work clothes. But people with a certain work experience acquire the pride and dignity of a skilled worker. They keep their clothes and work-place clean and neat and take care of their instruments. Young workers don't give a damn. They come just to kill time until the dances begin.

D. So after a few years, workers acquire a certain professional pride?

S. A few years isn't enough. This pride comes after ten years. The worker knows he is a professional. That's true even on the assembly line. Of course, it depends. Sometimes, even young people behave with dignity, while an old drunk is an old drunk.

D. Is there a lot of turnover on the assembly line?

S. The majority leave. Of course, that varies too. Some stay only three days.

D. And how long did you stay?

S. I held out for four years. Of course, I worked at different jobs on the line. When the others went off to the army, I enrolled in the evening *tekhnikum*[2] where I graduated after two and a half years as a mechanic-technician. During that time, I continued to work on the line, and it was hard also to study in the evening. Everyone fell asleep over their books.

D. Did you ever get used to work on the line?

S. Yes. The first months, you're hurrying, running, all the time and you can't keep up. You're always waiting for the line to stop. Sometimes you get caught up in a contest with the soulless machine. It's you or the line. It's a very curious condition. I think all the workers experience it, whether they are drunks, thieves or just ordinary people. Then you have the sense of elation when you've beaten the machine. You know that any time you like, you can walk away to joke with a friend and when you return you will have no trouble catching up. You develop a precision in your movements, a dexterity. Your muscles work on their own.

I had been working about four months when this man came with a camera and asked if he could photograph me. I was working with a pneumatic wrench attached to a long hose. Have you ever seen a shepherd with a whip? You don't feel like dragging that hose. You flick it, and it goes where you want. When you develop this movement, it is very elegant, and it attracted the correspondent's attention. But this was my personal victory. I had beaten the machine and I didn't want to pose for the public. That's why you've never seen me on the cover of *Ogonek.*[3]

D. You were saying you could walk away and talk with your friends.

S. The relations between workers on the line are sometimes very interesting. For example, we were installing the front seats, I the left and he the right. The car is at waist-level. We're jabbering all the time. He'd fall behind and you're already on the next car. Then he appears again, and you take up where you left off. We even developed our own language, variations on anecdotes that I won't repeat here or just interesting ideas. You would think them up at home and come to the factory not so much to work as to socialize with your friend. Sometimes we'd laugh until our sides ached. This happens to everyone, especially when you find an interesting friend you get along with well.

Of course, even with experience it isn't easy. Sometimes a worker will be absent, and the foreman asks you to do the work for two. For example, installing the track for the seat and the seat too. It's possible, but very hard. After a while, you fall behind. Everything is swimming before your eyes, and you feel nauseous. I remember one day I was given a new job that involved using an automatic screw-driver. I tried to work conscientiously, but the thread on the screws was bad. Everything is garbage here – the screws, the thread. The screws wouldn't go in, and I had to use force as if it were an ordinary screw-driver. I strained all my muscles and the next day I couldn't move my hand. But they made me work anyway. I was crying, but no one believed me. It happens that people cry on the assembly line. They fall and faint too. All kinds of things happen.

D. Is that when it's hot?

S. Yes. There's no air-conditioning, of course. In the winter, it is pretty well heated but there are draughts, since there are no heat curtains. But it is cold in the spring and especially in the autumn when there is an unexpected cold spell and the heating hasn't yet been turned on. We have a plan, after all. If it says the heat goes on 15 November, even if snow has fallen on 15 October, they won't violate the plan. So we steal pieces of the foam material they use for the seats. We cut out holes for the neck and arms and make jackets.

D. What about air pollution?

S. It is bad around the paint shop. It's supposed to be enclosed in glass, but the glass is often broken. Around the acid baths it is really sickening.

D. Does the assembly line's speed vary? Has it changed over the years?

S. The speed really isn't that important. I think it is probably slower than in the West. What matters is what you are doing, how many operations. If they see someone leaving to take a smoke or earning too good a wage, they give him an extra operation. The intensity has actually changed. When I came in 1970 and until Andropov, piece-rates were reduced every year. After Andropov, there were some attempts to introduce innovations. We couldn't make any sense of them.

When they increased the intensity, it was presented as gains in productivity. Every year the ministry ordered us to cut the number of workers. This is supposed to happen on the basis of new machinery, right? But what can you think up on the assembly line? They simply cut. The director would order the department head to cut twenty workers out of two hundred. With no change in technology. They would eliminate a job, divide up the operations and distribute them to other jobs. But they didn't increase the wages of the people who got the extra operations. In that way, rates fell, though take-home pay might have risen somewhat because every year the plan rose. They would tell you that you have to do 150 every day. Next year, 154, next, 160 and so forth. And we are running faster and faster.

D. This was under Brezhnev?

S. Yes, Maybe under Stalin too, for all I know. And come to think of it, it happened under Andropov too. I remember now that they reduced the number of workers by something like 12 per cent. Anyway, by a lot. But they increased the wages of the remainder. Starting from 1984, our new director raised the wages.

D. Are you organized in brigades?

S. In theory, there are brigades, but they were organized artificially and nothing depends upon them. The assembly line is simply divided into several sections. Wages are individual.

D. How are the jobs distributed? Are there better jobs than others?

S. We have two shifts now and two lines in each. We used to have three shifts and they are introducing a third one again with the new model car. The master distributes the jobs. The workers really know only that some operations are harder than others. But, yes, they do also try to get those that pay a bit more. No one ever came by with a chronometer. It happens like this. You're working on a somewhat easier job. Then another job is cut, and the operations are distributed among the others, and you get part added to your job. At first you say, 'No way! I won't do it!' They answer, 'You will or you can leave. We don't need you.' Everyone resists at first, and either 'sliding' workers or the foreman himself does it.[4] But in the end, some worker will do it.

D. Don't workers threaten to quit?

S. The administration doesn't fear that too much. They just say, 'Go. Others will come.' They aren't really afraid of the workers' threats. They have many ways to deal with them.

D. Can you give some examples?

S. In order to meet plan targets, we have to make more cars towards the end of the month. The bosses quietly speed up the line. The workers finally notice that they can't keep up even though they are running. They get mad and begin to shout, 'They increased the speed again!' The bosses deny it. This occurs at the level of

155

department heads. The director, on the face of it, opposes such practices. When the workers complain at a meeting, he says, 'Tell me who increased the speed and I will punish him.' And this happens all the way down the line, even though the administration at all levels is in on the speed-up. They all lie to the workers, who have difficulty seeing clear in this complicated mechanism.

D. What ways do the workers have to protect themselves against increasing intensity?

S. When a norm-setter comes up to you and says, 'We've been watching you and we have to add some operations to your job', you have to shout for all your worth, 'You can't, I'm already overloaded!' That's the only way a worker struggles. You have to know how to shout, turn red, go nuts, so that they'll fear you.

The norm-setter, of course, is under tremendous pressure from his superiors. He is told to seek out productivity reserves, to cut back on the work-force. If you are a quiet, conscientious person, you might object a bit, 'It's too hard, I can't'. But you'll end up doing it, and they'll pour it on until you die or leave. I finally left.

D. How long were you on the line?

S. Four years. I continued working one year after finishing the *tekhnikum* because there wasn't any work in my specialty. I wanted to become a foreman, but when I saw more clearly what that work entailed, I realized it wasn't a sweet life. The hardest thing in a foreman's work is to ask workers to do overtime. Three or four times a month you have to ask them to work on days off or in a third shift. The second shift simply continues to work into the night. Almost 16 hours on the assembly line is very hard, and, obviously, no one wants to stay. The foreman has to convince each worker. Some he threatens, for example, by saying, 'You were absent without a legitimate excuse, but I didn't punish you. Now help me out or the next time you will get punished.'

D. Is there a lot of absenteeism?

S. Not really. Basically they'll tell the foreman, 'My television is on the blink, and I called the repairman. He said he'd come sometime during the day.' Or else the mother-in-law has come, or he has to drive his wife to her mother, or meet the children. The foreman will say, 'OK, go and I'll put down that you worked today,' Such are the relations. The foreman lets you go, and when there is work at night or during a day off you help the foreman out. A worker understands it isn't the foreman's fault – the administration is forcing him. If the foreman doesn't succeed in convincing the worker, the senior foreman comes, then the party organizer, then the department head. One lad, Serezha, told me he had refused and the head of the personnel department came down and even climbed into the body of the car with him and embraced him as he tried to convince him to work.

D. Do they get time and a half for that?

S. More. In the 1970s, they paid 10 roubles for the extra shift. Later, it was raised to 15 and then 20, because workers wouldn't stay. Some get 25. It varies depending on how hard the work is, like in our department.

D. Do workers use this as a way to exercise pressure on the administration?

S. Yes. It is illegal to force someone to work overtime. The workers really don't threaten directly, but the foreman knows that if he angers certain workers, they won't come out. The foreman has to calculate all this when he is deciding whether to punish someone for a disciplinary infraction. So this is the hardest part of the foreman's job. But sometimes he gets fed up and tells the senior foreman or department head. There you are, working on a car, and these three are following you: 'Come on, help us. You know how difficult the situation is.' Their arguments are not rational. They are merely pestering you. The more you force them to pester, the more their insides are churning, and you know they are accumulating anger against you and will take it out some day. At some point, you decide that if you refuse, you'll definitely ruin the relations, so you yield. I was telling you about Serezha. He finally agreed to work the night. The next day, his 'good buddy', the department head, passed by and didn't even say hello. That's why I didn't decide to become a foreman when I finished the *tekhnikum*. I worked another year on the assembly line. I knew all the operations. It was hard, and I'm not so healthy. I saw strapping lads come and refuse the hard jobs. The foreman would give them to me. That's when I left.

D. Was the difficulty more physical or mental?

S. The most terrible thing is the psychological stress. If your health is normal, you get enjoyment out of the physical work. You don't get tired, you move without rushing, you joke. The movements have been mastered, and your muscles are developed. But the worst thing is when you are working and you know that there is

157

only a half-hour's worth of parts left and three hours remain until the end of the shift. As you pick up each nut you feel your heart dripping blood. When they are all gone, the assembly line will, nevertheless keep going. You keep telling the foreman that there soon won't be any nuts left, but he tells you to wait, something else is more urgent. The foreman is constantly running. They aren't allowed to try to organize production. They are like loaders, constantly carrying something. When you've tightened the last bolt, you shout, 'All gone', and the foreman knows it's time for him to run for some more. Meanwhile, the car is moving, and when the nuts arrive, you have to catch up. The end of the shift is approaching, and you're thinking about grabbing a shower stall. Otherwise you have to wait in line in your underpants. They keep you going and you yell, 'No, I won't! Stop the line!'

D. So you left at the end of your fourth year.

S. I had a very good friend who had studied with me at the *tekhnikum* and was working as a repair mechanic in the same shop in a section that repairs instruments and other devices used in the shop. He too didn't rise into the administration but stayed a mechanic. He suggested I join him. The pay was less, but the work was easier. My eyes had begun to hurt a lot. The assembly line had changed: the cars were lower. I had to stoop over more, and that was bad for my eyes.

D. Do workers get any compensation for work on the assembly line? Is it in the 'harmful' category?

S. No. they don't get money for harmfulness. But about seven years ago, a bonus was introduced for work on the line. After three years, they pay you 30 or 40 extra month. But if there is defective work, you lose your regular and your assembly-line bonuses.

D. I always wondered about that. How can they know if the worker is responsible for the defective work or if he received a bad part?

S. The struggle for quality goes in waves. I'll give you the latest case. We have a new model now that has handles with arm-rests. But they were designed in such a way that you couldn't get in to tighten the screw with any of the existing tools. So the cars were coming off the line with loose arm-rests. The workers and the foreman were called into the director's office. The head of production reads from a list: 'The arm-rest is not tight.' 'Whose job is that?' A worker gets up, 'I can't reach the screws'. Who is the foreman? Foreman, what is this worker saying?' 'What do you mean? There isn't any tool'. 'Who is in charge of tools?'

'Naumov'. That's me. 'Dock Naumov 50 per cent of his bonus for the absence of an instrument to tighten the screws'. Of course, I was fuming when I heard that. The designers and technologists hadn't foreseen this problem and I was hearing about it for the first time from the foreman. To cheer me up, he told me he had lost his bonus too, though for something else. 'We're both repressed', he joked. I said, 'Well, if he thinks we're going to work better after that, he's got another think coming.' We're always joking, because we don't give a damn.

D. But you must have lost 30 roubles.

S. Probably. I don't really know. To this day, I don't know how much my bonus is, because, say, we don't fulfil the plan for July and lose the bonus. A little later, the department head will write to the director, 'Please return the bonus for July', that is we get it a few months later. I get my pay stub, and there is no bonus. Then one month it will have three bonuses at once. And I can't figure out when and what for.

D. But is your average wage more or less stable over the course of the year?

S. Yes, my basic wage is 170 roubles a month and my bonus is 40. Sometimes there is an extra bonus, for exports, if the cars are selling abroad.

D. And how do you manage on that?

S. My wife works at another factory. She has a teenage son. We live from pay-packet to pay-packet.

D. So all the talk about Soviet workers having nothing to spend their incomes on is hot air?

S. As far as workers are concerned, yes.

D. Are you saying that you receive your wage and you don't know exactly how it is calculated.

S. That depends on one's character. I simply don't want to figure it out. There are workers who know everything: the export bonus, the quarterly bonus, and so forth. I'm just not interested. Of course, they can make a mistake; someone might have pressed the wrong key. But I simply have too many other interesting things to do. The newspapers have become so interesting, and I try to read them. That's why I feel a bit guilty before the factory.

D. Do you still work in the same place?

S. Yes, only now I am a foreman. We got a raise recently. They cut the number of foremen in the shop from twenty to sixteen and raised their wages.

D. Do you earn more than the workers?
S. Less than the workers on the assembly line. They make about
    200 plus about 70 in bonuses, though I'm not completely sure
    about the those figures. But with the raise, the foremen are
    catching up. Some foremen now get 185, without the bonuses,
    and the senior foremen get 200. That's pretty close to the
    workers' wages. In my instrument section, however, wages are
    low, less than what I make: 170, and that's with the bonus.
D. If a foreman earns less than an assembly-line worker, why
    become a foreman?
S. I can only tell you how I understand things on the assembly line.
    There are worker-operators and there are 'sliding' workers. They
    are paid more than an ordinary worker. There are usually four
    'sliding' workers in a section of about twenty to twenty-five
    workers. In practice, they usually work regularly on the assembly
    line as operators, except for one, who is on duty. But the foreman
    never writes that they are working regularly on the line. That
    would be stupid. He writes that they are all free. And in those
    squares of his report where there are no operators, he puts the
    names of three workers from a different shift and a different
    section. In this way, in the course of the month, they earn the
    foreman 90 roubles, which he splits with them.
D. Are there many women on the assembly line?
S. That depends on the line. Where they weld the body and attach
    the fenders and hood, there are only men. It's hard, dirty work.
    Women work, for example where the upholstering is done,
    where they install little things that require dexterity, like small
    lamps. Our technology is dated, and we glue on a lot of rubber
    seals and insulation. Only women can do that well.
D. Do they earn the same as men?
S. Yes, except that there are some jobs that women don't want to
    do. The work is hard, and so better paid. So you can say that men
    earn a little more.
D. Do women work in night shifts?
S. Yes, though it is illegal. And they get no special benefits. Of
    course, if they are pregnant, they are put on what is called light
    work.
D. What sort of women come to work on the assembly line?
S. Usually, they come when they are young. When I started at the
    factory, girls were coming from the villages. After military
    service, the men usually didn't return to the village. They'd go to

some big construction site, to build the Baikal–Amur railway in Siberia, or they came here. So prospective husbands were scarce. The girls left not only for Moscow but also for the nearby cities. They'd come to Moscow if they had a relative or friends here already. A girl would work a while on the line, get married, take maternity leave and stay with the child. Afterwards, she'd get a job at some factory in charge of a store room, that is, she'd try to get some decent work. If she failed to find any, she'd come back to the assembly line. But generally, after having a child, they look for easier work.

D. Can you say anything about their cultural level?

S. They have all completed high school, that is ten years of school. As far as I know, they like the cinema most of all, and some go to the film festivals. In the dormitories there are inevitably photos of actors on the wall. They don't go much to the theatre. It's hard to get tickets to good performances. Some girls who end up here originally came to Moscow to study at some institute of higher education but failed the entrance exams and are embarrassed about going home.

D. Are you married?

S. Unfortunately.

D. Why 'unfortunately?'

S. We don't get along so well. Last Sunday, Vitya invited me to a meeting of the 'Popular Front', and my wife hid my shoes. She wouldn't let me go. You know I have a lot of outside activities. We are at different cultural and political levels, and that leads to clashes.

But you were asking me what kinds of girls come to the factory. My wife works at a very old machine-construction factory in the stamping shops. Young girls come who had hoped to enter some institute. A few weeks go by, and they lose a finger or a hand. That happens a lot there because the equipment is in terrible condition. It is old. You are supposed to insert the metal piece in with special forks, but the women are in a rush and do it by hand. The older ones want to earn more, and the younger ones simply want to have a smoke. If the machines ran normally, nothing would happen. They will be inserting the detail as the press is rising, but it suddenly falls on their hand because it is out of order.

Protest and isolation

D.   Is there any protest?

S.   It doesn't go past shouting. It is smouldering anger. They don't see any way out. The traditions of struggle have been destroyed, and there is no experience. I think this is especially true of Moscow. There are no working-class traditions here. People come from the village. As far as I know, most cases of collective protest are over delays in paying wages.

 In our factory, management once declared a working Saturday, and about 100 didn't come out to work. They were sick of it. One young worker united them. Actually, it happens quite often that workers don't come out to work. Of course, it's frightening to do that individually. So some fifteen workers will agree among themselves to meet in the morning at the factory and go together to the movies.

D.   You said that management has ways of dividing workers. Can you explain?

S.   One time, as I said, it wasn't fifteen, but a hundred workers. They wanted to run two lines that Saturday but there weren't enough workers. The next day the foremen were writing down the names of the instigators. It was arbitrary – whoever had shouted the loudest, for example. The administration decided to fire seven people. They also promised to dock the rest their thirteenth month, that is the annual bonus.

 So the workers decided to complain to the central council of their trade union. They wrote a letter and collected signatures on the line. One foreman tried to grab it, so they hid it.

D.   When did this happen?

S.   About seven years ago. I wasn't yet a foreman. I also signed, even though I worked that Saturday. They got really frightened when I came to sign. They thought I was working for the administration. We all went together to the union's central council. We told the officials how hard the work was, how we were forced each month to work nights and days off. They gave us understanding looks, 'Can you believe that? And at such a renowned factory, too! What a disgrace!' Of course, they heard this every day from workers seeking justice.

 We waited for a commission of inquiry to come. Actually, I think they tricked us. They said it was a commission from the central council, but it was only a commission of the factory's own trade-union committee. We came, and I made a lot of noise. I told the administration that they were seeking guilty people among the workers, when it was the administration itself that regularly violated the law. We said that we didn't care if they violated the law by setting overtime, but don't dare punish those who refused to work. In the end, they didn't fire anyone.

But they gradually managed to isolate the lad who had organized the action. The foreman would come up to him and say, 'We called the KGB. They're coming for you, and your mother won't even know where you've gone.' Or, 'Did you see me walking over there with a man? He was from the KGB. They're interested in you.'

Gradually, his comrades began to avoid him. That's why I went up to him and told him that I would raise hell if they took him. I wouldn't abandon him. I wasn't trying to muddy the waters. I just was trying to understand, like you now, if the workers are capable of acting collectively for their rights. In my time, I spoke up and did a lot and received a lot of unpleasantness for it. But I eventually realized that I was alone. I always tried to find allies but I couldn't. That's why I went to him. The others were frightened. They knew that it would get back to the bosses that they were friendly with this trouble-maker. And since, as I explained before, workers always need some favour from the foreman – the mother-in-law is coming, or some wedding – you don't want the foreman to be angry with you.

They isolated him. He was also having family trouble and he finally left the factory, and Moscow too. Usually, the workers begin to fight when some common interest is threatened. They are solidarity for a time, but gradually they get scared and move away from you. It isn't a fate to be envied. This happens because over the course of seven years, informal relations have formed, that is, we don't live according to the formal laws that regulate worker – management relations, but according to informal agreements. Every worker has some favour to ask or some way to earn a little extra, and every boss also has ways of earning extra, for his summer home, for example. We are all linked together by these sins. And so when a fighter appears, and though you might really sympathize with him, you know you have some sin. Maybe in a burst of enthusiasm you will go shoulder to shoulder into battle with him. But you know that if you continue like that, they will inevitably dig up your sins.

D. What happens if they really succeed with their market reform, and there are no more sins? Do you think that will make it easier to struggle?

S. I really don't know how it is in the West. But there must be sins there too.

D. Do you still have close friends in the factory, like when you were a worker?

S. Sometimes you meet someone and then you lose sight of him. But you know, I have read an awful lot over the years, and gradually I drew away from the other workers. I would like to be friends with them, but if I start talking about Dostoyevsky, for example, they'd say, 'What sort of rubbish are you bothering with?' Their interests are different, and I promised myself at one point in my life that I would never again go with people who drink vodka out of tumblers.

D. Only out of liqueur glasses?

S. Yes. When it's out of a tumbler your only goal is to get drunk as fast as possible. So unfortunately, I started to move away. Then I became a foreman and they think I'm a loafer. You know, I'm in a white smock. They are working in blue overalls. I might come up to them to talk. They take that to mean that I've got a lot of free time on my hands. They don't understand that in the course of a workday, you can find five minutes. Of course, when the line stops, they play dominoes. But while it is going, they are always working. So they think my work is easy, when actually, it is hard. So relations become complicated.

The bosses' view

D. Have your own views of management changed since you became a foreman?

S. Well, I can understand their psychology better now. I also thought all the bosses were loafers. Now I understand that they are under pressure from above as well as from below. You have to experience that yourself to understand. They aren't loafers but they are forced to bother with things that they really shouldn't be doing. Take our department head, our boss. We aren't fullfilling the plan. The assembly line has been turned off because some part is missing. The director comes into the department and presses the button that restarts the line. Cars are coming off the line and piling up in the shop, unfinished. What can the department head do? He should be doing his work, but the director is standing there. So he runs out, jumps into a car and drives off in search of the missing parts that some other department or factory have not delivered on time. I feel sorry for him. He's like a little boy before the director, who can say to him, 'Don't come to work tomorrow'. I've personally seen that happen to foremen and senior foremen.

D. How does the department head see his workers?

S. They are some kind of rubbish.

D. You mean rabble?

S. No, something that makes life harder for him. His superiors are pressing him to get things done. He curses them, but accepts the situation as inevitable. It's like God. You can curse God for giving you a pug nose, instead of a classical one, but you know you have to live with it. The boss said to make 100,000 cars, and it's clear – the plan. But then you hear voices from down below, 'No, we won't make 100,000. We can't. Only 80,000'. He knows that 100,000 cars will get him his summer home built and a medal. And suddenly, someone down there is putting spokes in his wheels. He'd like to crush that voice from below.

He's not really a bad person. I sometimes catch myself with those attitudes when the department head comes and says, 'You mean you can't fix that machine? It's nothing. What sort of foreman are you?' I come in and see a mechanic smoking or playing dominoes. 'What's the matter, can't you fix the machine?' I ask. 'Give me the parts, and I'll fix it for you', he answers. I know I can't get the parts. But I also know it is easy to make them. But it isn't his work to make them, and the worker demands that I supply them.

So he sits and smokes. He can do that, But as foreman, I am responsible and I have no choice but to make the parts myself. Meanwhile, the department head is complaining about other things that I have to get done, but I'm busy making those parts. So I begin to think of that mechanic as someone who is making my life difficult.

That's my view of how a manager thinks. He will curse his superiors but he neither praises nor curses his workers. Rather, he says, 'Ah, the people, I support the people'.

D. Management maintains the workers, and not the other way around?

S. That's the attitude. You know it's the idea that the workers are stupid, that if you don't chase them out to work on their days off, they will die of hunger. The department head is like a military commander going to battle. Say some part is missing, and the line stops. He says to the foreman, 'What do you mean you don't have any? What's this?' 'That's for the left side. We need the piece for the right side'. 'Nonsense', he answers. He knows he could be prosecuted for it but he takes the risk. He's a real leader. And so when someone says to him, 'But that is not according to specifications', he's ready to wipe him off the face of the earth. And he does.

That is how it is on all levels of management. Very tough. Any manager can be called in by his superior to be chewed out in the foulest language.

D. Can the department head use foul language with workers?

S. No, he can only curse them in a friendly way, except of course in the privacy of his office without witnesses. They are very afraid of witnesses. They could be accused of violating the Leninist style of leadership. And department heads have a lot of enemies looking for a pretext to hurt them, although everyone knows that everyone routinely curses and yells. Of course, he can curse his immediate subordinate, the foreman, without fear.

D. And can the foreman curse the workers?

S. He can, but it is a subtle question of judgement when to yell and when not to. The foreman senses if the worker will let him get away with it or if he will answer back in kind. It's important for a worker not to show that he is soft, that he's mean, or else the foreman will walk all over him. Then the foreman will be afraid of losing face. He'll only choose weak people on whom to let out his wrath.

D. Do you use the polite form of address, the second person plural, or the informal address with workers?

S. The informal. It's friendly.

Two faces of the regime

D. You talked a bit about women workers' cultural level. What can you say about the men's?

S. None of us brought any books with us when we came to Moscow. We only listened to records of popular music. It was sad and boring: drinking, dances and nothing else. We were really living in Moscow illegally that half year. Factories like that – no responsibility. After that, those who remained were formally registered according to the 'limit', given three-year contracts, and moved to better dormitories. I immediately joined a library. Of course, I asked for science fiction.

But even so, I was somewhat different from the others, since I was an avid reader from childhood. My uncle, a driver, probably never read a book in his life. Same for my aunt. My father was an officer, who retired when I was young. We had no library at all in our house. But I borrowed books from the library. In the regular school, they taught literature, but not at technical school. The only reading that students from the villages had done was probably what they studied in school, and their parents too had no books.

But in the middle of the 1970s a book 'boom' began in the Soviet Union. Books even became black market items. People began to collect them and so did my worker friends. So you can't say everything stood still. Of course, that doesn't mean they read everything they bought. It was a sort of fad. Sometimes they just stood on the shelf. As for me, I eventually got access to a certain writer's private library and so to books and authors my friends had never heard about, including some published before the Revolution.

D.   When did you become interested in social and political issues?

S.   When I grew up in the 1960s, I believed Khruschev had done away with Stalinism, that we had freedom and that no one was any longer imprisoned unjustly. Then we learned that Khruschev had retired. Hints began appearing in our school textbooks that Khruschev had not been such a good leader. Also at that time, my father bought a radio and sometimes listened to the Voice of America. There I heard that Khruschev had been forcibly removed. I was really surprised. And I began to see that our papers can lie. Still, I listened to the foreign broadcasts mainly for the rock music and whatever I heard on the newscasts left little impression.

But then I came to the factory and I understood that there was a great difference between what I was seeing there and what was the papers wrote, that is I finally got a glimpse of real life. At the same time, I was hearing on the foreign radio that people were being arrested. I began to take more interest, and it seemed to me that what they were saying on the Voice of America was really about my life, while what was written in the papers was something else, false.

I was especially impressed by the economic commentaries. I would hear them maybe once a month. The international situation, on the other hand, didn't interest me much. And I thought, 'The Voice of America tells the truth once a month, while our papers in the course of a whole year don't write anything I can agree with'. And then there were the arrests and persecutions that I learnt about from the foreign radio. So I simply rejected the regime; I began to feel they were bad people.

I wanted to share this with my friends. They listened to me patiently and asked questions. But I saw that it didn't really concern them. They didn't care that someone had been arrested, beaten or died in camp. They were interested in beer and soccer. Sometimes they got into fights with other workers. I didn't like hooliganism.

D.   And didn't you find any older workers with whom you could talk?

S.   Yes, there were some older workers with whom I could talk. They cursed the regime, Brezhnev and Khruschev. They complained of the food shortages and they didn't like how the leaders spoke. But none of them spoke out about this publicly at meetings. When I tried to pose hard questions and ask what should be done, they fell silent. So although I respected them at first, I soon grew tired of their empty talking and complaining. I wanted things to change.

One of my first small attempts at protest was my refusal to come out to work on a Saturday. In 1970, when we were still at technical school, it was the hundredth anniversary of Lenin's birthday, and they organized a *Subbotnik*[5]. Singing songs, we collected the dirty rags and rusty iron from the yard. Some *Subbotnik*! No one thought to keep the yard clean all year round. I couldn't understand what this had to do with Leninism.

A year later, when we were already at the factory, they organized another *Subbotnik* in Lenin's memory. I really had lost any taste for it. But we came out to work on the assembly line. It was announced that the first secretary of the Central Committee of the Komsomol was coming with a delegation to participate also in the *Subbotnik*. Closer to noon a group of healthy strong and handsome young men appeared. They were given clean smocks and white gloves. We worked without gloves. And where one of us worked, they put three of them. The first secretary was given the job of putting on the wheels, which normally involves removing the nuts, putting the wheel on the axle, replacing the nuts and tightening them with a wrench. But he was given the task only of removing the nuts.

They worked an hour or an hour and a half and then disappeared. The rumour circulated that they had gone to eat. They had a separate table in the cafeteria. Then I read in *Komsomol skaya pravda* that the first secretary had worked alongside the workers on the *Subbotnik*.

When next year's *Subbotnik* came along, I was already studying in the evening *tekhnikum* and working in the first shift. We were supposed to come out for the night shift. Well, I was studying, and after all that had happened on the previous *Subbotniks*, I decided with a group of friends that we weren't going to work. But the foreman found out about this, and the pressure began – from the administration, the party organizer, the trade union. Each in their turn came over to talk and pester. It was very strong pressure.

In the end, I decided it would be simpler to come out. And it was a strange thing. I was seething with anger when I began to work. But for the *Subbotnik*, everything had been carefully prepared. The necessary quantity of parts was on hand for the line to run smoothly. Work conditions were good for a change. Gradually, almost against my will, I fell into the swing of things and even felt a joy in my work. It was not only my sense of mastery over the machine but the simple enjoyment of being able to work normally and to do good work, something that is so rarely given to a Soviet worker.

MOSCOW, DECEMBER 1989

The limits of reform in production

D. Tell me, Kolya, why do you think the economic reform is proceeding with such difficulty? Does it have anything to do with the undemocratic nature of the reform process itself?

S. Well, Gorbachev was never a democrat. He only imagined he was when he compared himself to the others in the Politburo, who were complete idiots and morons. In their company, he was a real radical and liberal and naturally he told himself that if he became leader, the country's fortunes would greatly improve. He would love the people, rule wisely, and the people would respond in kind.

My own experience at the factory might help you to understand the situation Gorbachev finds himself in. After I left the assembly line, I worked as a mechanic in the instrument section. My boss was a moron, a drunkard and a crook. One day, not long after I had begun to work for him, he called me into his office and said: 'Kolya, would you like a little drink of alcohol?' Well, I was thrilled that the boss had noticed me. He poured me a glass, added some water, stirred the mixture and then repeated the operation for himself. 'Let's drink', he said. I drank and thanked him. But his glass was still full. So I said, 'And you, Ivan Fedorovich?' He said, 'I'll sit a bit. I don't quite feel like it right now'. I got up to leave, but he told me not to hurry and offered me a cigarette. I sat a while longer and finally I said I really had to return to work. 'Of course,' he said, 'Go ahead. I'll drink mine in a little while'. Satisfied with myself, I told the story to the manager of the store-room, a desperate alcoholic. He told me that Ivan Fedorovich often invited him into his office for a drink without himself drinking. 'I know he's testing the alcohol on me – wood or grain. But I figure – if I croak, I croak'. So the bastard had kept me in his office while he was observing the effects of the drink!

D.   What is the connection with Gorbachev?
S.   That was fourteen years ago. I was just a beginning mechanic. When I came to see how this person, who was drunk each day and who sold instruments right and left, ran the shop, I began to think to myself, 'Surely if I became department director, I could put things in order'.

My time finally arrived: I became foreman. For two or three years, I beat like a fish on ice. I killed myself running about the factory from the time I arrived in the morning until 6 or 7 o'clock in the evening. I kept telling myself, 'Just a little more effort and you'll have everything running smoothly'. I paid left and right out of my own pocket to get things done. Three years passed. By then, I had established my ties, I knew who to pay off with some tool, who with money, who with alcohol. And gradually, instead of working, I began to read a few pages of a magazine or a book. Sometimes I spent almost entire days reading. And my mechanics began to say about me what I had said about Ivan Fedorovich, 'He's a lazy bastard. He only reads or plays chess'. Of course, no one knows that I sometimes take a nap for half an hour. That would be a big scandal. But my mechanics say, 'He doesn't do anything. He's a boss. And so why should we work?'

D. Are you sure they say that about you?

S. Let's say that I suspect as much, because to my face, of course, they appear to respect me.

D. Why were you unable to change things?

S. Where does one start? Before I became foreman, there was one instrument section under Ivan Fedorovich. Actually, he was senior foreman, but he called himself director of the instrument department. The problem was that all the machines stood in one part of the section, and when the department was divided, Ivan Fedorovich got the machines, and we got nothing. But I have twice as much work as he does. To get something milled or cut, I had to give his workers alcohol or money.

D. You mean you couldn't use the machines?

S. He wouldn't allow me to.

D. And you didn't complain?

S. Sure I did. I went to the chief engineer and to the director of production and explained the situation. They said they couldn't give me the machines because if they did, they would have to set some kind of plan for them. I asked how come Ivan Fedorovich had machines. They said that they were not officially there: he kept them illegally.

D. Why did the chief engineer lie to you like that?

S. Because he did not want to have any trouble with Ivan Fedorovich, who is a relative of the factory's director. It would have drawn the director's attention to them if they took away or divided up his machines. And no one wants to remind the director of one's existence at the factory any more than is absolutely necessary.

D. Why was the section divided in the first place?

S. We weren't meeting the plan, and they decided to make two sections with two bosses because it is easier to manage smaller sections.

D. Did they increase the number of workers?

S. No. But the increase in managerial and technical personnel is a rule, even under Gorbachev. They have added two bureaux to the department of labour and wages at the factory.

D. And how many workers was Ivan Fedorovich left with?

S. Two. And imagine! He had a factory car and driver. When he

171

drank himself into a stupor, they would load him into it and drive him home.

D.   Why did he have the car?

S.   Sometimes we have to bring parts, instruments, polishing materials, and so forth from the warehouse, which is a few kilometres away. When he needs something, he takes the car. But when I need something, I have to ask him. He says, 'I can't give it to you now'. Of course, I know why he can't: his driver took the car to fill it up at the factory pump and then drove it around to the lot where the employees' private cars are parked to sell it to them. He is always driving somewhere on his private business. So when I asked for the car for half a day, I was actually taking 25 roubles out of his pocket. I would have had to give him a present equal to that amount.

Of course, I couldn't. So I made a formal complaint. The director of production called me to his office. He got all worked up, shouted that Ivan Fedorovich's behaviour was outrageous, impermissible. He called in the department head, Ivan Federovich's boss, and threatened him with the direst consequences if it happened again. The next day I went to Ivan Fedorovich and asked him for the car. I told him I had spoken the the director of production. He replied, 'So, you complained? Out of my sight! Now you'll never see that car'. He has the director behind him.

In the first years, I was really burning with desire to put things in order. I would go to the department head, and make suggestions. He would answer, 'You know what? My headlight is broken. Do you think you can fix it?' So I found a turner, paid him out of my own pocket in the hope that the department head would help me. I came back to him and told him my ideas about improving work organization. He said, 'You know, the handle fell off my car'. Or, 'I need a hole made in this detail'. All he was interested in was his car or his summer cottage. He didn't give a damn about my suggestions. He didn't even hear them.

I think that Mikhail Sergeevitch, before he became first secretary, must have had thoughts similar to mine before I became a foreman. And now everyone in the shop hates me.

D.   Surely, you exaggerate.

S.   Well, maybe a little. For example, we have an automatic screwdriver. In 1983 I filled out an order for a new one. Six years have gone by, and we still haven't received it. The most you can work with one is two years.

D. And your workers blame you for that?

S. Well, yes. I repair the tools, because I am conscientious. Ivan Fedorovich has probably already thrown away ten wrenches, while I am still working with the same one, because I repair it. I am sure that I have received many times fewer tools than him because I take care of them and repair them. But life is good to him, he receives tools and sells them, earns money for alcohol and to pay some clerk to write off the instruments as worn out, and his workers are satisfied.

D. Is he still there today?

S. Yes.

D. And what do you do when you need to use a machine?

S. I ask one of his mechanics – they all secretly hate him – and I say that I will pay. In my opinion, I pay them too much.

D. How do you pay?

S. It varies. Sometimes, I go to the director of the department of labour and wages and ask them to pay, and they do. But sometimes I pay out of my own pocket. The workers try to do the work when Ivan Fedorovich is not looking, because he wants things to go badly for me. He wants the higher-ups to see that he can work better than me. Meanwhile, the machines stand idle in his shop. Complain as I might, no one will help. Sometimes, to get a detail ground, bored or milled, I have to spend the whole day running around the factory asking the machine operators. And the department heads keep changing. Just when I have finally explained the situation to one, another one comes and gives me jobs to do.

D. How many workers are there in your section?

S. There are five. Actually, I am supposed to have eight, but I could theoretically manage with three.

D. How is that?

S. I would often go to the bureau of the department of labour and wages and complain that I can't manage with the number of workers I have. I also inflated the value of the equipment.

D. What is your interest in having extra workers?

S. If I officially should have eight, I get five. When I said I could manage with three, I meant three skilled workers who really want to work and maintain the equipment. In practice, because wages in the shop are so low, I know I can't get capable, motivated workers. They'll send me an alcoholic, who can't get a job anywhere else, an invalid or a pensioner. And it takes eight of these weak, unskilled, unmotivated people to do the job. Sometimes it is less trouble for me to do their work for them.

D.   Why are wages so low?

S.   Compared to the assembly line, for example, the work is cleaner, less strenuous, there aren't any draughts. So I get cooks and barbers and I have to train them. But no sooner are they trained, then they quit and someone else is sent. I am the most skilled and experienced person. There is no job I can't do. So in the end, I say to myself, 'If I am so experienced, they can maintain me for my experience. I'll read the paper. If anything happens, I'll make sure the job gets done'. That's how I've come to justify my reading.

D.   Why didn't you try to organize your shop into a contract brigade?[6] You could have raised wages by reducing the number of workers.

S.   You might ask why Gorbachev hasn't been able to organize a market. I have tried. The head of the bureau of the department of labour and wages always answers, 'Kolya, I'll think about your suggestion. It's interesting. But right now I have to calculate these things here'. Wage rates are constantly changing. Either it is a new model or the speed of the assembly line or something else. And she is constantly calculating and recalculating. Or maybe she just doesn't want to be bothered with me. I go to her about once a year with my request. To go more often would risk getting her angry, and I am dependent upon her goodwill. I mentioned, for example, that she sometimes gives me money that I use to pay workers in other shops to do jobs for me.

Not long ago, I paid a couple of workers in another department to help me steal a drill press that we desperately needed. I keep it hidden in a hole I made in the wall. This is one of the sins that you have to commit if you want to do your job. But any administrator who wanted to take revenge on me could use those sins. That is why I am not at the forefront of the rather small group of people fighting for change at the factory.

D.   You mentioned that Ivan Fedorovich sold instruments. Have you done that?

S.   No, I give them away. Not expensive ones, of course. Anyway, I don't have his connections. But a worker will come to me and say, 'Kol, I really need these flat-nosed pliers'. It's not a big deal. Everyone does it.

D.   Are theft and the use of factory time and equipment for personal needs common?

S.   Well, for the majority, if they don't carry something off, even if only a rusty nail or a bolt, it's as if the day has been wasted. Their feet don't want to carry them though the gate. That's a joke, of course, but it contains a measure of truth. And it is considered natural to use factory equipment during work time to make things you need at home. No disgrace is seen in that.

Opening up debate

D.   Are the workers really interested in maintaining the situation you have described at your factory?

S.   There are some thoroughly corrupted elements. But most would like to change things if they saw a way. Attitudes are changing. Last summer, I sat in on a meeting between the director and workers in the 'red corner' of the assembly shop. The issue was the work schedule for 1990. Until then, there had never been any discussion of schedules. This year, the administration proposed that the labour collectives decide what labour regime they preferred: two shifts of 7 hours 40 minutes or two of 7 hours 50 minutes. In the second case they would have a smaller number of 'black Saturdays'[7]. Most shops had voted to have fewer 'black Saturdays'. Some even proposed to work 8 hour shifts in order to reduce the 'black Sundays' to a minimum.[8] Management wanted to keep the old schedule.

D.   What is their interest?

S.   With 7 hour 50 minute shifts, the second shift would finish work well after midnight. Even now, with a 7 hour 40 minute shift, workers quit a little early in order to catch the suburban trains. Moscow is growing, and there are people who travel an hour or an hour and half to work. The time to get washed and changed is not included in the work time. Of course, there are also some lazy-bones like myself who just want to leave a bit early.

  That's why management didn't want to confirm the 7 hour 50 minute schedule and lose work days. Management calculates that they can produce 2,500 cars each of these Saturdays. This is because the assembly line can be idle for entire days. They need the Saturdays to be sure to meet the plan, since they cannot guarantee a regular pace of production. So in order to get the work collectives to change their minds, the director decided to meet with them.

I can still see his hulking figure. He barely gets the words out from between his teeth. He's tired. Instead of the planned 120,000 cars for this year, we will make only 60,000. He's tired from running around the ministries and Gosplan, asking them to 'correct' the plan down to 60,000. He can't admit to the workers that he lied to them and to his superiors when he accepted the plan. That's probably why his tone is so sad and disgusted.

D. Why the huge difference?

S.   He blames it all on the factory's reconstruction and expansion that are behind schedule. Some say the mafia is warming its hands behind his back on the huge construction sites. Lately, management has been laying the blame on the poor training and lack of professionalism of the adjusters of the machine assembly works.

It reminds you of the seances of the 'extra senses' they have started showing lately on TV. You have a telepath sitting up there and he is pressing morally on the audience. The director is really casting a spell over the workers. I wonder if they have such seances in the West.

The same thing happens at the various progressive meetings devoted to different anniversaries. It makes people sick, but they are assembled and not allowed to get up and leave while they are being pressed. You could write a dissertation on it. After an hour or so of this, people become brutalized and look at the world with total cynicism, the same cynicism with which management pours out this false garbage before their eyes. It's a rare occasion that some pure soul shakes himself awake. But they publicly quash him as the others cowardly look on. Then you have the low-lives in the front rows who help: 'What do you know! An honest person! Sit still and don't drag it out. Everybody wants to go home.' It's always like that at our meetings. Only it was different this time.

The workers become aggressive. Someone asked, 'Why does the speed of the assembly line vary?' It happens that a whole shift is idle, and the next day they speed up the line to make up for the lost time. Then the next day, the workers are idle again, because the departments and factories that supply the line are in any case late with their deliveries. The director's answers, which show management's inability to organize production in a normal way, only get the workers angrier. They call him a liar. They propose to make cuts in the white-collar personnel. They believe that they will be able to raise their wages that way.

In the end, they voted for the 7 hour 40 minute shifts. After that, the director was afraid to organize a meeting with our department.

A recent trade union conference was similarly stormy. One of the issues raised was the purchase of machinery in France and Italy for the factory that turned out to be completely unsuitable. At the conference, it was alleged that this occurred because the director's son had been sent instead of engineers and workers who would be working on the machines and knew the specifications. The director defended himself, arguing that he wasn't even in his post when this occurred. Nothing came of all this, of course, but even a little while ago such a discussion would have been unthinkable.

In that sense, things are changing. But the power structure is in general the same. There is a labour-collective council, but the workers don't show much interest in it, probably because its sphere of activity is so limited. The factory paper still writes the same garbage. My impression is that self-management, if it exists anywhere in the Soviet Union, it is on a few islands.

D. The demand to cut technical and administrative personnel is very popular among workers. And judging by your own story, they really must seem to workers to be an obstacle to more efficient production.

S. The press and officials often blame workers for everything. That's pure demagoguery, when you realize that workers have no say in how things are run. I was very disappointed when Abalkin said 'As we work, so we live'[9]. The workers feel he is mocking them.

As for the technical and administrative personnel, it varies really. There are bastards and there are honest people among them. A few real fighters, who want to improve things, have appeared lately at the factory and they have the workers' support. But generally, the workers see them as parasites, and relations have become very tense. This is not only because the workers see the number of technical and administrative personnel growing and their wages rising faster than their own, but also because they see a lot of corruption.

The factory's new model is a big seller. The employees have

their own separate queue to purchase it, and now several dozen are sold each year compared to maybe ten in previous years. Of course, to start with, the price is enormous, something like 10,000 or maybe more, I don't know, and the average worker is somehow convinced that no one could come upon such a sum honestly. But that's neither here nor there. The obvious corruption starts when the employee whose turn has come wants special treatment for his car. In order to get it painted with metallic paint, which is in short supply, he shells out some 500 roubles to the appropriate department head. He does the same thing to have the welding done with four points instead of the usual two, to have two coats of rust-proofing instead of one, and so forth. He even pays management a bribe to get a safe, enclosed place to leave the car overnight while it dries out. After all, it is a very good car, and the mafia is well-informed about everything that goes on. More than one such car has been stolen right at the factory. This spread of corruption provokes a lot of anger among the workers.

D.   What do you think the future holds?

S.   Sometimes I feel really disillusioned when I see nothing changing and the workers still inert. I think sometimes of leaving the factory. But I don't know. There is a potential there and, in the end, I love these people, the way they keep their wonderful sense of humour even under the most adverse conditions, their natural intelligence and resourcefulness. I sometimes think of the workers in my home town. Incredible people. They would arrive at the factory in the morning bursting with energy and go to tremendous lengths, organizing the most complicated operations and running great risks – including prison – just so that at the end of the day they could buy some vodka, sit around, hug each other, maybe end up punching out each other's lights, and then hug again and make up. If this talent and energy could be put to positive use, it could make miracles.

      I'll stay for now. I'll manage whatever happens. The religious values I inherited from my mother and grandmother give me stability. But I'm worried more about you, with your socialism and faith in the workers. How will you survive a disappointment?

NOTES

1 To control population movement and the growth of cities, the Soviet regime introduced a system of residence permits. Because of the labour shortage, factories in the large cities were assigned annual 'limits' of workers they could recruit from the outside. These *limitchiki* were given temporary residence permits that after a certain number of years could become permanent. They are equivalent to the West European *Gastarbeiters* of the 1960s. In 1986 the *limita* was officially closed in Moscow.

2 A *tekhnikum* is a technical school, intermediary between high school and institute.

3 *Ogonek* is the equivalent to *Life* magazine.

4 'Sliding' workers are not permanently assigned a job on the line but take over when line workers have to absent themselves.

5 First organized under Lenin, *Subbotniks* are formally voluntary working Saturdays, during which people do such jobs as cleaning up and beautifying their neighbourhoods, or, in the case of workers, they donate the money earned to a political cause.

6 Under the contract brigade system, very much encouraged in the late 1970s and first half of the 1980s, the brigade enters into a contract with management. The brigade furnishes a certain quality and quantity of work by a certain time and in return it receives the materials, tools and total wage which is divided among the brigade members. Thus any economies of labour should mean higher wages.

7 'Black Saturdays' are worked Saturdays.

8 The work week is forty-one hours.

9 Academician and Vice Prime-Minister Abalkin is a liberal economist and one of the architects of the market reform.

6

A VIEW FROM PRODUCTION
The Hungarian transition from socialism to capitalism

Michael Burawoy

Since the mid-1980s we have seen the violent crushing of the democracy movement in China, the disintegration of 'communist regimes' in Nicaragua, and the dramatic questioning of the tenets of communism within the former Soviet Union itself. Why have we had to wait until 1989 for the collapse of regimes in Eastern Europe if they always had the same class character, if they always suffered from the same crises of legitimacy? How far can one rely on unreconstructed analyses of earlier generations of Marxists to provide plausible accounts for these recent events? In order to answer these questions we have to comprehend the character and significance of lived experience in 'socialism on earth'. We have, in particular, to enter the hidden abode of socialist production but we do so armed with Lenin's theory of the transition to Communism.

The Third Lenin

Lenin was not only the great architect of the Russian Revolution. He also accomplished a revolution in Marxism. It is virtually impossible to comprehend the state of Marxism before Lenin, so enormous and influential have been his contributions. For the purposes of this discussion we can say that Lenin moves through three theoretical phases corresponding to political and economic developments in Russia and the wider international context. The first phase concerned the theorization of the vanguard party, the relationship between party and working class. *What is to be Done?* was written in 1902 when an industrial working class had begun to flex its political muscle but in a context of political repression. The second phase is the theorization of imperialism, showing how capitalism's demise can be understood only at a world level. He tries to comprehend the outbreak of the Second World War and the support that socialist parties gave to their respective national bourgeoisies. Why did socialist parties break with working-class internationalism? The third phase is the theory of the transition to communism, corresponding to the collapse of Tsarism in February 1917 and the rising fortunes of the various socialist parties, in particular the Bolshevik Party, in Russia. While the First and Second Lenins have been hotly debated, the transition from socialism to capitalism calls for a reinterrogation of the Third Lenin, the Lenin of *State and Revolution*.

Lenin's theory of the transition from capitalism to communism involves two stages: a revolutionary transition from capitalism to socialism and an evolutionary transition from socialism to communism. The first transition is revolutionary because it involves destroying the capitalist state – the instrument of capitalist rule. It necessarily involves suppressing the capitalist class and establishing a new form of state – the dictatorship of the proletariat. But why is the second stage evolutionary? Why does the dictatorship of the proletariat 'wither away' leaving us with communism – a society in which people receive what they need and contribute according to their abilities? What is this transitional stage of socialism?.

It has three features which distinguish it from capitalism. First, it is **rational**. The pursuit of profit in the market based on private ownership of the means of production leads to polarization of wealth, wastage and continual crises. In socialism, planning assures the maximization of the welfare of all based on collective ownership of the means of production. Second, it is just. Capitalism rewards people first and foremost on the basis of their relationship to the means of production while socialism rewards people according to their contribution, their labour. Third, socialism is democratic. While capitalism is quite compatible with forms of parliamentary democracy in which popular participation is restricted to the election of representatives, socialism requires a much more radical democracy. The dictatorship of the proletariat involves dismantling the repressive apparatus of the state and subjecting leaders to the direct control of the led.

This third component is crucial. It is not an afterthought or a flight of fancy on Lenin's part. He well knew that it is one thing to suppress the capitalist class but it is quite another matter to prevent the rise of a new class. When Lenin insists on dismantling the state and arming the people, when he proposes that elected officials be subject to instant recall and receive an average worker's wage he explicitly recognizes the danger of the emergence of a new bureaucratic class.

Democracy is valued not only for its own sake but also because it enables those who produce the surplus to control its appropriation and distribution.

The status of this theory of the transition has to be clearly understood. It is a logical model rather than an historical account. *If* we are to arrive at communism *then* we must first create a transitional stage of socialism. In *State and Revolution* Lenin is not concerned to examine the conditions under which such a transition is possible. As regards the latter, Lenin argued that a socialist revolution in a backward country such as Russia could not fulfil its mission without support from socialist regimes in the West. What then happens to a socialist revolution made in a backward country? None of the pillars in Lenin's model of socialism – rationality, justice and democracy – was ever consolidated. Instead of the dictatorship of the proletariat, that is a workers' socialism, we have a state socialism, a dictatorship over the working class. In the absence of radical democracy, rationality and justice undergo significant distortion and turn into their opposite.

STATE SOCIALISM

State socialism has four features. First, without radical democracy, *a new class emerges which appropriates and then redistributes surplus*. This new class, variously called the *nomenclatura* or 'bureaucratic caste' or 'teleological redistributors', is placed in opposition to the class of direct producers. The two classes are antagonistic because the producers of surplus do not control its appropriation or redistribution by this new dominant class. To advance and deepen such a class analysis it is necessary to delve into the nature of planning under state socialism.

The original orthodox view of planning saw it as central stipulation of production targets which enterprises would fulfil. In practice the rationality of the plan directed from above gave way to a *bargaining relationship within the dominant class between the enterprise director and the state planning agency*. The enterprise develops interests of its own *vis-á-vis* central planners revolving around the incentives to fulfil plan targets. Like workers on piece-rates, when the targets are too difficult enterprise directors call attention to this by restricting output. Equally when the targets are easy then enterprises don't overfulfil plans for fear that the targets will be increased. Instead they bank the excess product and distribute it privately or use excess capacity to produce something else.

It is also difficult for a central plan to establish indices for evaluating output that will lead to the production of exactly what is needed. The production of nails may be evaluated on the basis of their weight but then enterprises will tend to overproduce heavy nails. Planning based on physical targets can be effective when the product is homogeneous and quality is not too important, particularly in the early phases of industrial development. With the development of sophisticated machinery the quality of products becomes more important and physical planning becomes increasingly irrational. The transition is then from physical planning to fiscal planning. The Hungarian economic reforms of 1968 largely did away with evaluating performance of enterprises on the basis of plan fulfilment and introduced fiscal criteria. The bargaining between state and enterprise now involves pricing policies but at least there is greater sensitivity to the needs of the consumer. A rudimentary market emerges among state-owned enterprises.

Of course, once the relationship between enterprise and state is understood as a bargaining one rather than unidirectional command, it is in the interest of the enterprise directors to increase their bargaining power. They do so by making themselves indispensable, which is accomplished by expansion, by trying to obtain as much investment from the state as possible. With this objective in mind it enters into intense competition with other enterprises. Since enterprises don't go bankrupt there are no internal barriers to expansion. This continual thirst for supplies (machinery, raw materials and labour) leads to shortages, which lead to hoarding, which leads to further shortages. The state socialist economy is a shortage economy in contrast to the capitalist economy which produces surpluses. Each has its own irrationality.

The bargaining relationship between enterprise and state does present a rationale for the *triple alliance between management, union and party within the enterprise*. The enterprise must present a united front to the central planners in the interests of the enterprise as a whole. Some of this might trickle down to the direct producers. But this should not obscure the other side of the triple alliance, namely class domination over the direct producers who are deprived of any institutionalized way of defending their interest against managerial despotism. This is the third feature of state socialism. Party and trade union are more or less automatic signatories to managerial edicts, whether these concern bonuses, transfers, wages or working conditions. If workers have power it is because they control production and management depends on their co-operation.

This brings into focus the final component of state socialism – *the ideology which justifies the central appropriation and redistribution of surplus*. Under capitalism the appropriation of surplus is mystified by the wage form. Capitalism is compatible with a wide range of ideologies none of which are essential for its functioning. Under state socialism, the state is the transparent appropriator and redistributor of surplus and therefore has to justify its exploitation. State socialism requires an ideology which legitimizes appropriation as being in the interest of all. This ideology is, of course, Marxism, or Marxism-Leninism, which claims that socialism is rational and just. It pretends that the programme formulated by Lenin in *State and Revolution* is being realized. As I shall try and show, how different classes experience the gap between ideology and reality holds the secret to the dynamics of class struggles in state socialism as well as the secret of its demise.

PAINTING SOCIALISM

It is difficult to comprehend the lived experience of workers in state socialism from the outside. In a workers' state the interests of the working class become a political and ideological football. The dominant class claims that it represents the interests of workers, which compels opposition or dissident intellectuals to deny this and declare their own interests as those workers. But the debate goes on over the heads of workers since there is no organ to represent their interests. Workers are spoken for, they don't speak for themselves except in unanticipated strike waves. Therefore, in order to begin to understand what it is to work in a workers' state one has to by pass intellectuals and enter the hidden abode of production directly.

I worked at the Lenin Steel Works in Miskolc, Hungary, as a furnaceman for six months in 1985, for two months in 1986 and for two months in 1987; I have been back to talk to my workmates twice a year since then. The Lenin Steel Works employs some 12,000 workers and produces around 1 million tons of steel, which makes it a very inefficient enterprise by international standards. It is one of three steel mills in Hungary.

It was a freezing February morning in 1985 when I began my first shift at the huge basic oxygen converter. There was a lull in production and I was casually talking to Feri, whose job was to clean the oxygen lance, when Stegermajer, the plant superintendent, came up yelling at us to get on with sweeping the place clean. The look of disgust on Feri's face made it clear what he thought of the idea. Who'd ever heard of keeping a steel mill clean? And anyway it was not his job. But there was no arguing with the menacing look on Stegermajer's face so we lazily took up our brooms and began brushing away at the railings, creating clouds of dust and graphite that would descend elsewhere to be swept again by someone else's broom. Aggressiveness and shouting seemed a way of life here at the Lenin Steel Works. The bosses were always on edge. What were they so nervous about?

No sooner had we brushed the railings to reveal a dull green and yellow than painters appeared, brightening up the surroundings at least for a few minutes until the dust and graphite descended once more. 'Was this normal?' I wondered. The next day the painting continued and I heard that some delegation would be visiting but no one cared who, why or when. As became clear in succeeding days, this was to be no ordinary visit. No less a person than the Prime Minister himself would be visiting. The automatic chute that used to send alloys from the bunkers over head down into the ladle below, broken now for many weeks, was being repaired. We would no longer have to shovel the alloys into a wheelbarrow and tip them down the chute ourselves, choked by clouds of silicosis-producing dust as we did so. Thank God for the Prime Minister.

On the Friday before the Tuesday visit of the Prime Minister, production had come to a standstill. Welders were out in force with their tanks of acetylene, resting uncomfortably near to the converter. New silver-painted doors threaded by water pipes to prevent warping were being erected to fence off the converter. Hoards of young lads from neighbouring co-operatives were swarming around to give the converter its final touch. Preparations were as elaborate as for a satellite going into orbit. Soldiers were shovelling the snow away from the entrances below and cleaning up the debris that they uncovered. It seemed that the entire land had been mobilized for the visit of the Prime Minister.

I found Józsi swearing in our eating room. 'This is a steel mill not a pharmacy.' He'd just been told to change into new overalls, with a new hat and gloves. I looked at him in disbelief, assuming I had not understood him properly. 'You won't even be working when the Prime Minister comes', I said. He looked at me as though I'd come from the moon. 'What's that to do with anything? Everybody has to conform. This is window-dressing politics.' So we all trooped off to get our new outfits, and came back mockingly giving our hard hats a final polish. Five minutes later, let alone next Tuesday, we would be filthy again.

Today was our turn for a communist shift. In aid of charity, such as support for a children's hospital or the National Theatre, we work an extra shift. It's a socialist form of taxation. We were assigned to paint in yellow and green the slag drawer, a huge machine that skims off slag from the pig iron as it passes on the way to the converter. There were not enough paint brushes to go round. I could only find a black one. What could I paint black? What better than the most treasured of the furnaceman's tools – his shovel? I had hardly begun this critical task when Stegermajer came storming over, with his hand behind his back and his hard hat bobbing, his head bowed for combat. 'What the hell are you doing?' 'Painting the shovels black', I replied as innocently as I could. But he was not amused so I added, 'Haven't you got any more brushes so I can help the others?' No, there weren't any others. 'So I can't help build socialism?' I continued, somewhat riskily. My mates cracked up, amused at the thought of their 'American professor' building socialism. Even Stegermajer caved in when Józsi interceded, 'Misi, Misi you don't understand anything. You are not *building* socialism you are *painting* socialism. And *black* at that.'

The 'painting' continued on Monday when we hauled out the always ascending graphs demonstrating the superiority of the converter over the old Siemen's Martin furnaces. Party slogans and directives for the forthcoming party congress as well as photographs of earlier visits by dignitaries were displayed at resting points on Tuesday's scenic tour. At noon on Monday Stegermajer came over to me with an embarrassed look, 'You know the Prime Minister is coming tomorrow.' I nodded and smiled. 'Well, why don't you take a holiday.' They surely didn't want their yogurt-eating furnaceman upsetting the visit.

I assume that the Prime Minister came. I saw his picture in the newspaper peering into the wondrous converter. When I returned on Wednesday, the flags were down, the graphs returned to their storeroom together with the party directives and photo. The filming was over. Once more we were a steel mill, at least until the next painting.

Workers looked upon the painting as just another instance of socialist waste and deception. 'This is the communist sector', begins the furnaceman's joke, 'If there's pig iron then there's no scrap. If there's scrap then there's no pig iron. If there happens to be both then someone must have stolen something.' Socialism, it seems, can conjure up an image of efficiency only by calling on its workers to collaborate in desperate and farcical cover up. Painting socialism calls attention not only to the irrationality of socialism but also to its injustice. 'Money doesn't count, the Prime Minister is coming' expresses the powerful resentment toward the Red Barons who direct society, whom we have to entertain with these charades. Furnacemen are fond of the joke about the contribution to socialism of three men. 'The first receives 5,000 forints a month. He builds socialism. The second receives 15,000 forints a month. He directs the building of socialism. The third receives 50,000 forints a month. For him socialism is built.'

I am told how 'connections' dictate membership of the famous inside contracting systems – self-selected, self-organized worker collectives (VGMKs) which receive specific lump sum payments for the completion of specific tasks outside normal working hours. Pay can be three or four times their normal wage which could easily double the pay a worker received each month. Karsci related the story of the VGMK assigned to clean up the roof of the Combined Steel Works: it contained the party secretary, the trade union secretary and the communist youth secretary. How often did we berate Hegedus, the day foreman, for being more concerned about his VGMK work that his formal duties. When we were on afternoon shift we would see him wandering around, sometimes supervising, sometimes opening bags of cement, as his token contribution to the VGMK which rebuilt the walls of the ladles.

Resentment is not levelled at inequality *per se*, since everyone wants to be rich, but against undeserved wealth accumulated through the exploitation of contacts of scarce skills without corresponding effort. Moreover there are those who, in the eyes of the steel workers deserve to be poor, such as the half million gypsies who, despite government assistance, I am forever being told continue to malinger and steal, live in a cesspool of poverty because they know no better, and thereby heap disrepute on to a nation of honest, decent and hard-working people.

Socialism compels compliance to its rituals of affirmation. Painting *over* the sordid realities of socialism is simultaneously the painting *of* an appearance of brightness, rationality and justice. Socialism becomes an elaborate game of mutual pretence which everyone sees through but which everyone is compelled to play. It is an intermingling of a desultory reality and fabricated appearance in which the appearance takes on a reality of its own. If we have to paint a world of efficiency and justice then we become that much more sensitive to inefficiency and injustice. This ritual juxtaposition of the real and the imaginary is not confined to exceptional moments. It is part and parcel of factory life: the union elections, the product conferences, competition among socialist brigades and the communist shifts. Because it is embedded in real practices, the pretence unwittingly assumes a life of its own, a spontaneous critique of existing society and a potential force for an alternative society. By failing to live up to the ideals that it preaches, state socialism generates a rudimentary socialist consciousness in its working class.

The capitalist game is very different. In advanced capitalism workers spontaneously consent to its directing classes by *obscuring from themselves* its *system* of domination and inefficiency. Here private appropriation of the product and wage labour establish the basis of consent to capitalism. In a fully developed *hegemonic regime* we find the co-ordination of the economic interest of workers and capitalists through the dependence of the former on the latter. That is to say, workers co-operate with capital in order to keep their jobs when profits are threatened and to extract concessions when profits are increasing. At the same time in the work-place, workers are constituted as individuals with rights and obligations defined by the production regime. Consent presupposes force which at the level of production ultimately rests with the employers right to hire and fire. In a hegemonic regime the application of force is itself the object of consent, bound by certain rules. Individual workers are disciplined or fired for violations of the regime's code but they can appeal against the employer. Here the rule of law applies but in lay-offs the rule of profit applies. Capitalists engineer consent to closure on the grounds of their right to make profit. So in capitalism the relations of production are *hidden* through participation in production whereas in socialism the relations of production become the central concern of workers and managers. Under socialism we are *called on deliberately to cover up* injustice and irrationality and to paint a vision of justice and rationality.

But why does everyone carry on playing the game? Enterprises have an interest in participating in these rituals. There is a rationality behind the irrationality. The growth of a capitalist enterprise depends on its profitability; growth of a state socialist enterprise depends on state dispensed investment funds. There are three steel mills in Hungary. Their common interest in expanding the resources available to the steel industry is broken up by an intense rivalry over the distribution of what is available. Each has to demonstrate its worthiness to receive investment. Since there are no clear objective criteria to assess the efficiency of firms, it is important to create the appearance of conformity to socialist values of rationality and justice. That is precisely why management has to paint the Lenin Steel Works when the Prime Minister visits. He had to be convinced that the Lenin Steel Works was at the forefront of the building of socialism. Thus, by its own logic building socialism turns into its painting, reminding all of the gap between what is and what should be, deepening the critical consciousness of workers and managers alike.

It is one thing to talk of a class consciousness; it is quite another matter to talk of class mobilization. Here Hungary and Poland in 1980 are at opposite extremes. Hungarian workers could advance their interest by individual participation in the second economy after normal hours whereas in Poland workers were more likely to be standing in queues to buy basic goods. The Hungarian second economy atomized its working class. Furthermore, Hungarian workers were bereft of resources for collective mobilization. In Poland after 1976 intellectuals played a critical role in forging links between different sectors of the labour force while the Church provided an arena in which collective identity could be forged. In Hungary intellectuals and the Church were far removed from working-class organization. Instead of a collective memory inspired by nationalism and Catholicism, binding society into a force hostile to the state. Hungary is a fragmented society, ambivalent about its past, driven by individualism and entrepreneurship. Hungarian workers have learnt to manoeuvre within the socialist order rather than revolt against it. They are contemptuous of the Solidarity movement which plunged Poland into economic chaos. 'They got what they deserved. Unlike we Hungarians who work for our living the Poles expect to have meat on their table by striking.' From being a land of brothers and sisters overnight Poland became a nation of loafers and hustlers. Their collective mobilization sent shivers down the Hungarian spine.

THE COLLAPSE OF STATE SOCIALISM

We have now discussed how painting socialism engendered class consciousness among workers and in the case of Poland class mobilization, but how did this contribute to the collapse of state socialism? It is often assumed that the regimes of Eastern Europe were swept away through popular revolts from below. To be sure there were popular movements from below, particularly in East Germany, Romania and Czechoslovakia but there have been much stronger popular movements which did not end with the collapse of state socialism. Why the difference? The most common answer is the Soviet factor, namely that perestroika and glasnost meant the end of Soviety domination of Eastern Europe. While obviously true, this assumes that the Soviet Union is somehow external to Eastern Europe whereas the same challenges are being experienced there too. What is remarkable is how peaceful these changes have been, with the notable exception of Romania. Communist parties lost the confidence and the will to rule. The collapse of state socialism was a collapse from above.

Here we have to look at painting socialism from the standpoint of the dominant class. The gap between ideology and reality, ritualized in painting socialism, refused to narrow despite repeated attempts at reform. Popular revolts from below but particularly the Solidarity movement, which after all was a workers' movement against a 'workers' state', made that gap painfully obvious and threatening to the ruling class. At the same time the membership of the ruling class was becoming more professional and more educated and less tolerant of an ideology so patently at odds with reality. Whereas previously this gap had led to attempts to change reality, through economic reforms, now it led to the rejection of ideology. In the end even the most degenerate form of Marxism – Marxism-Leninism – proved to be subversive of state socialism. Unable to bridge the gap between ideals of socialism and the reality of state socialism the ruling class finally turned against the ideology. Marxism was abandoned in favour of new ideologies which in different combinations celebrated nationalism, democracy, profits and the market.

What the new ideologies all share is an uncompromising anti-communism. The elections of spring 1990 in Hungary highlighted the strength of anti-communism. The victorious party – the Hungarian Democratic Forum – campaigned on a national popular platform while the second most popular party – the Free Democrats –

campaigned for a new capitalist order. Each side sought to outbid the other in their anti-communist rhetoric. So powerful was the anti-communist consensus that no party dare defend the interests of workers *qua* workers for fear of being labelled 'Stalinist'. The social democrats jumped on to the anti-communist bandwagon and failed to demarcate themselves from the others while the old communist party renamed itself from the Hungarian Socialist Workers' Party to the Hungarian Socialist Party. Commitment to workers was viewed as an even bigger liability than socialism!

Apart from the exclusion of the working class, anti-communism had another consequence, namely hostility to planning and indeed state intervention. The rallying cry for the election was privatization. Already before the elections legislation was enacted to recognize multiple forms of property which made it possible to create limited companies and joint-stock corporations or to turn state enterprise into private companies. The last socialist government was already enthusiastically pursuing what has come to be called spontaneous privatization, that is privatization based on initiatives from below. State enterprises must decide themselves on their own privatization plan.

But who would buy these state enterprises? First foreigners received tax incentives for investing in Hungary. Foreigners have indeed been investing but it still does not amount to much. Another possibility was the old *nomenclatura* class, which was encouraged to buy shares in new privatized companies by making investments tax deductible and by offering privatization loans at low rates of interest. In the name of spontaneous privatization the old dominant class has begun to turn its political capital into economic capital. Because it was not clear who actually owned state property, that is who should be paid, and because there were no effective ways of valuing assets of state enterprises scandals continually erupt. Collusion between managers, state officials and foreign capital have defined the pattern of privatization so far. We can look in detail at the example of the Lenin Steel Works.

The Lenin Steel Works (LKM) was officially transformed into a joint-stock corporation in January 1990. Because LKM had been a loss-making company it had been brought under direct state control. There was no enterprise council and according to the Transformation Act there was no need to raise the founding capital by 20 per cent or 100 million forints. Nevertheless, as we shall see, LKM did seek outside investment through the creation of internal 'limited companies'. When it was turned into a joint-stock company, the state became the major shareholder of its 11 billion forint assets.

LKM faced seemingly impossible barriers to profitability under hard budget constraints. Raw materials had to be imported at increasing prices, much of its capital was antiquated, it suffered from considerable overmanning and however hard it tried it could not effectively enter Western markets because world competition was so intense. These constraints were real and operated quite independently of its management. The government continually bailed LKM out so that its management could present their operations as profitable. Nevertheless, at the beginning of 1990 the new corporation faced an accumulated debt of the order of 2 billion forints.

The company was essentially bankrupt but desperately needed new capital for reconstruction. It had difficulty obtaining credit from national banks or government and so turned to the new source of finance provided by the privatization legislation, namely foreign capital. It managed to attract about 1 billion forints worth of investment from several companies, mainly Austrian and West German. However, partly because of political and economic uncertainties, they would invest only in particular parts of the enterprise such as the continuous caster, the foundry, the electric arc furnace, the rolling mills and so on. By the middle of June 1990, the corporation contained twenty-six limited companies and joint-stock companies.

Why were foreign enterprises prepared to invest in LKM? Surely there were more lucrative outlets for their capital? The foreign investors came in with strings attached. They were not concerned about the viability of LKM but with guaranteeing returns on their own investments. Some were able to exchange their investment for control over the distribution of the LKM's products while others extracted either guaranteed income returns on investment or guarantees on the profitability of the units in which they invested. The latter could be assured through the manipulation of internal prices. Moreover, it was to the advantage of the central corporation to boost the profitability of internal companies where there is foreign investment since that gave greater tax relief.

If some hoped that foreign investors would bring in new management and begin to reorganize LKM then they were to be disappointed. They left the organization of steel production in the hand of the existing management. Two things, however, did change. First, there was a multiplication of managerial hierarchies since each internal limited company had its own general director and managerial structure. Moreover, they received very high incomes for their new positions. At the same time lay-offs still seemed to be unacceptable. Apart from natural attrition, management decided to cut the number of employees in the central organization – employees who were now clearly redundant. Instead of laying them off, however, they were sent to the various limited companies, boosting their already swollen administrative ranks with what came to be known as 'parachutists'. This was not a way of increasing profit but of redistributing increased losses.

The second change also intensified problems of the past. By creating internal companies based on profits tensions increased between units over the distribution of costs and the determination of internal prices. The old conflicts between say the rolling mills and steel production or between the continuous caster and the converter intensified. Struggles were more focused on the manipulation of internal prices, determined by the bargaining strength of the different units. Pressures on internal prices were so great that a 'Price Censorship Committee' was created which regulated prices in the 'interests of the Company as a whole'. Still power relations and not market relations governed the relationship between the interdependent units within the steel mill. The introduction of profit centres did not and indeed cannot give rise to greater efficiency or reduce costs where the units are part of a single integrated production process.

LKM managers soon realized that the creation of internal limited companies exacerbated rather than diminished old problems. The units which top management had once controlled now assumed an autonomy that was legally based. Still what could they have done? They were trapped by the logic of spontaneous privatization. They could obtain external financing only by seeking assistance from foreign capital which entailed limiting market manoeuvrability, multiplying managers and disrupting production. Short-term survival came at the cost of long-term viability. They were left to their own devices without any clear guidelines from above. There was no national industrial strategy because that would be tantamount to planning – a dangerous regression towards communism.

In the case of the transformation of LKM only about 10 per cent of the shares are held by foreign enterprises – the remainder being held largely by the Ministry of Industry. An alternative solution is to enter into a joint venture with foreign capital such as occurred at OZD. There the West Germany steel consortium, KORF, bought out 60 per cent of OZD Steel Works. OZD was probably the weakest steel complex and has essentially lost control of its future.

There is another alternative which some enterprises, like the sister plant supplying iron ore to LKM and OZD, are pursuing. Rather than lose control of the enterprise to the state or to foreign capital they are thinking of selling shares to their own employees. This is becoming an increasing popular idea among managers, although no company has yet succeeded in doing it. There are a number of reasons for the popularity of employee ownership. In the first place it is to retain control of their enterprise when threatened with state or foreign direction. They would also stand to gain materially if shares are distributed to employees in accordance with their income and seniority in the company. In other instances, management seeks to establish itself among its workers by making employee ownership a concession. The collapse of the *nomenclatura* system, and thus of support from on high, has left them vulnerable to worker rebellions from below. We turn now to such mobilizations.

WORKERS' RESPONSE

What is the response from the working class? Excluded from the political process they stand and watch from the sidelines. For the majority the only significant change has been rampant inflation and the multiplication of managerial hierarchies that privatization has brought about. For the time being, at least, there is still little unemployment.

Nevertheless, in places, workers' councils have sprung up to represent the interests of workers, As of the end of June there were about 160 legally recognized workers councils. Although they take different forms they do share certain traits. They usually emerged in response to some blatant injustice, such as huge management bonuses. Workers protest to the trade union which fails to come to their assistance. The workers then set up a workers' council as a 'real trade union' which will represent the interests of workers both as individuals and as a collectivity. They collect dues but they are retained for the benefit of the membership and not to maintain some remote bureaucracy.

At this point workers' councils are very much rooted in production and are wary of extending links beyond the enterprise to other enterprises. Among them is the workers' council at the blast furnace of what was the Lenin Steel Works and soon to be registered are councils in the foundry and in the Combined Steel Works. Hearing about other workers' councils and helped by a Hungarian Democratic Forum lawyer an old-time leading operator began organizing a workers' council in the blast furnace. He recalled the importance of his experiences in the 1956 council when he was 17 and a young employee at LKM. He and his fellow organizers had taken the constitution of the workers' council at the famous Herend porcelain factory as their own and presented it to the court for registration in January 1990. Although the court was able to put up some obstruction in the end it could not stop the formation of the workers' council which was finally given legal approval in the middle of April. In June 1990, of the 300 workers in the blast furnace, 120 were members of the workers' council, 80 were still enrolled in the old trade union, while 100 were not a member of either organization. From the blast furnace the idea has spread to the converter and the foundry. The struggle with management for extending the rights of workers is only just beginning.

What motivated the formation of the workers' council at LKM? As elsewhere, the most basic impetus is opposition to the old-style trade unions who colluded with management to defend the interests of the enterprise rather than workers. The subordination of the trade union was symbolized by its automatic signature of any managerial decree, whether or not it was in the interests of workers. The workers' council vows that it will defend individual workers against arbitrary managerial sanctions. Its most ardent supporters go further and want to see workers' councils exercising control over management and even organizing elections of managers. Finally, workers' councils are interested in promoting employee ownership although they are not sure yet exactly how this is to be accomplished. In this last regard they differ from the council ideas of 1956, which usually took for granted state ownership of the means of production.

The workers' councils signify four features of Hungarian society in transition. First, the separation of state politics and production politics. With the autonomization of parliamentary politics and the legal apparatus and the collapse of the party so there has been a corresponding autonomization of enterprise politics. Moreover, spontaneous privatization has made the enterprise the locus of decisions concerning its own future. The enterprise becomes the locus of important struggles in which competing interests clash. Second, in rebelling against the official trade unions the workers' councils are highlighting their irrelevance in the new production politics. With the declining importance of bargaining between enterprise and state so it makes even less sense for trade unions to ally themselves with management. Since the official trade unions seem unable to restructure themselves it is not surprising that new forms of representation emerge to defend worker interests. Third, in being excluded from wider political processes and having no institutional channels through which to express their interests as workers, they have to rely on the one source of power they share, namely their power in the work-place. The dependence of managers on their spontaneous co-operation gives rise to demands for a radical democracy springing from the shop-floor.

Last but by no means least, the workers' councils are the legacy and embodiment of the critical socialist consciousness they developed through participation in the rituals of painting socialism. At the core of their project is the commitment to 'rationality' that is the efficient organization of production and to 'justice' that is the reward for labour, although at this point they conceive of this only in terms of the factory and not in terms of the organization of the wider society.

CONCLUSION

State socialism is a degenerate form of Lenin's democratic socialism. It is a class society legitimized by the socialist ideals of justice and rationality. The gap between ideology and reality gives that society its political dynamic, explaining its collapse and the birthmarks of the new society. Beneath the cloud of Marxism-Leninism very different regimes of state socialism existed in different countries with different degrees of success. Just as we should not be deceived by the socialist ideology of state socialism so also we should not be deceived by the ideology of the transitional society. It not only shapes but also obscures a multiplicity of alternative visions of the future, including the one based on workers' councils.

The collapse of state socialism is a blow only to socialists who believed that the Soviet Union was the incarnation of the real and only socialism. Devotees of the Soviet Union were blind to the gap between ideology and reality. They were not able to comprehend the significance of painting socialism. They therefore did not grasp alternative forms of socialism nor the dynamics of existing state socialism. They couldn't see that Marxism was at odds with the class character of state socialism and indeed that Marxism in the end proved to be the undoing of that society. The collapse of state socialism liberates Marxism from a continuing association with despotic rule. It liberates it to search for alternative conceptions of socialism, to explore and develop Lenin's original model.

What we have learnt from Eastern Europe is that the absence of the third element of socialism – radical democracy – gives rise to the distortion of the first two. The rationality of planning becomes the irrationality of bargaining within the dominant class (between enterprise directors and state managers) instead of the supervision of the dominant class by the subordinate class. The justice of reward according to contribution becomes the injustice of reward according to political position.

We have also learnt that such a radical democracy while going much further than parliamentary democracy requires the bourgeois rights of parliamentary democracy. Radical democracy requires a multi-party system; it requires the protection of basic individual political, social and civic rights. But bourgeois democracy is not a stage en route to radical democracy since the former effectively undermines class mobilization toward the latter. Rather, if radical democracy is to develop at all it will do so alongside the development of bourgeois democracy.

Part IV

CHINA

INTRODUCTION

While the former Soviet Union and the countries of Eastern Europe have long been judged conservative and reactionary in their labour process practices, China has been viewed quite differently. As Paul Thompson points out in Chapter 8, Braverman (1974:13) and Gorz (1976) were only two of many Western writers on the left who interpreted the Chinese experience as a break with hierarchy and despotism in the work-place. Cooley (1972), for example, produced an early critical discussion of the deskilling effects of Computer Aided Design and the need for engineers to maintain craft unity with manual workers, which owed its intellectual origins to the Cultural Revolution (Smith 1987; 1991). Undoubtedly the events in China in the late 1960s had positive effects on the debates on the nature of work, the division of labour and bureaucracy in the West. But these effects have to be separated from the actual nature and experience of the events themselves, which were a complete disaster for the Chinese economy and political reform process. Like the current glorification of Japanese work organization by Western managerialists, in looking at China we need to unveil reality from appearance, fact from image, the actual process of reform in the work-place from officially proclaimed objectives. Both the chapters in this part of the book are careful to do just that.

From the late 1970s China has been encouraging more liberal economic measures in order to break away from Soviet-style industrialization and modernize its economy. The results of these economic changes encouraged, in the late 1980s, demands for political reform which were eventually brutally crushed in June 1989 with the massacre of students and workers in Beijing. Such repression has been the state's response to previous reform movements in Eastern Europe – Hungary in 1956, Czechoslovakia in 1968 and Poland in 1981. China therefore still appears locked into a reform and counter-reform cycle

201

characteristic of an earlier stage of state socialism, and relatively immune from the more thorough-going effects of 'de-totalitarianism' evident in some, but not all, Eastern European societies.

We have noted in previous chapters the way that *ad hoc* reforms tended to reinforce existing problems and contradictions, rather than change the nature of the regime. The reason for this is that reforms did nothing to alter the undemocratic nature of the state, being attempts at piecemeal change within the political contours of the existing power structure. Chapters 7 and 8 emphasize different aspects of this same process in China. They look inside the economic reforms as they affect management and workers, Jude Howell focusing on joint ventures and Paul Thompson on a state-owned, but foreign-invested, auto factory.

Jude Howell's argument in Chapter 7 is that while formally more autonomous than state-controlled enterprises, foreign firms, whether wholly owned companies or partially owned joint ventures, are in practice obliged to conform to the labour process, employment and managerial policies within the dominant environment. Foreign capital was encouraged to enter China after 1978 to diffuse managerial skills, technological capacities and new labour standards. The fact that such 'innovations' are not occurring reflects the ability of the existing regime to subvert externally derived reforms. This highlights a conclusion central to other chapters in this book, namely that reform cannot be grafted on to a dominant regime, all that happens is that novel and radical processes are forced to conform to existing arrangements.

Howell develops her argument by examining the micro-political processes operating within the foreign-invested firm, and contrasting these to the official rules guaranteeing the independence of these firms. Compared with state-owned enterprises, joint ventures – the main mechanism of significant foreign investment – have considerable formal authority to set their own budgets, control wages, welfare and employment, 'hire' and 'fire' workers according to their requirements and design their own managerial structures. In practice, however, these formal freedoms are the subject of local and micro-political *bargaining*.

Howell reveals the conflict between Chinese and foreign partners over a range of issues. Foreign capital is attracted to China because of the size of the internal market, but the Chinese state needs foreign currency, and therefore wants the products of joint ventures to be exported. This is also necessary to keep inflationary pressures under control. In this area, however, the Chinese government seems to be losing out: Howell quotes several examples where the 100 per cent export policy was far from being achieved. However, in other areas, such as the composition of boards of directors and labour management, Howell refers to instances of conflict over attempts to impose new work disciplines or sack workers, and some trends towards 'Sinification' of joint ventures. Foreign partners lack political power in the system, and there is often an implicit reproduction of the social contract between managers and workers of the typical state-owned enterprise within the joint venture. While organizational conflicts are normal in all joint ventures and clashes between host and foreign partners endemic to this form of ownership. Howell rightly suggests that the conflict in China is between rival *systems* not just nationally distinct ways of working. Her conclusions are that for the foreign-invested enterprise to act as a *genuine* source of innovation, there is a need for there to be tighter controls over, and guarantees of, their operational autonomy. Unlike Thompson, she sees moderate institutional reform, rather than major macro-economic and political change, as a feasible precondition for a more 'effective' utilization of the foreign-invested firm in China.

Thompson's chapter offers both a general account of the economic, labour market and labour process reforms that began in China in the late 1970s, and the effects of these within a Beijing auto factory. He argues that political reform is essential for successful economic reform, and that without democracy and major instutional changes in the society, especially a shift towards centralized welfare provision, then reforms will accommodate themselves to prevailing practices and structures. Indeed, he suggests that piecemeal reform results in the worst of both worlds: the anarchy of the market without the discipline, while continuing the dead hand of the command economy at the same time as breaking the 'iron rice bowl'. The result – 'disorganized socialism', a hybrid and unstable system.

The top-down reforms aimed at ending an egalitarian reward system and total job security, through labour market segmentation and new incentive systems, have not succeeded in altering the way enterprises operate as mini-welfare states. Increasing the number of contract workers, numbering 10 per cent of a 100 million work-force, only *appears* to have broken employment security and introduced labour flexibility and increased managerial control. In practice these reforms have not brought about fundamental change, as contract workers are also able to obtain housing provision and other welfare services from their enterprises. In other words, the conditions of the majority of core employees, are applied to the minority or periphery. No one in the auto plant he studied had been made redundant. Where duality exists, this is not novel, but the traditional divide between urban and rural workers new to industry or the cities. Moreover, like the situation in the former Soviet Union, women workers suffer more from peripheral status, and have experienced the inequalities of reform, without the economic benefits.

While recognizing the ideological adjustment necessary for treating labour as a commodity, Thompson suggests that it is not ideas or traditions, but the lack of appropriate institutional mechanisms which make the transition to market socialism difficult in China. The chapter constantly stresses the ability of the system to *absorb* new developments. Thus, some writers have argued that scientific management has been penetrating the labour process on the back of economic reforms. However, Thompson says that this has nothing to do with Taylorism, because the continued uncertainties of the regime require that production workers be adept at repair and maintenance functions, thus inhibiting the detailed division of labour and bureaucratic control system needed for Taylorism. He concludes by suggesting that following the massacre in Tianenmen Square, the party has been increasing its control over the enterprise and centralizing authority at the local and regional level, retrenching any loss of power the reforms may have created. The society remains locked in the past and will remain so as economic, legislative and administrative powers remain so tightly integrated through the one-party state.

REFERENCES

Braverman, H. (1974) *Labor and Monopoly Capital* London: Monthly Review Press.
Cooley, M. (1972) *Computer Aided Design: Its Nature and Implications*, Richmond, Surrey: TASS.
Gorz, A. (1976) 'Technology, technicians and class struggle', in A. Gorz (ed.) *The Division of Labour: The Labour Process, and Class Struggle in Monopoly Capitalism*, Brighton: Harvester.
Smith, C. 1987 *Technical Workers: Class, Labour and Trade Unionism*, London: Macmillan.
Smith, C. (1991) 'Engineers and the labour process in C. Smith, D. Knights and H. Willmott (eds) *White Collar Work: The Non-Manual Labour Process*, London: Macmillan.

7

THE MYTH OF AUTONOMY
The foreign enterprise in China
Jude Howell

The adoption of the 'Open Door Policy' at the Third Plenum in December 1978 signalled not only the expansion of China's economic relations with the West and Japan but also the introduction of foreign direct investment for the first time since Liberation. During the 1980s over 30,000 foreign-invested enterprises, involving US$ 22 billion of pledged foreign investment, have been established in China.

In order to attract foreign investment the reformist leadership headed by Deng Xiaoping has granted foreign investors not only numerous incentives in the spheres of taxation, land use fees and domestic sales but also considerable autonomy in the organization and management of their enterprises. The realization of this autonomy implies a distribution of power and resources within the foreign-invested enterprise different to that in state-owned enterprises. The likely beneficiaries are foreign capital, Chinese directors, managers and technocratic cadres while the potential losers are the party, trade unions, labour and external bodies.

This chapter argues that the actual implementation of policies designed to promote the autonomy of foreign-invested enterprises has been strongly informed by the conflict and co-operation between potential 'winners' and 'losers' both internal and external to the foreign-invested enterprise. Moreover, although the reforms in state-owned enterprises entails a similar redistribution of power and resources, the micro-political processes in foreign-invested enterprises are distinct in that they involve an additional actor, namely foreign capital. As a result of this conflict and co-operation between competing actors the degree of autonomy enjoyed by a foreign-invested enterprise has often been less than promised. This has important implications not only for our understanding of the policy-making process but also for the feasibility of reforms in state-owned enterprises, which draw inspiration from the example of foreign-invested enterprises.

The chapter is divided into three sections. The first briefly outlines the nature of the autonomy granted to foreign invested enterprises. The second section focuses on the bargaining process between foreign capital and the Chinese partner(s) in the implementation of policy in joint ventures. The final section examines the continued influence of external bodies in the affairs of the foreign-invested enterprise.

THE AUTONOMY OF THE FOREIGN-INVESTED ENTERPRISE

Before looking at the policies granting foreign-invested enterprises (FIEs) greater autonomy, some background information on the concept of a FIE as well as its organizational structure is first provided. There are three types of FIE in China, namely the equity joint venture (EJV), contractual joint venture (CJV), and wholly-owned foreign enterprise (WOFE). These vary according to the degree of foreign ownership, the distribution of profits, export sales, taxation and the length of the contract.

In an EJV the Chinese and foreign partners jointly invest in and operate the corporation sharing the profits, losses and risks. Aware of the dangers of majority ownership, the Chinese leadership has tried to limit the equity participation of the foreign partner to a maximum of 50 per cent. In CJVs Chinese and foreign partners co-operate in joint projects, sharing output, earnings or profits according to the contract.

Although the reformist leadership has consistently shown greater preference to JVs and in particular for EJVs, it has nevertheless permitted on a restricted scale the establishment of wholly owned foreign enterprises. In a WOFE the foreign investor provides capital, equipment, management and marketing and is responsible for all the profits and losses. Although a foreign investor in a WOFE may enjoy greater control over the enterprise than in a JV, this is still within the bounds of national policy. For example, WOFEs are required to be 100 per cent export-oriented. Moreover, the management practices adopted in WOFEs are subject to the same labour regulations as JVs.

The organizational structure of a FIE differs markedly from a Chinese state-owned enterprise (SOE). The Sino-Foreign JV Law of 1979 and the 'Regulations for the Implementation of the Sino-Foreign JV law of 1983' provided official guidelines for the organizational shape and legal obligations and rights of the EJV. As laws specific to WOFEs and CJVs were not passed until April 1986 and early 1988 respectively, these forms of FIE have tended to follow the guidelines for EJVs.

The highest body of authority in the FIE is the Board of Directors. In a JV the chairman of the Board is to be selected by the Chinese partner(s) and the vice-chairperson/people by the foreign side.[1] The Board of Directors then selects the general manager and assistant manager who may be either foreign or Chinese. The departmental heads are appointed by the general manager of the JV.[2] In a WOFE the Board of Directors is made up solely by foreign capital. The general and assistant managers are most probably foreign while middle management and supervisory positions might be occupied by Chinese personnel.

In a SOE, however, authority is shared between the factory director and party committee with the latter enjoying greater power. Recent experiments such as the factory director responsibility system have aimed at strengthening the power of the director in economic matters *vis-à-vis* the party committee. Other senior figures in the SOE, such as the managers and chief engineers, are all administratively appointed by the party committee and superordinate body responsible for the SOE. Senior personnel tend also to be party members.

The Board of Directors in an EJV enjoys, in theory at least, far greater autonomy than the factory director of a SOE in organizational production matters. First, the Board decides the overall production plans, budget and expansion projects. Second, it determines the wage, welfare and employment system. It has the legal authority to hire and fire employees. Moreover, it can appoint the general and deputy managers, the chief engineer, the chief accountant, treasurer and auditors and determine their terms of employment. Third, it can decide the overall organizational structure of the enterprise. Finally, it can make long-term investment and financial plans as well as decide the distribution of profits.[3]

While the Board of Directors deals with the overall development of the enterprise, the general manager handles the day-to-day operations and management, and not only represents the EJV to outside bodies but also has the power to appoint and dismiss subordinate personnel.

In a SOE, however, the production plans budget and major investment projects are administratively determined by the respective central and/or local authorities. The total wage bill and the allocation of labour the appointment of technical and professional staff are administered through the local labour bureaux in accordance with provincial and national plans. Long-term investment and financial plans require the approval of local and often central authorities. Moreover, SOEs enjoy little autonomy in the distribution of the profits, though the introduction of the profit retention system has witnessed an increase in the use of their profits.

The greater autonomy of FIEs compared to SOEs is matched by a more restrictive role for trade unions. While trade unions are permitted in JVs, there is no legal provision for workers' congresses. Trade unions can participate in Board meetings in JVs as non-voting delegates on labour-related issues and discussion of general plans.[4] Although their exclusion from other topics implies a restriction of their powers, trade unions in SOEs are likewise left out of overall policy decisions. Trade unions are permitted in WOFEs, but they cannot send delegates to Board meetings.

In a SOE the trade union deals with the allocation of housing, the provision of medical care and welfare benefits, ideological education as well as training. The trade union has historically been subordinated to the overall interests of the party, although there have been leaders such as Li Lisan who have pressed for greater autonomy.

The new structural arrangements in JVs and WOFEs entail a distribution of power between particular political forces within the enterprise and between the enterprise and external bodies, which departs from that in state-owned enterprises. As redistribution implies 'winners' and 'losers', it is likely that conflicts between 'old' and 'new' beneficiaries will emerge. One might predict that the likely losers are the external bodies related to the enterprise and within the FIE the party, trade unions and labour while the potential winners are the Chinese directors and managers, technocratic cadres and foreign capital. However, the boundaries between 'winners' and 'losers' may not be so clear-cut. Thus the 'losers' might seek ways to minimize their losses while the 'winners' might have to make some compromises to reap other gains. The next section focuses on the conflict and co-operation between foreign capital and the Chinese partner(s) in a JV.

CHINESE AND FOREIGN PARTNERS:
DIFFERENCES IN OBJECTIVES

The implementation of policy in the foreign-invested enterprise is partly determined by the conflict and co-operation between the foreign investor and Chinese partner(s). Tension between foreign capital and the Chinese partners has arisen over issues relating to differences in objectives such as domestic sales, the composition of the Board of Directors, the organization of the enterprise and the management of the labour force. Each of these will be dealt with in turn.

Domestic sales

The bargaining process between foreign capital and the Chinese partner has in part been informed by fundamental differences in objectives regarding participation in the venture. The primary objectives of the Chinese partner in establishing JVs may include one or several of the following: the introduction of foreign technology and management expertise, increases in foreign exchange through export earnings and a supplementary source of capital. The objectives may vary as the 'Chinese partner' in JVs may be one or several partners with converging and/or competing interests. The 'Chinese partner' frequently incorporates a government financing body such as the newly founded quasi-state Investment and Trust Corporations and a local factory.

The foreign partner may be primarily drawn by the prospect of selling in the huge Chinese market. However the goals of foreign capital are likely to vary according to national and sectoral priorities. Small-scale investors from Hong Kong, for example, are concerned to secure an economic niche in their future homeland while American and European companies may be driven by the lure of China's huge domestic market.

Tensions related to these differences in objectives have been manifested in a range of policy issues such as domestic sales, foreign exchange remittances, technology transfer and marketing and supply. These differences have surfaced most prominently at the time of contract negotiation and have been resolved through a process of bargaining between foreign capital and the Chinese partners.[5] This process will be examined in relation to domestic sales.

After a decade of foreign direct investment, it has become clear that

China has had to concede larger proportions of domestic sales than it orginally intended in order to attract more FDI.[6] Concessions on domestic sales are thus becoming increasingly perceived as a necessary trade-off for a rise in the level of FDI. These concessions have been restricted in policy to companies which are either introducing advanced foreign technology or engaged in import-substitution.[7] The relaxation of policy towards domestic sales has reflected an implicit bargaining process between foreign capital and the Chinese state.

Although the policies issued by central government linked domestic sales to technology introduction, import substitution and firm performance, it has nevertheless been left up to the partners in the enterprise to decide upon the actual proportions at the time of contract negotiation. From interviews carried out with JV companies in Xiamen SEZ, Fujian Province, the proportion of domestic sales was stated to be one of the chief areas for protracted discussion.

In Fujian Hitachi JV, which involved a Japanese company, the Fujian Electronics Bureau and the former Fujian Electronics Equipment Factory, the level of exports was fixed through a bargaining process. It was finally agreed in the contract that the JV would 'gradually increase exports to 50 per cent'.[8] However, in practice the Japanese side underlined the word 'gradually' to delay the implementation of 50 per cent exports as it was primarily interested in the domestic market.

Similarly, in the Sino–US JV Tianjin-Otis the American partner reported considerable pressure from the Chinese partner, the former Tianjin Elevator Company, to agree to a specified level of exports. This was perceived as the cost of admission to the Chinese market. As Otis had already satisfied existing markets, it was not willing to concede this condition. A process of bargaining between the two sides led to an agreement whereby Otis was not required to purchase a fixed quantity of products for export and the Chinese government was not required to guarantee conversion of Renminbi profits.[9] Although details are not available, it is likely that the Chinese partner was under pressure from local authorities to ensure adequate forex earnings though export.

There is thus a contradiction between the policies concerning FIEs which have been generated by the central leadership and their actual implementation at the micro-level. As no clear guidelines have been given regarding the amount of permissible domestic sales by JVs, the decision then becomes a matter of protracted bargaining between the two partners. Hence there is a widening gap between policy and its actual implementation. As foreign capital becomes more deeply entrenched in China, the contradictions emanating from fundamental differences in motives and interests between the Chinese state and foreign capital may intensify. The outcome will depend not only on the urgency for foreign capital of expanding into the China market but also on the primacy attached by the Chinese government to acquiring foreign technology by means of FDI.

Composition of the Board of Directors

As well as conflict between the foreign and Chinese partners related to different objectives, tensions have also arisen over the composition of the Board of Directors. The structure of a Board of Directors was intended to heighten the autonomy of the FIE by diminishing the role of the party, trade unions and external bodies in the affairs of the enterprise. In practice, however, the party and external bodies have tried to minimize their potential loss of power in the JV by securing positions on the Board of Directors.

According to Henley's survey of thirty-four JVs in Shenzhen SEZ in 1986, administrative departments connected to the JV have sought representation on the Board of Directors. The chairman on the Board of Directors has frequently also been the head of the superordinate body to the JV.[10] In some cases the Chinese factory could not even get representation on the Board.[11] Henley also found that many of the Chinese members of the Board had no direct business experience and were appointed as a reward for past service to their respective administrative bodies. As a result, the Board then becomes a 'small government of China', with directors representing interests external to the enterprise.[12]

The tendency reflects the attempt by outside bodies not only to maintain control over the operations of the enterprise, but also to minimize their potential loss in power implied by the greater autonomy granted to JVs. To the extent that these directors owe allegiance to their own original units rather than to the JV, their dual responsibilities may interfere with them playing an active role in the JV. Similarly, to the extent that the foreign partner in the JV owes loyalty to the parent company, the interests of the JV may be treated as a secondary. This lack of loyalty to the JV is underlined in the following extract from an article in a well-known Chinese economic newspaper:

During a difficult period, fundamental contradictions that are usually concealed will surface because the personal interests of each member of the management staff are closely linked to their own company and not to the interests of the JV enterprise itself.[13]

The process of decision-making in the JV thus becomes infused with the competing interests of external departments and the overseas parent company. It might be argued, however, that having Chinese directors with close ties to important external administrative bodies could actually facilitate the operations of JVs, especially with regard to accelerating or bypassing bureaucratic processes.

Organization of the enterprise

Although a FIE has in theory the autonomy to decide on its own internal organization, in practice this will be shaped by different concepts of enterprise organization. As the Board of Directors is a new organizational form in China and as many of the directors and the chairperson are likely to be senior cadres from administrative organs, one might expect that they will harbour certain conceptions and expectations about the functions and methods of the Board and the management of an enterprise which may not always accord with those of the foreign partner.[14] These conceptual differences in management approach were highlighted in an American business journal:

> Chinese managers assumed that the joint venture – like its Chinese predecessor – would continue to be driven from the top down by the state planning system and have as its main concerns engineering, manufacturing and maintaining the same number of employees in the plant. The concepts of financial discipline and market competition were outside their experience.[15]

Similarly, American businesspeople have particular expectations about the management of a plant:

> They (foreign managers) did not realize that Chinese managers have never developed a corporate strategy or coordinated the activities of the various departments – finance, marketing, personnel and production – necessary to achieve it.[16]

Another example of how different expectations about the operation of a company can lead to tensions concerns the level of horizontal integration and co-ordination within an enterprise. Just as at the macro-level central planning has led to vertical integration with a concomitant absence of horizontal integration, so too at the micro-level of the enterprise there can be considerable lack of co-ordination between departments. In the Tianjin-Otis JV, for example, two different departments took the inventory simultaneously for different purposes despite requests from the foreign manager that they co-ordinate their activities.[17] The inability of the foreign partner to achieve departmental co-ordination also draws attention to their lack of authority within the JV.

The importance of these different expectations concerning the management of an enterprise was highlighted in a Chinese economic newspaper:

> Internally, both the Chinese and foreign parties of a JV enterprise cannot help but run into disagreements and opposing ideas and methods in the course of the day-to-day management of the enterprise and in decision-making.[18]

While differences in enterprise organization have bedevilled JVs all over the world, the issue is more acute in China, where JVs represent the confluence of two fundamentally distinct politico-economic systems.[19] The continued appointment of cadres from outside bodies to JVs as well as the reported lack of authority of the foreign partner in the management of the enterprise suggest that the JV is subject to pressures from particular interests within and without the enterprise to behave like a SOE. This potential 'Sinification' of the FIE has implications both for the implementation of policies granting FIEs autonomy in the management of production as well as for the realization of enterprise reforms. If FIEs are to serve as models of a new form of enterprise to be applied elsewhere in China, then to the extent that interested parties try to preserve their influences in the enterprise and interpret policies to their favour, then the effect of reforms in SOE is likely to be considerably diluted.

Management of the labour force

Compared to SOEs foreign companies in China enjoy considerable autonomy in the management of their labour force. According to the JV law of 1979 FIEs are permitted not only to 'hire and fire' employees according to their 'production needs' but also to determine the pay scale, wage form and bonus.[20] The circulation and exchange of labour in FIEs is thus to proceed according to market principles rather than administrative fiat. Stricter supervision of employees as well as payment according to work performance portend greater managerial control over the work-force.

Despite the official sanctioning of the rights of FIEs to 'hire and fire' workers and set their own wage levels, the implementation of these policies has in practice been much harder to realize. Conflicts between the foreign and Chinese partners over the management of labour have surfaced in issues such as work discipline and dismissal, wage rises and bonus distribution, and management techniques.

For example, in an electronics FIE in Xiamen Special Economic Zone (SEZ), Hong Kong managers tended to resort to dismissal as a means of discipline far quicker than would mainland managers.[21] According to the Chinese deputy general manager relations between management and workers were much stricter under Hong Kong management than in a Chinese enterprise, where management and workers were like a 'family'. He felt that FIE regulations did not take 'human feelings' into account. In the end the Hong Kong managers were replaced by Chinese managers.[22]

Similarly, although FIEs have more autonomy in the remuneration of their work-force than SIEs, this has been constrained by pressure from the work force on local managers to distribute bonuses equally regardless of differences in individual performance. An official in an electronics JV in Xiamen SEZ commented:

> Egalitarianism is common in SOEs. Although now we are a JV,
> it is still difficult to change the previous situation completely. . .
> Traditional thinking can influence JV affairs.[23]

Some FIEs have circumvented this by paying workers in individual sealed wage packets so that no worker knows what the other is being paid.[24]

Where Chinese leaders in JVs have agreed to differential payments in JVs they have sometimes been forced to backtrack because of the tensions created both within the JV and between workers in JVs and SOEs. In a Sino-foreign cigarette factory in Xiamen SEZ, for example, the higher earnings of contract workers in the JV workshop became a source of tension with the permanent workers employed in the rest of the SOE. This tension was also in part fuelled by the differences in age, as the permanent workers tended to be older than the newly recruited contract workers. In order to appease the permanent workers, these were also permitted to work in the export-processing section of the factory on a piece-rate basis to increase their earnings, thus negating the intended effects of the contract system.[25]

This pressure from the work-force on management in relation to both stricter management techniques and differential remuneration points to the implicit reproduction of the social contract between managers and workers in SOEs. According to this contract managers secure the compliance of workers by adopting a more 'humane' approach to discipline which tolerated days off, lack of punctuality and a slower pace of work.[26] State provision of welfare facilities within the enterprises as well as the guarantee of job security were the costs for the state in securing the co-operation of the work-force. The FIE by contrast has fewer carrots to offer, while wielding the newly acquired stick of dismissal, non-renewal of contracts and bonus disparities.

This reproduction of the implicit contract between the state and the Chinese work-force is also facilitated by the frequent lack of authority of the foreign partner within the enterprise. This was seen in the failure of the Hong Kong managers in the electronics company in Xiamen SEZ to implement their stricter management methods as well as the inability of the foreign partner in Tianjin-Otis JV to co-ordinate departments, as mentioned in the previous subsection. As a foreigner is essentially an outsider in a JV, s/he has not had the time to build up 'factional ties', which according to Walder can be an important source of authority.[27]

The reluctance of some Chinese partners radically to reform management methods as well as the lack of authority of some foreign partners may reflect not only pressure from the work-force but also an implicit attempt by the party to retain some influence within the enterprises and in particular over the work-force. Although there are no official requirements that the directors or managers of FIEs be party members or that the party secretary have any formal role within the FIE, this does not imply that party members do not hold positions of responsibility or that party activities are not being conducted.[28] For example, fourteen out of thirty-five JVs operating in Tianjin had primary Party organizations and 13 per cent of JV employees were party members.[29]

The different formal structural position of the party within the FIE has the potential of reducing the party's control over labour. While in the SOE activists and model workers would be rewarded by the party and trade union with preferential treatment in housing, access to consumer goods, holidays and so on, the primary role of a FIE as a unit of production rather than reproduction effectively removes these economic sources of privilege. However, new sources of economic power could have emerged. For example, the party would still have considerable leeway in the selection of workers to go overseas for training and study. Moreover, to the extent that party members remain in positions of responsibility, there may be some continuities in the pattern of authority between SOEs and FIEs, which thus make the introduction of foreign management techniques more difficult.

As in the case of enterprise organization there is pressure from certain vested interests within the FIE, such as party members, politico-cratic cadres and some members of the work-force, to make the FIE operate like a SOE. Although the central leadership may see the introduction of managerial skills as an important objective of FIEs, the implementation of policies designed to this end becomes constrained at the micro-level of the enterprise. Whether or not new methods of labour management are adopted in JVs thus depends less on policy rhetoric at the central level and more on micro-political processes operating within the enterprise.

To conclude this section, it is clear that foreign capital is a significant actor in the political processes within JVs, which has to be negotiated with by the Chinese partner and authorities. China cannot compel foreign companies to invest in China. The need to attract foreign investment thus implies a process of bargaining both at the macro-level during policy generation and establishment and at the micro-level during policy implementation.

Furthermore, there may be pressure, whether deliberate or not, from potentially 'losing' social groups and political institutions within the enterprise to maintain their influence in the FIE by attempting to make the FIE operate like a Chinese SOE. To the extent that this 'Sinification' of the FIE does occur, it has implications not only for the realization of the purported autonomy of the FIE but also for the feasibility of carrying out reforms in SOEs.

THE FOREIGN-INVESTED ENTERPRISE AND EXTERNAL BODIES

The implementation of policy within the foreign-invested enterprise is not only affected by the conflict and co-operation between political forces within the enterprise but also by the interactions of the FIE with outside bodies. Although the JV and WOFE are supposed to operate autonomously, evidence exists of the continued involvement of the immediately superordinate body, the local government and other administrative bodies in the economic affairs of the enterprise. This section examines the nature of and reasons for this continued involvement and the implications thereof for the implementation of policies granting FIEs autonomy in their management of production.

JV and the superordinate body

A Chinese SOE will fall under the administrative charge of a higher authority such as the municipal electronics bureau. This superordinate body will set the targets of production and profit for the enterprise, appoint managerial and supervisory staff, arrange supplies of raw materials and manage the sales of the final products.

In a JV, however, many of the functions carried out by the superordinate body are taken on by the enterprise itself. A JV thus has the right to determine its own production plans, distribute its profits, arrange its supply of inputs, market its own products overseas and appoint its own managerial and supervisory staff. As the autonomy of a JV is in theory greater than a SOE, the control to be exercised by the superordinate body over the JV is diminished. At the same time, however, the superordinate body continues to perform its usual role with regard to other SOEs under its auspices. One might hypothesize that the superordinate body would be likewise compelled to exert control over the JV, particularly where the original Chinese factory previously fell under its charge.[30]

There is considerable evidence to suggest that the superordinate body attempts to maintain its involvement in the operations of JVs, thus limiting their autonomy. This has been manifested, for example, in the appointment of senior staff. The superordinate body seeks to maintain its influence within the JV by appointing its senior cadres to positions of responsibility. Although the vice-chairperson and deputy general manager may be selected from both sides of the venture it has been found in practice that the Chinese deputy general manager and middle managers are appointed by the department in charge of the JV.[31]

Moreover, where the Board has not selected a general manager from the superordinate body, there have been cases of direct interference by the department-in-charge. For example, in April 1986, at the US Sino-foreign JV Hubei-Parker Company, the Provincial Bureau of the Machine Building Industrial Corporation, which was in charge of the factory, dismissed the Chinese director and deputy director of the JV without consulting the Board of Directors.[32] Although the US representative challenged this decision, the provincial bureau refused to reverse it. As a result production slowed down. In response the provincial government intervened and reinstated the director and deputy director.

Underlying this example is a complex web of competing political forces. On the one hand, the superordinate body attempts to gain control within the JV by usurping the power of the Board. In this moment the interests of the foreign and Chinese enterprises coincide. They thus challenge the gauntlet thrown down by the superordinate body and win the backing of the provincial government. As this occurred at a time when central government was seriously considering ways to improve the overall investment climate, one might hypothesize that the reformist elements within the government interpreted this as a favourable moment to set a precedent. The provincial government certainly would not have wanted a major conflict in a JV at a time when the central government was looking closely at the management of FIEs.

The superordinate body has attempted to secure its power within the JV not only by influencing the appointment of directors and managerial staff but also by intervening in other issues such as wages. Although the level of wages of the staff and workers of a JV is limited to a lower ceiling of 120 per cent of the wage of their counterparts in SOE, according to article 9 of the 'Provisions of the PR China for Labour Management in Chinese-Foreign JVs', the Board of Directors, is, within the limits described, empowered to set the system of wage standards, the type of wages, bonuses and subsidies.[33]

There have been cases, however, where the superordinate body has intervened in the Board's ability to determine wages. Thus a JV that planned to triple top salaries, introduce merit bonuses and a profit-sharing bonus scheme, which would have been paid directly to the workers rather than to the general welfare fund, was prevented from doing so by the department-in-charge of the JV. Wages were considered too high and bonuses had to be cut. Although the municipal labour bureau and even the labour ministry in Beijing agreed with the policy of the JV, they were not able to overrule the department-in-charge.[34] In the end a compromise was reached whereby workers would no longer receive a bonus until further notice.

However, it might also be the case that the municipal labour bureau and central labour ministry did not really support the proposals but felt compelled to adopt an apparently conciliatory approach towards the JV. On the other hand, it would also have been impossible for the bureau and ministry to agree to tripling top salaries and raising the actual received wage of the worker because of the potential political and economic implications of this for SOEs. Substantial increases in wages in JVs might not only make workers less willing to work in SOEs but also might increase inflation through demands for higher wages. This state intervention in wage determination in FIEs was thus economically and socially well-founded.

In CJVs where the Chinese side takes responsibility for manage-ment, the foreign side may have little control over the distribution of wages. In some CJVs in Guangdong Province with Hong Kong companies, for example, the Hong Kong partners pay the wages directly to the department-in-charge which then distributes this to the workers in the factory. Where workers have urban residence, they receive 60 per cent of the wage while the factory retains 40 per cent. There have been instances, however, where the department-in-charge reduced the workers' wages for no apparent reason and even deducted night shift allowances already paid by the Hong Kong partners.[35]

Although JVs are supposed to enjoy autonomy in their economic operations, there is evidence pointing to the continued involvement of the superordinate body in the affairs of the enterprise. While this involvement may be economically well justified as for example in controlling large wage increases, at times it may border on illegitimate interference, as in the case of the Hubei-Parker Sino-US JV. However, it also should not be overlooked that the parent company of the foreign partner may likewise involve itself or indeed 'interfere' in the operations of its JV. The production plans, market-ing channels as well as the prices of raw materials and components are frequently determined by the overseas parent company.

FIE and other administrative bodies

The autonomy of the JV has been affected not only by the superordi-nate body immediately responsible for that enterprise but also by other administrative organs with which the JV has operational relations. In a Chinese SOE departments within the enterprise will be vertically related to municipal and/or provincial administrative bodies outside the enterprise. The labour department of a Chinese enterprise will, for example, be answerable to the Municipal Labour Bureau. Similarly , the finance department will be accountable to the municipal finance bureau.[35] As a result the loyalties and interests of departments are split between the enterprise and these vertically related external bodies. Not only does this bifurcate allegiances but also it dislocates horizontal cohesion within the enterprise.

These vertical obligations to outside administrative bodies have also shaped the pattern of relations within the FIE, particularly in JVs where the Chinese partner is a pre-existing SOE. The appointment of directors in JVs by outside bodies has, for example, affected the functioning of the enterprise in several ways. Foreign investors have, for example, complained about the frequent changes in directors who may be transferred at any time by the government agencies to which they belong, thus affecting the continuity of the Board of Directors.[37] As mentioned earlier the predominance of directors appointed by external bodies increases the range of competing interests at Board meetings with the result that decision-making can become a long, tedious affair. This is illustrated in the following quote of a Hong Kong investor:

> It takes us five days to hold a meeting with the Chinese members of our Board of Directors because they have to ask their leaders for instructions whenever they come across problems.[38]

The appointment of managerial and supervisory staff by external bodies likewise bifurcates allegiances and retards decision-making processes. In order to reduce the involvement of external administrative bodies, the foreign manager in one joint venture restricted the time spent by Chinese managerial staff dealing with vertically related external administrative bodies.[39] These vertical ties with outside administrative bodies thus lead to competing interests within the JV. As departments in the JV may be responsible both to the JV and its related external administrative body, it may be subject to conflicting targets and demands.

Although FIEs are in theory supposed to enjoy the 'right' to 'hire' employees according to its choice, this has on occasions been affected by the competing interests of external bodies. When a certain glove-making WOFE was seeking a location in Xiamen, the first site was offered free of charge on the condition that the enterprise employ all the staff in that factory. When it later acquired a factory site in Huli Industrial District, the Labour Service Company pressurized it to hire workers from the displaced land in Huli. There is thus a tendency for the Chinese administration to pressurize FIEs to take on unnecessary staff, in part due to an ideological reluctance to shed labour.

As well as trying to control the source of employees to FIEs the Labour Service Company has also on occasions attempted to make FIEs approximate SOEs more as units of reproduction. In the glove-making FIE in Xiamen SEZ, for example, the Labour Service Company stated that any expansion in production would have to be covered by employing rural workers. In this case the foreign enterprise would be required to provide housing. This pushes the foreign enterprise into adopting some of the features of a Chinese SOE such as providing accommodation. In another instance the Labour Service Company requested the glove-making foreign company to supply workers with cold drinks in the summer, a practice common in SOEs. Although the foreign company agreed, it stressed that this was not written in the contract. There is thus pressure from both work-force and local labour institutions to make FIEs observe the implicit social contract pertaining between management and the work-force.[40] This implies a drive towards the reproduction of the socio-economic dependence of the worker common to the SOE in FIEs.

Although the involvement of outside bodies may sometimes be detrimental to the autonomous operations of FIEs, there are nevertheless instances where it has justifiably sought to control some less desirable effects of FIE 'autonomy', particularly regarding the right of FIEs to 'hire and fire'. The mushrooming of commune factories engaged in compensation trade and CJVs in the rural areas of Guangdong in the early 1980s led to a withdrawal of labour from agriculture and absenteeism from schools.[41] This then engendered conflicts in Dongguan Commune between the propaganda department of the party brigade and the party brigade secretaries. The former wanted to make the pupils return to school, if necessary by firing them from the factory. However, as the pupils obtained their jobs through connections, it was not possible to effect their dismissal. Although the party brigade was not able to prevent the continued employment of young people in these CJVs, it nevertheless provides an instance of a 'socially justifiable' intervention on the part of the bureaucracy.

This section has highlighted the impact of external bodies on the implementation of FIE policies. Although JVs and WOFEs are supposed to operate autonomously and according to market principles, there is evidence to suggest that external bodies such as the immediate superordinate body, the Labour Service Company and other administrative bodies seek crevices of power and influence within the FIE. This thus implies a divorce between central government policy and micro-level practices. Although reformist leaders may have responded by reiterating the need for outside bodies to withdraw from the economic affairs of FIEs, this clearly requires considerable support from local authorities and personnel within the FIE. However, to the extent that outside bodies try to exert their influence in FIEs through, *inter alia*, controlling the appointment of key personnel in the FIE, then the development of a layer of personnel committed to the implementation of policies granting FIE economic autonomy is inhibited. On the other hand, to the extent that the implementation of those policies redistributes power and privileges to manager, technocratic cadres and non-Party member workers, the social base of support within the FIE for the implementation of, *inter alia*, existing labour policies may grow.

CONCLUSION

According to the Sino-foreign JV law of 1979 and subsequent regulations, FIEs are supposed to enjoy autonomy of operation in China. This autonomy implies a different distribution of economic and political resources both within the enterprise and between the enterprise and particular external administrative bodies. The beneficiaries in the FIE are the directors and managers, foreign capital and those with professional expertise, while the losers are the party, trade unions and labour. However, these divisions are not clear cut as losers may attempt to minimize their losses while the potential winners may have to accept some compromises.

Although the reforms in SOEs entail a similar redistribution of power and resources, the micro-political processes in FIEs are distinct in that they involve an additional actor to be negotiated with, namely foreign capital. Tensions between foreign capital and the Chinese partner(s) have surfaced in issues such as domestic sales, the composition and functions of the Board of Directors, enterprise organization and the management of the labour force. The resolution of these issues has been through a process of bargaining between Chinese and foreign partners. The micro-political processes lead in turn to widening discrepancies between centrally formulated policy concerning FIEs and local level policy practice.

The process of policy implementation has been affected not only by this bargaining process between the Chinese partner and foreign capital but also by the conflict and co-operation between other social groups and political institutions within the FIE. Although Chinese directors and managers might welcome greater power over the work-force, they may at the same time be constrained by the 'willingness' of the work-force to 'play the game' according to a new set of rules, which offers less 'carrot' and more 'stick' than the SOE counterpart. Moveover, in order to minimize their losses, the party might attempt to maintain its influence within the FIE both through the appoint-ment of its members to key positions and possibly by supporting workers *vis-a-vis* management. To the extent that particular social groups and political institutions attempt to resist new policies and minimize their losses, there is pressure on the FIE to conform to relations of production characteristic of the SOE.

The implementation of policies granting FIEs greater autonomy have been shaped not only by mico-political processes within the enterprise but also between the enterprise and external bodies. The parent company of the foreign partner may pursue its own interests, different to those of the particular JV, while the superordinate body of the JV might also harbour different goals from those of the JV. The appointment of cadres from external bodies to the Board of Directors reflects a strategy to maintain the influence of these bodies in the JV. As a result the implementation of policy in JVs becomes permeated by the competing interests of various external parties. Hence decisions may not always be made which are either economically rational or beneficial to the JV. This in turn contributes to a widening disparity between policy rhetoric and practice.

To the extent that the implementation of policy is the outcome of bargaining, there is an element of arbritrariness in the policy process. This might on the one hand reduce the attractiveness of the foreign investment climate to foreign investors and on the other hand reduce the level of control of central policy-makers over the operations of FIEs. Moreover, the element of arbitrariness could also work to the favour of foreign investors, particularly with regard to issues such as domestic sales.

If FIEs are to serve as conduits for the transfer of technology and management expertise as well as earners of foreign exchange through exports, then there is clearly a need not only for greater policy guidance from central and provincial authorities to those involved in negotiating and operating FIEs, but also perhaps for the creation of appropriate supervisory bodies which monitor the implementation of policy at the micro-level. However, whether or not the autonomy of the FIE can become less of a myth and more of a reality will depend both on the continued commitment of reformist leaders as well as on the relative strength of interested parties such as the managers and directors within the FIE.

NOTES

1 Henley and Nyaw 1988: 12.
2 It is likely that the process resembles that in SOEs where department heads are assigned either though external, administrative bodies or through promotion within the enterprise.
3 See Sino-Foreign JV Law, 1979, in Foreign Languages Press 1982: 1–7.
4 See Henley and Nyaw 1988: 12; for the regulations see for example Almanac of Xiamen SEZ Economy Editorial Board (1986), Articles 98 and 99. pp.285–6.
5 According to studies carried out by McKinsley & Co., Coopers and Lybrand, seven out of ten JVs fell short of expectations or are disbanded. Although some of these were disbanded because they had achieved their goals, many were disbanded because they failed to resolve conflicting goals (see Auster 1987).
6 In August 1983, for example, JVs introducing new technology were permitted to sell some of their products on the domestic market (Beijing 15 August 1983 in *SWB/FE/7417/C1/1*). In June 1984 a further relaxation of policy occurred when JVs were permitted to sell goods on the domestic market once a set quota of forex had been earned (Xinhua 22 June 1984, in *SWB/FE/7682/B11/4*). In January 1986 new regulations were issued, offering concessions on domestic sales to high-tech products and internationally competitive products using advanced technology (Xinhua, 26 January 1986, in *SWB/FE/C1/1-3*).
7 The US company insisted on 'no Chinese equity participation, no technology transfer and no exports'. For details on this, see Brown 1986: 107.
8 Interview, Fujian Hitachi, June 1987.
9 Hendryx 1986a: 59.
10 See Henley and Nyaw 1988: 6.
11 ibid.
12 ibid.
13 See *Shanghai Shijie Jingji Daobao* 11 May 1987.
14 This is related in part to the different motives of Chinese SOEs. According to a World Bank study it was found that Chinese enterprises had a combination of five main objectives, namely the maximization of family income and benefits, expansion, introduction of technology, compliance with higher authorities and profit. The main driving force of a capitalist, however, is profit maximization. Moreover, the economic behaviour of a factory director in a SOE differs to a foreign manager in a foreign company. Thus the director of a SOE will tend to hoard labour and raw materials whilst the foreign manager will keep inventories to a minimum and will react to price signals as an indicator of relative scarcity.

15 See Hendryx 1986b: 81.
16 ibid.
17 ibid.
18 ibid.
19 On general problems in JV, see Gomes-Casseres (1987), who argues that while some see the instability of JVs as indicative of their proneness to failure, survival may not always imply success.
20 Foreign Languages Press 1982: 1–8.
21 Interview, Xiamen SEZ, June 1987.
Note: Xiamen SEZ is one of five special economic zones in China.
22 ibid.
23 Interview, Xiamen SEZ, July 1987.
24 Interview, Fujian Hitachi, June 1987.
25 Interview, Xiamen Cigarette Factory, July 1987.
26 This was particularly so in the 1970s following the disruption of production during the Cultural Revolution and the inability of managers to raise wages or restore bonuses (See Walder 1986: 205–10).
27 Walder 1986: 175–9.
28 According to *Shanghai Shijie Jingji Daobao* 11 May 1987, 73, all administrative relations (Party, trade unions, etc.) *temporarily* belong to the Foreign Investment Bureau so that the Party is in theory extracted from the enterprise.
29 See Horsley 1988: 52.
30 'In fact, however, in their business activities many enterprises still have to seek instructions from the competent departments, interventions in enterprise decision-making power occur from time to time, and the role of the board of directors is often weakened', in *Shanghai Shijie Jingji Daobao* 11 May 1987, 71.
31 Hendryx 1986b: 83.
32 Renmin Ribao, 26 September 1986, in *SWB/FE/8384/B11/7*.
33 See Foreign Languages Press 1982: 20–4.
34 Hendryx 1986b: 83.
35 *Hong Kong Kuang Chiao Ching* no 93, 16 June 1980, in *FBIS* 21 July 1980, 130–4.
36 Hendryx 1986a: 64.
37 Henley and Nyaw 1988: 6.
38 *Hong Kong Zhongguo Xinwen She* 9 January 1987, in *FBIS* 13 January 1987.
39 Hendryx 1986b.
40 See Walder 1986.
41 See Foreign Languages Press 1982: 20–4.

REFERENCES

Primary sources

BBC, Summary of World Broadcasts, Far East, China
Hong Kong Kuang Chiao Ching
Hong Kong Zhongguo Xinwen She

Renmin Ribao
Shanghai Jingji Daobao
US, Foreign Broadcast Information Services, Daily Report, China

Secondary sources

Almanac of Xiamen SEZ Economy Editorial Board (1986) *Almanac of Xiamen SEZ's Economy, 1986* China Statistical Publishing House.

Auster, E. R. 1987 'International corporate linkages: dynamic forms in changing environments', *Columbia Journal of Business* XX11(2): 3–6.

Brown, D. G. (1986) *Partnership with China: Sino-Foreign Joint Ventures in Historical Perspective*, Oxford: Oxford University Press.

Foreign Languages Press (1982) *China's Foreign Economic Legislation*, vol. 1, Beijing: Foreign Languages Press.

Gomes-Casseres, B. (1987) 'JV instability: is it a problem?' *Columbia Journal of World Business* XX11(2): 71–101.

Hendryx, S. R. (1986a) 'Implementation of a technology transfer JV in the P.R. China: a management perspective' *Columbia Journal of World Business*, spring: 57–66.

Hendryx, S. R. (1966b) 'The China trade: making the deal work', *Harvard Business Review* July-August: 81.

Henley, J. and Nyaw, M. K. (1988) 'The system of management and performance of joint ventures in China: some evidence from Shenzhen special economic zone', *Working Paper Series*, 88/15, Department of Business Studies, University of Edinburgh.

Horsley, J. P. (1988) 'The Chinese workforce' *China Business Review* May-June: 50–5.

Lieberthal, K. and Prahalad, C. K. (1989) 'Maintaining a consistent China strategy', *China Business Review* March-April: 47–9.

Walder, A. (1986a) 'Wage reform and the web of factory interests 1986' in D. M. Lampton (ed.) *Policy Implementation in Post-Mao China*.

Walder, A. (1986b) *Communist Neo-Traditionalism: Work and Authority in Chinese Industry*, University of California Press.

8

DISORGANIZED SOCIALISM
State and enterprise in modern China
Paul Thompson

The years 1990 and 1991 were ones of immense change in state socialism regimes. Despite being in the forefront of economic reforms for ten years and starting the political upheavals with the short-lived democracy movement in Beijing and other cities in 1989, China remains frozen for the time being in what has been dubbed 'market Stalinism'. While offering little comfort to the citizens of that great country, its preservation gives Western academics a chance to study the mechanisms of a mode of production and labour process fast passing into history elsewhere. This chapter aims to analyse the origins, development and ultimate failure of the most sustained and far-reaching attempt to reform state socialism from within. It deliberately minimizes attempts to draw broader conclusions about the functioning and collapse of command economies, as this has been done elsewhere (see Thompson and Smith, Chapter 1 in this volume).

CHINA AND THE REFORM PROCESS

The gradual integration of China into the world economy denotes an important step in the development of the international division of labour. With almost a quarter of the world's population it constitutes a massive new labour reserve where the cost is less than one fifth of its Asian rivals such as Hong Kong and South Korea, primarily because the costs of reproduction of labour power are met by the state (Chossudovski 1986). However, that country has occupied a central place in *debates* about the division of labour for a lot longer. For many on the Left in the early 1970s China was seen as embodying a development path which was consciously primed to avoid the mistakes of the Soviet model such as the imitation of capitalist science and technology and the emergence of new elites through the retention of the separation of mental and manual labour.

Early labour process writings (Gorz 1976) pushed this line and Braverman makes favourable passing reference (1974: 13, 23) before it got lost in more insular issues. That kind of interest was also partly killed by the defeat of Maoism, but the ghosts of those debates still rumble on. Recent issues of *Organisation Studies* have carried a vitriolic exchange in which documents such as Mao's 'Twenty Manifestations of Bureaucracy' have been brandished in order to prove whether the Cultural Revolution was a failed war on bureaucracy.[1] An assessment of that phenomenon is beyond the scope of this chapter, but I would argue that the ascribed theoretical significance is out of all proportion to the practical substance of events. Though the enterprise is a social-political unit which inevitably reflects in the turbulence of factional conflict, there has been too great a tendency to take theoretical pronouncements generated in political struggle as indicative of real changes in the labour process and other spheres. Too many commentators and visitors have been led or led themselves up the garden path and become victims to over-active imaginations.

The reason for highlighting this is that problems of gaining access to reliable information still remain in spite or perhaps because of the opening to the outside world. Old China hands gradually realize the limitations of the carefully controlled visit and the potential statistical manipulation behind the official slogan 'seek truth from facts'.[2] Others are not so wary, John Chowcat returning from a union delegation to pronounce that 'the rights of China's industrial workers to shape and control their lives are being massively extended' (*Labour Weekly* 20 January 1984). However, the 'victims' are changing as gullible leftists are being replaced by eager representatives of Western management schools on similar rounds of visits and interviews with senior managers and officials, compounded by genuine language and cultural barriers.[3] These problems should be kept in mind in the following account, which includes material gathered from workshop sessions with managers and a partly aborted case study of a Beijing truck plant, to supplement secondary sources from China and the West. We start, however, with a brief overview of the broader changes.

The basis of reform: re-shaping transactions between state and enterprise

The year 1978 and the Third Plenary Session of the Central Committee of the Chinese Communist Party (CPC) denotes the start of the economic reforms within the framework of the 'four modernizations' – industry, defence, agriculture, and science and technology. Change was certainly necessary. To add to a basically unreconstructed Soviet planning model and dual control between party and management in the work-place, there existed a particularly extensive workfare state dubbed the 'iron rice bowl' (or iron armchair for white-collar workers!) with its employment guarantees and social subsidies. Whatever advances had been made in the initial stage of socio-economic reorganization after 1949, subsequent performance was not impressive. As Van Ginneken observes, 'Industrial growth since 1957 has been achieved mainly by increasing the quantity of outputs (capital, labour and raw materials), rather than by increasing the efficiency with which they are used' (1988:60).

Furthermore the problems had been exacerbated by the damage done to morale, expertise and efficiency during the Cultural Revolution. One small illustration is that my own work unit, then called the Beijing College of Commerce, was simply closed from 1968 to 1976. This period brought to the fore some of the most debilitating elements within the Chinese version of state socialism; big-push development, excessive use of normative incentives and sanctions and ultra-egalitarianism ('eating from the same pot').

With this depressing situation and the influence of reforms in Hungary in the background, the CPC leadership began cautiously with experiments in particular regions and in rural areas (see Child 1987 for more detail). By 1984 progress was sufficient to persuade them that they could significantly up the pace and include all state enterprises in the new measures. What then were the key elements? At the centre was a combination or administrative and economic decentralization,[4] with a guiding philosophy of 'control the big things, disperse responsibility for the small'. Administratively we saw the streamlining of the state apparatus itself (e.g. the number of ministries), and the delegation of powers over investment and other areas to provinces, cities and other branches of the local state. Planning was supposed to become indicative rather than prescriptive in nature, backed up by a new macro-economic framework in which state-regulated markets would guide enterprise activity. The detail of this hybrid 'socialist planned commodity economy' included a shift towards taxation rather than profit delivery for enterprises; a new central banking system to control credit price reforms which allowed some to float while retaining state specifications of others; and provisions to allow bankruptcy and mergers.

Economic decentralization in the form of the 'enterprise responsibility system' is aimed at expanding enterprise decision-making powers, centred on enhanced discretion over purchase, sale and pricing of products; choice of suppliers; use of funds for investment; and the recruitment, reward and dismissal of workers. In return they will ultimately be solely responsible for their own profits and losses. This is supplemented by a further responsibility system focused on the factory director, in which he or she is charged with delivering whatever contractual arrangements are made with higher administrative bodies. An increasing number of enterprises are extending the contract process to include all employees through the sectional units they belong to, thus increasing accountability and the link between rewards and performance. Taken together the goal is to change culture and practice from production to business unit and from bureaucrat to manager. It should be noted, however, that though the scope of the mandatory plan has been reduced, there remain definite contraints in a whole range of areas as we shall explore in later sections.

Another significant aspect of the reforms has been the opening to foreign capital begun in 1978, but codified in the sixth five-year plan 1981–5. The establishment of Special Economic Zones has received the greatest attention. Begun again on an experimental basis in areas of southern China such as Shenzhen with its close proximity to the resources of the expatriate bourgeoisie in Hong Kong, the zones have been extended to many of the coastal areas. Joint ventures have been the most common form of investment combining domestic land, labour and buildings with foreign technology and management. Arrangements of this nature are openly admitted by the CPC to be state capitalist, but the exploitation is justified on the grounds that it is controlled and necessary for the modernization process. Zones are, however, only part of a wider trend. During 1979–85, the authorities approved throughout China, 300 joint ventures, 3,700 co-operative projects, and 120 foreign-run enterprises employing 150,000 workers (Leung 1989).

Finally, we should note the goal of shifting the balance between different forms of ownership within the traditional hierarchy of state enterprises, collectives (often run by township of village authorities) and private. The official rationale is that 'The existence of many different levels of the forces of production requires a corresponding multiplicity of forms of the system of ownership and of modes of management' (Liu Guoguang 1987: 166). Some success has been achieved. The collective sector has grown in new areas of consumer goods and services, while private ownership and self-employment has rapidly developed in retailing, reducing the state share from 91 per cent in 1978 to 46 per cent in 1985 (Lockett 1987: 14). But in the economy as a whole new forms of ownership remain relatively insignificant, individual and private economies accounting for only 2 per cent of GNP in 1989 (Zhang Zeyu 1990). The state sector still produces about three-quarters of industrial output and the 7,000 large and medium-sized enterprises supply about 80 per cent of the national budgetary revenue. If the reforms are to make an impact, it must be here amoung the elite of permanent state sector workers and this will be our focus in the following more specific sections looking inside the enterprise.

SHIFTING DECISION-MAKING PROCESSES

The transformation of decision-making has two elements, the increased autonomy of management and the factory directorate in particular, and the increased role of worker participation through workers' congresses and trade unions. To an extent both depend on and assume a corresponding reduction in the role and influence of the party apparatus. I shall examine each in turn.

Autonomy

Degrees of autonomy are conditioned by a variety of factors, including in the case of the Beijing motor vehicle plant that I studied (subsequently described as Motorco), ithe form of ownership. The plant has in recent years become designated as a foreign investment company (as opposed to direct ownership from abroad or a joint venture). Such enterprises can opt-out of the mandatory plan or choose a proportion of its production to remain within it. In this case the management evaluates the situation on a year-by-year basis, but has always chosen to work partly inside the plan given that they will receive guaranteed markets and prices as a fall-back to its other transactions on the market. Foreign investment companies also receive special tax dispensations – none in the first two years, rising to 55 per cent of the normal amount after five years. These new relations can be expressed as shown in Figure 8.1.

One of the most extensive general examinations of the issue was carried out in an inter-related study by Child (1987)[5] and Campbell

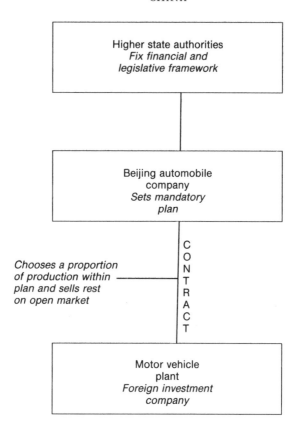

Figure 8.1 Planning relationships

(1987) of six Beijing manufacturing plants. Forty-eight indices of decision-making autonomy were used parallel to the Aston criteria of the degree to which powers are passed down the hierarchy. The results appear to confirm that many of the aims of the reforms are being achieved. In fact Child says that the sample 'displays a comparable level of overall decision-making autonomy to the Canadian and later English sample, and a higher level than the other Western samples' (1987: 38). A follow-up by Child and LuYuan (1990) argued that while enterprise reforms had secured additional autonomy, the process was both uneven and uncertain.

I'm not convinced that comparisions of the relations between state holding companies and subsidiaries and Western models of parent company branches and their equivalents are wholly meaningful, particularly since the holding companies themselves operate within far more restrictive frameworks than their capitalist equivalents. But there is little doubt that autonomy in areas such as decisions on internal organization, products, and purchasing have been increasingly decentralized and the non quota elements of production have expanded; a fact confirmed by complementary studies of the commercial sector (Brewster et al. 1988). A more detailed reading of the findings, however, reveals considerable variations and constraints.

There are variations by type of *plant*, many of the larger and in strategic sectors remain subject to greater controls, for example the stipulation that they buy from and sell to other state companies: and by the *content* of decision, with key parameters such as the determination of investment, pricing of products and size of employment establishment are examples of things more likely to be still decided by higher authorities. As Campbell admits, while the pace of reform has accelerated, 'the amount of discernible change can be exaggerated' (1987: 69). There is another sense in which the expansion of *formal* enterprise powers does not always tell the whole story. Far more attention has been paid to decision-making within state-enterprise transactions than to the equivalent *internal* processes.

Negotiating the 'web of interests'

External contracts still have to be operationalized inside complex structures and networks. One mechanism of doing this is through internal or 'all-round' contracts, which though not legally-binding, aim to produce monitoring and decision-making mechanisms that tie the goals and rewards of all groups to the broader responsibility system. Motorco had initiated such a process, shown in Figure 8 2.

The contract system has led to improvements in performance and more effective integrative mechanisms such as the Evaluation Group to deal with new responsibilities and forms of differentiation. But considerable problems remain. During the preceding period there had been a number of sharp conflicts within the contract process, especially those arising from disputes over setting and delivery of targets between groups. If anything the reforms are likely to add to the general potential for conflict, for they add new uncertainties to those that remain from the command and shortage economy.

Existing formal mechanisms have never been able to deal with the decision-making conflicts and problems related to those uncertainties

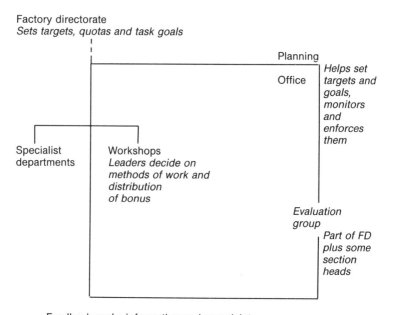

Figure 8.2 The Motorco monitoring and decision-making process

and despite the new procedures, informal bargaining and lobbying is a significant factor at Motorco and in Chinese enterprises generally. Within the web of interests that such activities flow through, the power of work-groups and their leaders is important and perhaps one factor of continuity with the Cultural Revolution (Child 1987: 38). Of course these are not specifically Chinese phenomena. The systemic uncertainties that arise from the bureaucratic environment need to be dealt with in part by internal labour market transactions that promote flexibility of task allocation and rewards. As Stark (1986) demonstrates this can take place through shadow or 'transactive' bargaining in which the key actors are informal groups, membership of which is determined by social position in shop-floor networks. Given that the conditions of exchange are complex and particularistic they cannot, unlike internal labour markets under capitalism, be subject to bureaucratic rules.

This scenario is certainly compatible with the importance of personal connections (*guan-xi*) in Chinese culture and the way that the CPC has promoted the work-group as a feature of social affiliation and distribution. But as I argued earlier we have to be careful not to generalize too extravagantly across state socialist regimes.[6] Informal transactions and bargaining will take distinct forms, reflecting factors such as organizational structures. For example China has traditionally had a large overlap between some staff section and line (production workshops) responsibilites. The ensuing friction and duplication of efforts, exacerbated by the tendency to pass decisions upwards has led to overload of the organizational hierarchy (Lockett 1988). One of the consequences has been a prominent role for the party secretary and committee in mediating within the web of interests and many decisions are still referred to them. This is not *supposed* to happen under the new responsibility system. If any interest groups were to enhance their power, it was to be workers' congresses and trade unions. So it is to the relations between the three that we now turn.

Interest group changes: workers' congress, unions and party

Participation has been a much used term in Chinese industrial development, notably the 'two participations' – workers in management and management in labour – to 'worker management teams' in the Cultural Revolution. Whatever advances were made were quickly swallowed up by the use of such structures as means of political factionalism and mobilization (see Lockett 1983). **Workers' congresses** are now the chosen vehicle. Though reactivated in 1978, they've been around in one form or another since shortly after liberation and have their roots in the workers' conference system. These were modelled on the Soviet system of production conferences and appear to have been largely formalistic exercises in endorsing the decisions of party and senior management, summed up by a CPC leader in 1957; 'The director makes the report, the party committee gives instructions, the trade union issues the call, and the masses give the pledge' (Li Xue-feng, quoted in Chossudovsky 1986: 85). Since then their chequered history has followed the ups and downs of Chinese industrial-political development – downgraded during the brief period of 'one-man management' in the early 1950s, resuscitated though with little real influence from the mid-1950s to mid-1960s, only to be shut down during the fervour of the Cultural Revolution.

The current phase appears to denote a more serious intent and was first signalled by Deng Xiao-Ping in a 1978 speech to the official unions (ACFTU). Deng talked of the need for workers to elect section heads and other junior management; of major issues being discussed by congresses or membership meetings; the right to suggest replacement of leading personnel and of the need to safeguard the legitimate rights of employees. A further speech the following year spoke of the director responsibility system under the leadership of the congress rather than the party. Key elements of this were embodied in the 1981 Provisional Regulations which specified the election of more senior management and described congresses as 'organs of power'. Finally in 1986, the State Council accounced further regulations, which though they were situated in the context of 'extending socialist democracy and socialist rule of law'; shifted the emphasis to issues of monitoring management and protecting legal rights.

Evidence from official Chinese sources indicates a rapid, if uneven, spread of workers' congresses throughout the above period. The *People's Daily* had claimed 200,000 by 1982 and 'almost all' state enterprises by 1986, with over half a million administrative heads being elected (see Leung 1989). Even after the suppression of the democracy movement, the official press is still trumpeting 'success stories' such as the Shoudu Iron and Steel Company (*Beijing Review* 11–17 December 1989). Evidence on the ground, especially from more sceptical Western observers, is patchier (Littler and Lockett 1984; White 1987; Child 1987). Congresses are more likely to operate in the large cities and in old industrial strongholds such as Wuhan. The reporting system through local union officials encourages a vast inflation of the actual numbers. Even where officials have been elected it tends to be at the lower levels. None of the directors of the six Beijing enterprises visited by Child had been elected and the practice had even been stopped for work-group leaders.

Even where congresses exist, whether it indicates anything about the *content* of these processes is another matter. Though one of the more favourable commentators, Lockett (1983: 617–18) reports Chinese criticisms of congresses being held only for the sake of formality and being used as rubber stamp bodies. In many instances they will deal just with social issues such as distribution of housing, or become operative only in periods of sharp conflict. In my own experience of talking to workers and managers there was little evidence of congresses being taken seriously. Certainly there was no sign of any significant role being played at Motorco, where a congress was established in 1982 and usually meets once a year. Its functions are focused on social welfare issues and its leadership is 'selected by democratic election under the leadership of the party committee', and is restricted to people who follow the four cardinal principles (leading role of the Party, Marxist-Leninist thought, etc). As for elections of staff, even work-group leaders are *appointed* by the factory director.

One of the major limiting factors has undoubtedly been an evident confusion and tension of roles and of goals. An early theme was to unleash employees' creativity and enthusiasm in a system that even Deng admitted was in reality based on 'ownership by party secretary and factory director'. This was accentuated by the increased managerial powers under the responsibility systems, *China Daily* commentating that workers have little or no participation rights and 'contractors and leaseholders simply regard themselves as bosses and treat their workers as subordinates' (3 March 1989). The article went on to say that the authority of managers could not be established without workers' support, emphasizing the point that congresses and allied measures have more to do with restoring managerial legitimacy than extending democracy.

However, the monitoring functions embodied in the latter were also aimed at improving the competency and efficiency of the cadre of enterprise officials, with elections a counterweight to patronage and political favouritism (Lockett 1983). For all the talk of congresses giving flesh to the traditional slogan of workers as 'masters of the enterprise' instrumental factors have unquestionably been dominant. While such issues are entirely legitimate, they run right up against existing power structures. At best we could endorse Henley and Nyaw's judgement that they can be 'a consultative forum that imposes limited obligations on top management' (1987: 144). Being enmeshed in existing power structures does not refer only to management, but to a tripartite institutional relationship in which 'the functioning of the workers' congress system depends upon the joint efforts of the party committee, the trade union and factory management' (Ng and Lansbury 1987: 153). At Motorco there is a joint meeting every three months between representatives of the party, the youth league, workers' congress and factory director to discuss the progress of the factory plan.

The trade union apparatus is officially charged with carrying out the functions of the congress between meetings. Given the nature of trade unions in state socialist regimes this obviously raises severe doubts. Nowhere has their role as welfare assistants and junior enforcers of party and plan been clearer than in China. Yet **trade unions** with their 93 million members out of a work-force of 120 million, have also had a similar chequered history under CPC rule. For instance in the early 1950s the party leadership had to close down union papers and purge leaders accused of 'economism' – putting the short-term interests of workers before the long term interests of the nation (Leung 1989). During the One Hundred Flowers campaign in 1956-7 union leaders were conned, like many others, into raising their voices, in this case for more independence from the party. They were subsequently uprooted along with other 'right-wing weeds'.

To some extent China's rulers could afford to sit on such demands while the iron rice bowl remained intact. But problems inevitably accompanied the post-1978 reforms; after all if labour was to become in part a commodity, then interest group politics would surely follow. The CPC soon officially recognized rumblings of discontent as workers used to primitive egalitarianism and seniority-based rewards began to complain of unfair income distribution inside the enterprise and excessive rewards accruing to new entrepreneurs outside. Foreign management in the special zones were also 'persuaded' somewhat reluctantly to allow unions a more active monitoring and representational role (*Shanghai Focus* 7 May). It was also clear that the lessons from other state socialist countries had been learned, notably the emergence of Solidarity in Poland in 1980–1 (See Lockett 1983 for details).

The party leadership, embarrassed by widespread descriptions of unions as irrelevant, waved the theoretical magic wand to designate some different social interests as non-antagonistic. Practically, they could point to the enhanced role for unions alongside workers' congresses in the new decision-making structures. But in 1989 they complemented this by announcing draft laws to give unions 'sweeping new powers to take a greater part in the running of the country' (*China Daily* 5 February). This consisted largely of rights to propose new laws for legislation, rather than new powers in the enterprise. In fact the right to strike was explicitly ruled out.

Some progress was made. Committees to stop unfair wage distribution were set up in some districts, and union leaders, particularly in the heavy industrial regions, were drawn more into the web of interests through consultation and channelling grievances. But the effects were still limited and unions continue to be spoken of with contempt or cynical amusement by most employees. Such limitations are hardly surprising. It is hard to shake off the habits of decades where unions were 'humble' dependants of enterprise management and government departments', as one leading official put it. More importantly there is an obvious tension between expanding managerial discretion in various aspects of the employment relationship and at the same time encouraging trade union structures to interfere with the results.

Then there are the political constraints of acting as a transmission belt for the party, which can be illustrated through events during the democracy movement in 1989. The headquarters of the ACFTU was on the bus route between my work unit and the city centre and most days you could see large crowds of workers gathered outside to lobby for support for the protests, particularly during the hunger strikes. For a short period the pressure was successful. A large cash donation was made and the union banner was taken on one of the massive demonstrations. One of the reasons for the small shift was the emergence and increasing popularity of the Beijing Autonomous Workers Federation which had set up its tents in Tianenmen Square. Though small it undoubtedly articulated the desire of employees for genuine independent organization and representation in policy-making, as well as more conventional economic grievances. One worker remarked that 'I came because the ACFTU is completely useless. If we wait for them then the time will never come' (quoted in Leung 1989: 8). The ACFTU has been prominent in the subsequent extensive repression of the Federation activists not killed on 4 June.

As long as **the party** remains the sole significant force in Chinese society any freedom for trade unions is contingent on political conditions. It does not necessarily follow that it is as powerful in enterprise decision-making. Officially the internal party organization is now restricted to giving support to the work of the director/ate; guaranteeing and supervising the implementation of party and state plans; and carrying out ideological and organizational work among employees. Some Western observers (Brewster et al. 1988. Laaksonen 1988; Child and Xu 1989) partially back claims of a reduced role, the former study saying that, 'the previously powerful party secretary was only in evidence in a few of the organizations we visited. Our impressionistic view is that their power has declined' (p.284). Child and Xu argue that at the high point of reform in mid-1988, the party's role had contracted so sharply that it was not even fulfilling its supervisory role. Where party secretaries exercised influence, it was because their activities and expertise had become managerial in nature. Previous studies are said to be either out-of-date or not based on empirical observation.

While it may be true that the party's direct role in production has declined and that considerable variations exist in activity by size and type of enterprise, there are many reasons for believing that the above view is naive. Difficulties abound in measuring observable party influence on formal decisions, or in focusing too specifically on the secretary. There are two spheres of activity the party cannot or will not give up. First is its *apparatus of political control*, most conclusively identified by Walder (1984). In many work-places 10–15 per cent of employees will be party members, organized often in a parallel administrative hierarchy, thus giving them their own chain of command and communication. That power is used primarily to influence the appointment, promotion, removal and reward of personnel.

Whether formally or informally, the party apparatus is still likely to perform an extensive review and screening role (Chamberlain 1987; Walder 1989). Appointments by the factory director, even of workshop leaders, have to meet with the approval of the party committee within Motorco. In general the party apparatus draws on the surveillance and intelligence potential of study reports from the endless series of political meetings (my unit generally held at least two per week for all employees), and files kept by the party personnel department. The party leadership in the enterprise (sometimes through its control of the satellite of 'mass' organizations of youth, women, unions, etc.) may control the allocation of titles such as 'model worker', so distribution according to loyalty can still have crucial effects on rewards (Henley and Nyaw 1987: 141). It is true that political compaigns at work had declined in recent years and that many workers ritualistically go through the motions at meetings. But the process remains a strong mechanism of social control and can be easily reactivated on full power as the post-Tiananmen events indicate, as Child and Xu admit.

The other sphere is what may be called the party's *co-ordinative* role, in that party membership and structures still perform essential linking and mediating functions. Enterprises are still highly dependent on external planning bodies and the party secretary may examine and approve business plans. Given the web of interest we talked of earlier and the tendency to pass decisions upwards, the party secretary is often the final arbiter in disputes and has the final say on important decisions. The overlap of memberhip between senior management and party obviously facilitates these processes. Outside of the appropriate networks you may be in trouble. Child (1987: 44–5) gives the example of the director of an electrical switchgear plant whose non-membership meant that he had not even taken up the formal powers available under the responsibility system and who still deferred to the party secretary about anything significant.

To conclude this section, while new roles were sorted out in theory for management, party, unions and workers (through congresses), in practice they are confused and overlapping partly because fear dictates that each acts as a counterweight to the other. Furthermore, reforms aimed at transforming and redistributing decision-making powers have faced major external and internal constraints. The fragile and largely instrumental basis of the initiatives ensured that they remained highly dependent on political and economic circumstances which have never been very favourable to substantial change, despite the existence of differing strands of opinion inside the party, unions and congresses.

REDESIGNING REWARD SYSTEMS

Reforms to decision-making **processes** must also connect to specific issues of **content** and one of the most important of those is reward systems. The principle underlying official state policy has always been 'from each according to his ability to each according to his work'. But that notional link between rewards and quantity and quality of labour has proved impossible to implement under the iron rice bowl and 'eating from the same pot'. As a popular Chinese saying puts it, 'You work you get 36 (yuan). you don't work you also get 36' (quoted in Leung 1989: 67).

Colloquialisms, however, do not tell us how the system works. Though set in motion after 1949, the first unified national wage system was consolidated in 1956, again based on the Soviet model. Though it varies a little by sector an eight grade wage system – based on standardized rewards for types of work, with pre-fixed differentials – covered almost all manual workers, while there were fifteen for technical and twenty-five for cadres. Within wage bands there are also work grades, steps based on specified degrees of technological complexity, labour intensity and reponsibility. It was recognized that these rates needed boosting by regular bonus payments to get closer to 'each according to work'. On top of this came a range of supplements and allowances, including those for unsocial conditions and on a regional basis; plus normative incentives ranging from 'model worker' to 'advanced work group'. Finally , but by no means the least important are the range of fringe benefits and subsidies that constitute the social wage. Their significance lies partly in the fact that the CPC has explicitly pushed a low-wage, high-employment policy based on a mixture of wages and rationing. Walder lists those available to **state sector** workers (though on a bigger the unit, more available basis):

> subsidised enterprise apartments and dormitories, meal halls with subsidised breakfast and lunch, free kindergartens and day-care centres, factory hospitals and medical clinics, and recreational facilities. State labour insurance provides sickness and injury compensation, life insurance benefits, free medical care for the employed and partially subsidised care for dependents, disability and retirement pensions and injury compensation. (Walder 1984: 545)

A range of 'hïdden' advantages may also be conferred, including superior access to housing, transport and rationed goods.

The results of such a system were that pay in general acted as a poor motivator and low pay in particular a poor basis for effort control. For many the only way to get a pay rise was promotion, yet promotions were fixed according to national guidelines. Fixed and inflexible job classifications and wage rates undermined any extensive use of work measurement. As indicated earlier, in order to create differentiated rewards and flexibility managers had to circumvent rather than utilize the bureaucratic system. On many occasions they had to fall back on emulation campaigns and moral exhortation which had ever more limited effects, especially among younger workers (Lockett 1988).

When reforms were initiated, mainly in 1984–5, they therefore had a number of basic features and goals. All enterprises are allowed to retain a portion of their profits to distribute as bonus. This most frequently takes the form of a bonus fund at a percentage based on profits and taxes paid to the state (though limited to no more than four months standard employee wages). In turn this facilitates a 'floating wage system' whereby enterprises may let a proportion of the employee's wages be adjusted according to economic performance – the more above the profit quota specified in contracts, the more available for distribution. A further initiative during this period extended wage supplements and linked them to job reponsibilities and levels.

Clearly the aim is both to give managers greater discretion and genuinely to link pay and performance. An additional aspect is the

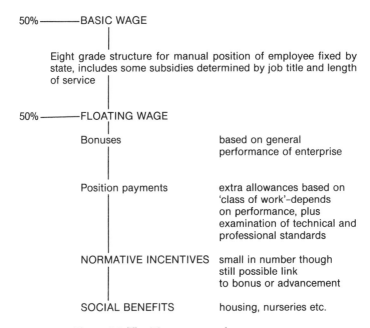

50% ———— BASIC WAGE

Eight grade structure for manual position of employee fixed by state, includes some subsidies determined by job title and length of service

50% ———— FLOATING WAGE

Bonuses — based on general performance of enterprise

Position payments — extra allowances based on 'class of work'-depends on performance, plus examination of technical and professional standards

NORMATIVE INCENTIVES — small in number though still possible link to bonus or advancement

SOCIAL BENEFITS — housing, nurseries etc.

Figure 8.3 The Motorco reward structure

attempt to shift the balance between types of reward, legitimizing multiple sources of income; reducing the social wage elements, with the eight grade system in effect becoming a minimum wage (Chossudovsky 1986: 112). A typical product of the changes can be seen at Motorco (See Figure 8. 3).

The new wage policies in the enterprise are not only failing to work effectively, but also contributing to wider problems in the Chinese economy. Since 1978 standard time wage as a proportion of total wages has declined from 85 per cent to 59 per cent, while bonuses have risen from 2 per cent to 12 per cent (Van Ginneken 1988: 72). In itself this is not problematic, but there are a number of defects in bonus arrangements. It is widely acknowledged (*Beijing Review* 28 August–3 September; Campbell 1987; Lockett 1988; Brewster et al. 1988), that the practice of distributing bonuses and subsidies far too indiscriminately and equally with little relation to performance or penalty continues to persist. There is a particular problem with cadres and administrators given that it is hard to utilize any criteria of performance measurement. However, that is part of a broader problem that bonuses are too frequently derived from **overall** rather than differentiated performance. Over-complexity is also an issue, there being a plethora of opportunities for bonuses, position payments and allowances. In this light it is also interesting to note that the level of non-wage benefits has substantially risen since 1977, with subsidies increasing from 6.5 to 15.2 per cent.

One of the basic problems, as Walder (1987) argues, returns us to the interrelationship between the web of interests within an updated version of plan bargaining. Managers and employees still have considerable opportunities to collude in maximizing incomes, the former continuing a tradition of buying co-operation through maximizing bonus and social spending with little cost to the enterprise. The fact that workshop managers often decide on bonuses and receive the average of the group is a contributing factor. For instance, in the last quarter of 1984 there was a 46 per cent increase in wages. This followed a Government announcement that 1985 wages were to be based on 1984 figures precipitating a rush to raise wages by every conceivable means (Leung 1989: 72).

The combined effects has been an explosion of incentive payments contributing to an over-heating of the economy. But it is not all a one-way process. Despite frequent claims that wages have outstripped prices since 1978, there is evidence that the growth in real income has been exaggerated and inflation underestimated (Van Ginneken 1988). The perception of state workers that they are chasing prices is exacerbated by hostility to aspects of the new multiple forms of income, particularly in some rural areas, among the new petty bourgeoisie and party elite; a process obviously not helped by prominent publicity given to endemic tax evasion and kick-backs. As a result the official press complains that 'The rational high salaries received by model workers, skilled technicians and enterprise managers fails to be understood and often inspires ridicule or slander' (*Beijing Review* 28 August–3 September 1989).

REORGANIZING LABOUR

We have seen that the organization of labour under state socialism requires a degree of flexibility in allocating rewards and tasks in order to overcome uncertainty and secure continuity of production, perhaps facilitated in China by some tradition of job rotation within small groups (Lockett 1983: 602–5). But labour utilization problems are still serious in Chinese enterprises and have also been the subject of attempted reforms. So as to enable possible comparisons with trends in Western business, I shall divide the initiatives into numerical and functional flexibility.[7] First, a reminder of the problems and issues.

The authorities themselves admit extensive surplus labour, 20 million in the state sector (*Shanghai Focus* 14 May 1989) or 15–20 per cent of jobs across the country (*China Daily* 8 May 1989). A number of factors account for this, most prominently the life tenure system of state employees, a policy aggravated by the tendency for families to place their offspring or children to inherit their parent's jobs; that is when they or the spouses of employees are not being found work in the 6,766 collective sector plants run by state enterprises for similar purposes (*China Almanac*, in Walder 1984: 546). There is also a tendency for management to want to 'own' those they have trained, even when they are not really needed. The mismatch between work needs and numbers has encouraged a growing tendency towards moonlighting, with one million second jobs in Shanghai alone (*Beijing Review* 6–11 November 1989). Even when those jobs are outside work, employees are often saving energy by not working within it.

A unique system of direct administrative allocation of labour made it impossible for a single enterprise to escape the consequent over-manning, the CPC having traditionally followed a labour intensive economic development policy. In part the centralized system through state labour bureaux was designed to manage the flow of workers from rural to urban areas, a particularly necessary influx during periods such as the Cultural Revolution when 17 million urban youth went in the opposite direction (Van Ginneken 1988: 66).

By the end of the 1970s great pressure was building up inside and outside enterprises. Undoubtedly the labour surplus was the greatest single obstacle to the raising of productivity. But contributory factors included some rigidity of function with a failure to relocate specialists where needed, plus a poor training record which means that 60 per cent of employees enter without receiving any (*China Daily* 31 March 1989). Externally a number of factors including the baby boom, a backlog of youths returning from the countryside and yet shortages in sectors such as textiles and construction were converging to make more flexible and diverse methods of allocation a political priority.

The policy goals of the new measures are summed up by White (1987). They are to increase allocative efficiency by a more flexible system, which having weakened the iron rice bowl could match supply and societal need and job openings with individual talent and aspirations. In future the state labour bureaux were to be restricted to setting overall proportions, channels of allocation were to be diversified and contract labour was to be introduced into state enterprises.

In the sphere of numerical flexibility managers were empowered by giving greater discretion over hiring and firing.[8] Dismissals were largely tied to the new *labour* contract system. Regulations issued in 1986 stipulated that any workers taken on would be employed for specified periods after which their contracts would be renewed or terminated because they no longer 'belonged' to the work unit. The previous 'all carrot and no stick' practices were replaced by the goal of insecurity as a motivator. In return individuals received the notional freedom to change jobs and a labour insurance system to cushion any period of temporary unemployment. Use of contract workers is not in itself new, but previously such people were in the *temporary* category on specific jobs (Jackson 1988: 357). But past practice does indicate that state enterprises had partly depended on core-periphery relations to meet the needs of flexibility of function and numbers, drawing particularly on rural workers without permanent status. Figures do demonstrate that the policies are having an effect. 1988–9 the number of workers under the contract system rising by 270,000 to 10.34 million, around 10 per cent of the total labour force (*China Daily Business Weekly* 23 April 1989). It is certainly 10 per cent at Motorco. Meanwhile 96,000 are reported to have resigned or been dismissed in Shanghai since 1987 (*Shanghai Focus* 14 May 1989).

Hiring powers could be adequately realized only by allowing managers to 'bid' for labour provided in a semi-market environment created by new agencies. Official policy refers to a 'three-in-one combination' consisting of the traditional labour bureaux, labour service companies and a variety of less formal measures which allow exchange or placement in sectors such as self-employment. An example of the latter is the Beijing Talent Exchange Centre which holds events such as the Spring Labour Fair, in 1989 bringing together 130 firms and 6,000 potential employees and resulting in 600 appointments (*China Daily* 17 April 1989). Initiatives of this kind supplement existing unofficial and specialized labour markets such as those for domestic servants from the countryside employed by the urban elite.

Labour service companies (LSC) – a curious amalgam of arm of the state and autonomous body, labour exchange registering those await-ing jobs, and job creation and training agency – are a more substantial policy direction. Set up initially by local labour bureaux to deal with under-employment, their role has been increasingly focused on translating training into the establishment of new co-operative/ collective enterprises. Whether intended or not LSCs have therefore become part of the process of changing the balance between forms of ownership. They have been especially active in the special economic zones (see Howell, Chapter 7 in this volume). Foreign ventures must employ staff through the LSC and pay a labour management fee which sustains its role as a social security agency. Other functions include manpower research and documentation, services for unemployed, arbitration and wage setting and negotiation (Leung 1989: 148–50). Management *choice* in the economy generally is further promoted by discouraging patronage and job inheritance, in part through more open recruitment procedures and in some cases public examination for highly prized (though at the moment largely white-collar) state sector posts.

A link between improving numerical and functional flexibility is the policy of *optimization of labour*. Interestingly the pressure on state-run and large collective units to reorganize the labour force comes out as realization that the practice of using bonuses to stimulate productivity had proved too expensive (*China Daily* 17 April 1989). Optimization refers both to relocating and retraining of workers in the most effective way and to the squeezing out of 'unnecessary' workers. As usual, there are extensive reports from the official media of large numbers of enterprises involved in optimization initiatives (Zhu Zhichang 1990: 15). In fact the government has sometimes set enterprise quotas of such workers to be removed from their posts. These policies are being backed-up by the launch of China's first national job training scheme to ensure that all new workers receive pre-employment help, plus a review and examination process which could lead to the rejection, transfer or demotion of those who fail (*China Daily* 31 March 1989).

One of the most controversial aspects of the reshaping of the labour process is the supposed growth of scientific management. One of the few remaining Western pro-Maoists, Chossudovsky (1986: 216), argues that the adoption of such methods is a key element in a drift into capitalist production relations. According to him, 'Scientific management in post–Mao China combines Confucian authoritarianism with Western Taylorism', departing from practices adopted during the Great Leap Forward and Cultural Revolution such as the emphasis in the *duo main shou* movement on multipurpose machines and diversified skills. It is true that during periods of political conflict workers occasionally adopted exotic titles, my favourite being the 'anti-Taylorist Combat team of the Red East Armed Corps of the Worker's Congress of the Beijing Toy Industry' (Locket 1983: 628). It is also true that it is easy to find officials calling for management to be treated as a branch of science; the newly formed Chinese Enterprise Management Association claiming that only by 'running the enterprise in a scientific way will it be possible to bring into full play the potentialities of the manpower and material resources, and to gain greater economic results' (quoted in Warner 1987: 76).

However, it would be wiser to treat both as either largely symbolic or as referring only to 'scientific' management in the most general way. Chinese workers may be being subject to greater discipline and controls, but that is far from identical with specifics of Taylorism. Child (1987: 38) observes that his site visits revealed very limited application and scientific management and cost techniques. As argued earlier, the very uncertainties in state socialist economies necessitate a level of functional flexibility, for example in getting production workers to engage in repair and maintenance activities. Stark correctly notes that as a result, 'many of the material and organizational prerequisites of strictly Taylorist work methods and payment systems are absent on the socialist shop floor' (1986: 495). If such methods are operational, they are fairly recent and limited in character, for example the 'full work-load method'.[9]

There has been some dramatic evidence of success in implementing the numerical side of reforms. In Shenyang, capital of north-east Lianong province 63,000 of the 300,000 workers that the authorities consider to be redundant were transferred or laid-off from state-owned enterprises in 1988 (*Far Eastern Economic Review* 19 January 1989), But it has to be said that this is not the general rule. White's judgement sums up the overall picture more accurately, 'progress in implementing new labour policies has been frustratingly slow and results disappointing' (1987: 120). Even LSCs have largely been creating new jobs rather than facilitating mobility within and between enterprises. While there has been a limited increase in the circulation in some groups and sectors, the situation is far from anything resembling a labour market.

With the exception of LSCs in the special zones, administrative allocation through state labour bureaux is still the dominant factor. For example, government job assignments still determine the job destinations of all but a few scientific personnel, technicians and university teachers; only 2 per cent of whom managed to change jobs in 1988 (*China Daily* 30 March 1989).

Those who do change are often opting out of the state sector. Earlier I referred to the 96,000 dismissed *or* resigned in Shanghai. In fact, the city leadership admits that many of those currently unemployed are people who gave up their jobs in order to search for the crock of gold at the end of this self-employed rainbow. More importantly, the quantitative advances made under the contract labour system are mainly illusory. Most of the workers taken on under the new arrangements are in *practice* permanent, regardless of the theory. Managers and employees alike will tell you that it is still difficult and often impossible to terminate someone's employment, except for some kind of 'extreme' behaviour. No one has ever been dismissed at Motorco except for having committed serious crimes. Normally contract workers will still have to be housed from the enterprise stock, therefore getting rid of the person is likely to risk losing the flat, to say nothing of the risks of harassment from the person's relatives. In fact the local government and police often put pressure on management not to dismiss workers because of the ensuing social control problems. (Ji Li 1990).

Despite the failure to significantly alter enterprise labour practices, what *has* happened is a reinforcement and extension of the existing pattern of dualism in employment structures and relations, laying the basis for a longer term shift towards a dual labour *market*. 'Peripheral' categories have been expanded involving more ex-rural workers, those working for many collectives and in temporary posts. One report indicated that some industries prefer to fill positions from rural applicants rather than urban labourers because the former are less demanding (*China Daily* 8 May 1989). Additionally there is a danger that more women will fall into marginal categories. Many of those that are laid off are women with young children, who may be offered a 'long vacation' on up to 70 per cent of base pay and there is wider evidence of increasing marginalization of women's job prospects, pay, promotion and training (Leung 1989: 82–3). Even women college graduates are 'facing a higher level of discrimination than ever before, with virtually all potential employers asking for men' (*China Daily*) 21 February 1989).

Why in general, however, has there been limited movement towards official goals? Simple caution is part of the answer. There are major ideological and practical adjustments to be made in beginning to treat labour as a commodity. Administrative expertise is limited and old commandist methods die hard as the experience of the labour optimization programme shows. Managers frequently used it for factional purposes, to favour their or other workers' relatives, or to merely go through the motions by casually re-allocating workers among existing posts (Zhu Zhichang 1990). Undifferentiated quotas did nothing to develop a meaningful voluntary and continuous process of reorganization. Management at Motorco still get their yearly quota to hire. There is also an understandable fear of giving up the capacity to control rural to urban flows. Such fears in the minds of the CPC leadership were worsened by the tendency of the large numbers of jobless and homeless collecting in the big cities to add their grievances to those of the students and workers during 1989.

We should not discount resistance. While the idea of workers as masters of the enterprise was always fiction, the reforms undermine one of the major benefits people got out of the system. For instance, those graduate students without *guan-xi* to fall back on have often been dubious about swappng job security for freedom of choice, particularly when many factory directors are being much more stringent about the numbers they are taking on. In a number of provinces similar attempts to Shenyang to lay off workers ran into heavy protests and accusations of exploitation and anti-communism (*Far Eastern Economic Review* 19 January 1989). Resistance is also fuelled by resentment at corrupt practices among recruiters who are using their new-found powers to demand money or presents such as colour televisions, or continuing to appoint on the basis of favouritism and family ties.

Shenyang itself worked only because the laid-off staff retained their base wages, state housing and other benefits, at least until they had been helped to find new jobs. This illustrates the point that the biggest constraint is the attempt to pursue labour reform independently of wider institutional change. As *China Daily* plaintively put it, 'One result of reorganization is that it has helped turn those who occupied work posts but had no work to do, into unemployed people. But the problem is who should care for them?' (17 April). Without a housing market there can never be a labour market. Without a *national* welfare state and adequate insurance and benefits replacing the enterprise as a mini-welfare state, labour mobility and acceptance of the end of the iron rice bowl will be a pipedream. Though the State Council promised to establish an insurance scheme for the unemployed in 1986, they fail to deliver in any comprehensive manner. Reform cannot go on being bought with the enterprise bearing the heaviest burden.

DISORGANIZED SOCIALISM: A FAILURE OF TRANSITION

Many of the goals of economic and enterprise reforms were both desirable and necessary. Even if all the goals had been successful, it did not represent, regardless of what the Western media or some commentators claim, a return to capitalism. Not unless markets and capitalism and socialism and central planning are regarded as indistinguishable. But they were not successful, the results either did not materialize or had unintended consequences.

Explanations of that failure are rightly multifaceted, but perhaps the most popular theme has been the failure to accompany economic by political reform. The events of April to June 1989 are a powerful confirmation of that. But it is a partial truth, for it can serve to deflect attention away from economic problems and failures. It is easy to point, as the Chinese press do, to a series of specific problems such as poor quality control or inflationary investment. But the underlying issue is the nature and management of the transition process from a command economy to a form of market socialism. We have already seen a major example of the inability to get that right in the failure to develop an adequate social and welfare infrastructure to accompany labour reforms.

The official line understandably tends to downplay the weakness of the general strategy, preferring to locate problems in the locality and enterprise. In analysing the reform of the state-owned system, the economist Liu Guoguang describes macro-economic management as scientific and rational, whereas success is determined by, 'whether micro-economic units are responsive to measures for macro-regulation and control, that is whether the foundation required for macro-management exists at the micro-level' (1987: 171). In truth weaknesses at both levels are mutually reinforcing, but as the old saying goes the fish starts to rot from the head. Too often the old reins have been let go without proper planning or thinking through the consequences with reference to the growth of excessive inequalities in rewards, *Beijing Review* comments that 'because the government's direct control over income distribution has weakened perceptibly, while the new indirect macro-control system and methods have yet to be established, the original problem of income

251

distribution has not really been thoroughly resolved' (28 August–3 September 1989).

In the absence of what Boisot (1987: 219) calls 'tested macro-economic controls that can be inserted into the existing institutional fabric to steer the economic agents in the desired direction' the most serious problem is *localism*. Many command powers have not so much been abolished or even seriously reduced, but have been redistributed from central to local state planners on provincial, county or city authorities. Before the reforms such bodies tended to operate as autonomous city states only interested in their vertical relations with higher authorities. The same parochialism is reproduced at enterprise level. New control over the levers of investment led to extensive funding of local projects. Central authorities found it difficult to exert controls in part because excessive decentralization was often a way of securing support of local political leaders who had their own interests to secure and who tended to be motivated by an ideology of quick results. Above all else they behave with a protection-ist mentality towards 'their' economic units: 'The rampant, almost blind investment of the past decade gave rise to many of inefficient township enterprises. Local authorities are unwilling now to abandon them, and this exacerbates the general strain on energy, materials and funds' (*China Daily* 1 March 1989).

'Investment hunger' had central planners realizing that the situa-tion was out of control by the end of 1984. But calls for cut-backs had little effect. The restructured state banking system, in the absence of effective fiscal or regulatory controls and under pressure of reciprocal obligations from local networks of peers and superiors was lending freely to enterprises and others (Lockett 1987; Boisot 1987). In addition there was a considerable amount of spare money floating round the system as a result of the reforms. The journal *China Business* reported that factories, colleges, government departments and other bodies had hoarded 170 billion yuan equivalent to 47 per cent of total bank deposits (*China Daily* 6 April 1989).

These developments had a disastrous effect on the wider economy, not least overheating and what was for China hyperinflation. Less obviously, localism in the context of excessive growth resulted in irrational forms of production and competition.

Because at first the reforms mainly concentrated on enlarging the decision-making powers, concession of profits and enliven-ing enterprises, the main cluster of interests was dispersed. This made for a marked increase in regional blocks, trade barriers and market division. Industrial structure within the regions took on similar characteristics. For example, various localities competed in investment, kept importing and blindly introducing production lines for luxury consumer goods, so that production far exceeded the available capital. (*Beijing Review* 4–10 September 1989)

New powers and their negative consequences remain unchecked, not just by inadequate regulatory mechanisms but by any serious penalties for poor performance. Some of the benefits of markets are being sought without some of the pain. It is interesting to note that the first bankruptcy of a state-owned enterprise – the Nanchang Motorcycle Factory – was announced in December 1989.

The factors above by no means exhaust the macro-economic problems, prominent of which is the two-track pricing system. Unwilling to let the market wholly determined prices, the CPC leadership allowed two prices for each product. As is now admitted, this situation, 'resulted in unbridled spending, unfair income distribution and official corruption' (*China Daily* 6 April 1989). In particular it taught enterprises to use price differentials to gain large circulating profits and to exchange low-priced products to their own advantage, particularly in avoiding taxes. The absence of a viable price system also made it harder for supervising authorities to evaluate enterprise performance (Boisot 1987: 220).

Within the resulting mess some groups have gained, notably those identified earlier – sectors of the rural economy, the new petty bourgeoisie in urban areas and sections of the party elite at local level. Marketization has gone much further in the countryside than in the manufacturing and commercial sectors. From 1978 to 1985 the proportion of household income from commodity (rather than collective) production rose from 27 per cent to 81 per cent (Nee 1989). The rich pickings from becoming self-employed, or 'economic individuals' as they are sometimes described, is reflected in the long waiting list for permits from local authorities. Meanwhile the party elite gains from manipulating the *interface* between command and market processes, as in the two-track price system. State subsidies go largely to managers and party officials who have privileged access to official resources, which they can then sell at the higher market price. In addition a number of local officials have used their command of resources and political influence to themselves join the ranks of new entrepreneurs, a characteristic of marketization in other state socialist regimes.

Despite these gainers, the effect on society as a whole has been profoundly destabilizing. A popular interpretation of the outcome is that China is now a perverse hybrid, described by Cyril Lin as 'market Stalinism'. Whether either Stalinist or market is a particularly illuminating term to use in the context of modern China is open to doubt, but he is right in his observation that 'Reforms since 1978 have not so much dismantled the fundamentals of the Soviet-type economic system as grafted market processes on to it (Lin 1989). It coincides with Kornai's (1986) view that partial reform brings out the worst aspects of both central planning and markets.

Regardless of what it's called, the effect it seems to me has been to create a kind of 'disorganized socialism'. The recent application of 'disorganized' to capitalism (Lash and Urry 1987) strikes me as a rather peculiar metaphor, but it fits China admirably. For the old arrangements are disintegrating from within as collectivist and statist structures are undermined by decentralization, opening up to the outside world, embryonic forms of interest group politics and cultural diversity. The disorder is not only economic, but also moral. This can be seen in increasing party warnings in the latter part of the 1980s about the tide of 'spiritual pollution', expressed in economic malpractice and 'bourgeois' life-styles, particularly among urban youth (Sklair 1987). It is easier to tackle the latter than the former, as corruption is endemic both to new forms of economic transaction and traditional forms of closed political power. In fact that particular combination gives the planners and officials a potential 'double dip' in redistribution and market opportunities (Nee 1989: 679).[10]

Decisive political leadership and change is required to deal with disorganization. It *is* possible to have economic modernization without political reform. Indeed that it is precisely the conclusion drawn by a section of the young modernizers around the now-disgraced party chief Zhao Ziyang who actively promoted the 'neo-authoritarian solution'; rapid modernization under guided leadership along the lines of their south-east Asian neighbours Singapore or South Korea. But it all depends on where you start from and in China's case political reform is a precondition for an effective transition to market socialism.

Prior to Tianenmen the CPC leadership did talk of political reform in terms of supervision of government and some separation of legislative, economic, political and administrative powers. But the party is incapable of delivering, as it proved when it was unable and unwilling to deal with even the more modest demands of the democracy movement. To deliver would mean unravelling that fusion of powers on which CPC rule depends. We have already seen the way that party subordination of trade unions and workers' congresses is simply too useful for them to be allocated the new and different roles devised for them in theory and in law. Such practices continue the old Maoist slogan of 'putting politics in command', state socialist societies representing a curious inversion of the Marxist base-superstructure framework.

Unable to go forward and traumatized by the economic and political fall-out from the events of June 1989, the CPC leadership appears to be increasingly pursuing a policy of *retrenchment*. Through the 1989–91 State Planning Commission plan and CPC internal documents we are seeing a partial return to commandist methods such as mandatory plans and fixed quotas; restrictions on private and collective industries (notably rural township firms) that compete with state-owned enterprises; re-imposed central controls over distribution of raw materials, a weakening of factory director authority in relation to the party secretary; and gradually ending the two-track price system by eliminating the floating market price (*Far Eastern Economic Review* 1989). On my return to China in May 1990, it was particularly noticeable that the secretary was always described as the 'number one' in work units and had a much more visible profile, a development also noted by Child and Lu Yuan, who comment more generally that 'the changing configuration of decision-making levels between 1985–88 was a reforming trend which will for the time being be halted and possibly reversed' (1990: 346).

Part of the motivation of such measures is an attempt to grapple with real problems, especially the budget deficit, inflation and uncontrolled expansion. But there is also a large element of a reversion to old ideological orthodoxies. These can be seen in the parallel campaigns recalling old heroes – the example of the humble soldier Lei Feng – and bogeymen – prostitution and pornography on the spiritual side and private entrepreneurs on the economic. It is no longer the case that 'to get rich is glorious', as Deng once said. But if the leadership cannot go forward, there are doubts on whether it can go back. For example, any attempt to roll back the collective and self-employed sectors is contrary to their role as mop-up agencies for surplus labour. The process is bound to be uneven, as the leadership is pulled in different directions, both by external events and internal power struggles between factions and regions with different economic needs. The recent and long-delayed decision to open a first stock market in Shanghai is one indication. China is now stuck somewhere between Eastern Europe and the few remaining bastions of old-style communism. The consequent paralysis will lead to new upheavals. Timing is the only question.

NOTES

Organization Studies

1 See 10(1), 10(2), 10(3) (all 1989). Orthodox organization theory with its preference for the eternal necessity of traditional bureaucracy is represented by Shenkar 1989a; 1989b, while Clegg and Higgins (1989), rightly in my view, downplay the significance of this supposed revolution against bureaucracy.

2 See William Hinton's account of his long relationhip with the model village of Dazhai (*China Now* Summer 1988).

3 See for example the report of a visit from Cranfield School of Management (Brewster et al, 1988).

4 This is not the first time that decentralization has taken place, but during the Maoist period it was confined to attempting to influence behaviour within the enterprise by administrative means, while leaving centralized planning and the command economy intact (See Walder 1981).

5 Child and Lu Yuan's follow-up study contains a useful and detailed account of the administrative hierarchy governing relationships between ministries, local regulatory bureaus and enterprises.

6 This is one of the limitations of Stark's analysis. Again the discussion draws heavily on the Hungarian experience, particularly in describing the switch to a form of internal subcontracting based on VGMs, or 'enterprise business work partnerships'.

7 Using these categories derived from Atkinson's flexible firm model in no way endorses the rather distorted claims as to the nature and extent of flexibility.

8 Regulations give foreign-funded enterprises even greater powers to hire and fire, the latter in theory without being subject to outside intervention.

9 The full-load work method was developed by a manager, Zhang Xingrang, after a visit to Japan. It rests on fairly convential management-worker goal setting to improve productivity and reduce manning levels (See Ji Li 1990 for more details.

10 Corruption is also made more likely by the Chinese preference for the use of personal connections – going through the back door – one of a number of examples of the way that traditional culture can reinforce economic problems (see Lockett 1988).

REFERENCES

Bian Yi (1989) 'Unemployment poses a serious threat to city', *Shanghai Focus* 14 May.

Boisot, M. H. (1987) 'Industrial feudalism and enterprise reform: could the Chinese use some more bureaucracy?' in M. Warner (ed) *Management Reforms in China*, London: Francis Pinter.

Braverman, H. (1974) *Labour and Monopoly Capital*, London: Monthly Review Press.

Brewster, C. Brown, R. and Burns, P. (1988) 'China: management in a time of change', *European Management Journal* 6(3): 280–5.

Campbell, N. (1987) 'Enterprise autonomy in the Beijing municipality', in M. Warner (ed) *Management Reforms in China*, London: Francis Pinter.

Chamberlain, H. B. (1987) 'Party-management relations in Chinese industries: some political dimensions of economic reform' *China Quarterly* 112: 631–61

Child, J. (1987) 'Enterprise reforms in China: progress and problems', in M. Warner (ed.) *Management Reforms in China*, London: Francis Pinter.

Child J. and Xu, Xinzhong (1989) *The Communist Party's Role in Enterprise Leadership: At the High Water of China's Economic Reform*, China–EC Management Institute, Beijing.

Child, J. and Yuan, Lu (1990) 'Changes in the level of decision-making in Chinese industry: a window on the progress of economic reform 1985–88' *Organisation Studies* 11(3): 321–51.

China Daily (1989a) 'Jobs crisis for women graduates', 21 February.

China Daily (1989b) 'China adheres to four principles', 3 March.

China Daily (1989c) 'Changing jobs still difficult', 30 March.

China Daily (1989d) 'Double prices no longer help reform', 6 April.

China Daily (1989e) 'Where does the money go outside the bank?', 7 April.

China Daily (1989f) 'Beijing Labour Fair finds jobs for 600', 17 April.

China Daily Business Weekly (1989) 'Workforce drops a million, but contract system grows', 23 April.

Chossudovsky, M. (1986) *Towards Capitalist Restoration? Chinese Socialism After Mao*, London: Macmillan.

Chowcat, J. (1984) 'China's new worker syndrome', *Labour Weekly* 20 January.

Clegg, S. and Higgins, W. (1989) 'Better expert than orthodox: reply to Shenkar', *Organisation Studies* 10(2): 261–6.

Delfs, R. (1989a) 'The iron rice bowl cracks', *Far Eastern Economic Review* 19 January: 63–4.

Delfs, R. (1989b) 'Power to the party', *Far Eastern Economic Review* 7 December: 24–5.

Ginneken, W. G. (1988) 'Employment and labour incomes in China, 1978–86' *Labour and Society* 13(1): 55–79.

Gorz, A. (ed.) (1976) *The Division of Labour: The Labour Process and Class Struggle in Monopoly Capitalism*, Brighton: Harvester Press.

Gu Chengwen (1988) 'Unemployment to rise as ten million join job seekers', *China Daily* 8 May.

Guo Zhongshi (1989) 'Ministry plans drive to educate workforce', *China Daily* 31 March.

Han Guojian (1989) 'Moonlighting craze hits China' *Beijing Review* 6–12 November: 21–3.

257

Henley, J. S. and Nyaw; Mee Kau (1987) 'The development of work incentives in Chinese industrial enterprises – material versus non-material incentives', in M. Warner (ed.) *Management Reform in China*, London: Francis Pinter.

Hinton, W. (1988) 'China's reforms economise with the truth', *China Now* Summer.

Jackson, S. (1988) 'Management and labour in Chinese industry: a review of the literature', *Labour and Industry* 1(2): 335–63.

Ji Li (1990) 'On China's reform in employment policies' Paper to ASTON-UMIST Labour Process Conference, April.

Jiang, Zemin (1989) 'Eliminate unfair income distribution', *Beijing Review* 28 August–3 September: 16–20

Kar-Nin Chen, P. (1984) 'A note on the new roles of managers of industrial enterprises in China', *Labour and Society* 9(4): 389–96.

Kornai, J. (1986) *Contradictions and Dilemmas: Studies on the Socialist Economy and Society*, Cambridge, Mass: MIT Press.

Laaksonen, O. (1988) *Management in China During and After Mao in Enterprises, Government and Party*, New York: Walter de Gruyter.

Lash, S. and Urry, J. (1987) *The End of Organised Capitalism*, Oxford: Polity Press.

Leung Wing Yue, Trini (1989) *Smashing the Iron Rice Pot: Workers and Unions in China's Market Socialism*, Hong Kong: Asia Labour Monitor.

Leung, Trini (1989) 'Workers for democracy', *International Labour Reports* 34/5 (July–October): 7–11.

Li Rongxia (1989) 'Economy develops amidst snags', *Beijing Review* 4–10 September: 15–24.

Li Rongxia (1990) 'Enterprise merger and grouping', *Beijing Review* 8–14 January: 25–6.

Lin, C. (1989) 'China's reforms caught in no man's land', *Guardian* 24 April.

Littler, C. and Lockett, M. (1984) 'Trends in Chinese enterprise management', in N. Maxwell and B. McFarlane (eds) *China's Changed Road to Development*, Oxford: Pergamon.

Liu Guoguang (1987) 'Problems of the reform of ownership relations in China', in M. Warner (ed.) *Management Reforms in China*, London: Francis Pinter.

Lockett, M. (1983) 'Organisational democracy and politics in China' in C. Crouch and F. Heller (eds) *Organizational Democracy and Political Processes*, London : John Wiley.

Lockett, M. (1987) 'The economic environment of management ', in M. Warner (ed). *Management Reforms in China*, London: Francis Pinter.

Lockett, M. (1988) 'Culture and the problems of Chinese management', *Organisation Studies* 9(4): 475–96.

Nee, V. (1989) 'A theory of market transition: from redistribution to markets in state socialism', *American Sociological Review* 54(5): 663–81.

Ng Sek Hong and Lansbury, R. D. (1987) 'The workers' congress in Chinese enterprises', in M. Warner (ed.) *Management Reforms in China*, London: Francis Pinter.

Shenkar, O. (1989a) 'Rejoinder to Clegg and Higgins: the Chinese case and the radical school in organisation studies', *Organisation Studies* 10(1): 117–22.

Shenkar, O. (1989b) 'Rejoinder to Clegg and Higgins: better expert than orthodox', *Organisation Studies* 10(3): 423–4.

Sklair, K. (1987) 'Capitalist efficiency without exploitation – some indications from Shenzhen', in M. Warner (ed). Management Reforms in China, London: Francis Pinter.

Stark, D. (1986) 'Rethinking internal labour markets: new insights from a comparative perspective', *American Sociological Review* 51 (August): 492–504.

Thompson, P. (1983, 1989) *The Nature of Work: An Introduction to Debates on the Labour Process*, London: Macmillan.

Van Ginneken, W. (1988) 'Employment and labour incomes in China, 1978–86', *Labour and Society* 13(1): 55–79.

Von Glinow, M. and Teagarden, M. (1988) 'The transfer of human resource management technology in Sino–U.S. cooperative ventures: problems and solutions', *Human Resource Management* 27(2): 201–29.

Walder, A. G. (1981) 'Some traces of Maoist legacy in industry', *Australian Journal of Chinese Affairs* 5: 21–38.

Walder, A. G. (1984) 'Worker participation or ritual of power? Form and substance in the Chinese experience, in B. Wilpert and A. Sorge (eds) *International Perspectives and Organisational Democracy*, London: John Wiley.

Walder, A. G. (1987) 'Wage reform and the web of factory interests', *China Quarterly* 109: 22–41.

Walder, A. G. (1989) 'Factory and manager in an era of reform', *China Quarterly* 118: 242–64.

Warner, M. (ed) (1987a) *Management Reforms in China*, London: Francis Pinter.

Warner, M. (1987b) 'China's managerial training revolution', in M. Warner (ed.) *Management Reforms in China*, London: Francis Pinter.

White, G. (1987) 'Labour market reform in Chinese industry', in M. Warner (ed.) *Management Reforms in China*, London: Francis Pinter.

Yuan Zhou (1989) 'State gives a voice to workers', *China Daily* 5 February.

Zhang Tingting (1989) 'Congress reviews union role' *Shanghai Focus* 7 May.

Zhang Xiaoguang (1989) 'Local authorities need new lessons', *China Daily* 1 March.

Zhang Zeyu (1990) 'Keeping private business on the right track', *Beijing Review* 22–8 January: 4–5.

Zhao Lijuan (1989) 'Reorganisation of labour under way', *China Daily* 17 April.

Zhou Guanwu (1989) 'Contract system stimulates enterprises', *Beijing Review* 11–17 December: 19–22.

Zhu Zhichang (1990) 'Labour combination optimisation: a report on the development in China's labour process and employment system', Paper to ASTON-UMIST Labour Process Conference, April.

INDEX

Aix Group 39, 40, 74
All-China Federation of Trade
   Unions (ACFTU) 235, 239
Anokhin, N. 123–4
anti-communism 190–1
Armenia 122
Assmann, G. 86, 90
automobile industry, USSR 105–7,
   149–79; assembly line 106–7,
   149–50, 153–8; equipment 121;
   living conditions 151–2;
   management view 164–6; and
   politics 166–9; production reform
   169–75; protest 162–4; wages
   158–60

Baron, J. N. 43, 46, 48
Bauman, Z. 11
Beijing Autonomous Workers
   Federation 239
Benton, L. 42
Bettelheim, C. 3
Beynon, H. 106
Bielasiak, J. 14
Bielby, W. 48
Blackburn, R. 6, 28
Block, F. 47
Bluhm, K. 94
Bogdan, J. 6
Boisot, M. H. 252, 253
Boltanski, L. 48
Bourdieu, P. 48
Braverman, H. 3, 5, 23, 46, 201, 228
Brewster, C. 233, 239, 243
Bulgaria 14
Burawoy, Michael viii; on collapse
   of state socialism 11, 17, 190–4,

196–7; on feudalism 3; on
Hungarian transition to
capitalism 13, 16, 17, 108, 180–
97; on Hungarian workers'
councils 16–17, 194–6; on Lenin
107, 180–2; on new technology in
Hungary 6; on 'painting'
socialism 96, 107–8, 184–9; on
relations in production 18–19; on
self-management 26–7, 27–8; on
state socialism 5, 7–8, 11, 17,
182–4
bureaucratization 43–61;
   redistributive 45, 50–61;
   regulatory 44, 45–50, 51–2

Callaghan, J. 20
Campbell, N. 231–2, 233, 243
Capecchi, V. 42
capitalism 45–8; and ideology 184;
   and informal economy 38–9, 41–
   66; innovation and the division
   of labour 39–40, 73–92; labour
   process 18–19, 22; Lenin's theory
   of transition to communism 181–
   2; relations of production 18–19,
   22, 188; and state socialism 3,
   37–40
Carlo, A. 18
Castells, M. 43, 48
centralization of planning 5–6, 50–2
Chamberlain, H. B. 240
Child, J. 229, 231–2, 234, 236, 239–
   40, 248, 255
China 201–4, 205–24, 227–56;
   collectives 230–1; Communist
   Party (CPC) 228–9, 239–41, 254–